SPY THRILLERS

INSIGHTS

General Editor: Clive Bloom, Senior Lecturer in the Faculty of Humanities, Middlesex Polytechnic

Editorial Board: Clive Bloom, Brian Docherty, Gary Day, Lesley Bloom and Hazel Day

Insights brings to academics, students and general readers the very best contemporary criticism on neglected literary and cultural areas. It consists of anthologies, each containing original contributions by advanced scholars and experts. Each contribution concentrates on a study of a particular work, author or genre in its artistic, historical and cultural context.

Published titles

Further titles in preparation

Spy Thrillers

From Buchan to le Carré

Edited by
CLIVE BLOOM
Senior Lecturer in the Faculty of Humanities
Middlesex Polytechnic

St. Martin's Press   New York

© The Lumière (Co-operative) Press Ltd 1990

All rights reserved. For information, write:
Scholarly and Reference Division,
St. Martin's Press, Inc., 175 Fifth Avenue,
New York, N.Y. 10010

First published in the United States of America in 1990

Printed in Singapore

ISBN 0–312–04245–0

Library of Congress Cataloging-in-Publication Data
Spy thrillers: from Buchan to le Carré / edited by Clive Bloom.
    p.   cm.—(Insights)
ISBN 0–312–04245–0
1. Spy stories, English—History and criticism.   2. English
fiction—20th century—History and criticism.   3. Buchan, John,
1875–1940—Criticism and interpretation.   4. le Carré, John, 1931–
—Criticism and interpretation.   I. Bloom, Clive.   II. Series:
Insights (New York, N.Y.)
PR830.S65S6   1990
823′.087209—dc20   89–49608
                                                            CIP

This one for Lesley – with love as always

Contents

Preface and Acknowledgements

This volume presents thirteen essays on the Spy Thriller in the twentieth century including a critical introduction to the subject. Each essay combines in a clear and understandable way formal, historical and aesthetic theory with sound practical criticism. Authors covered range from past masters such as Joseph Conrad and John Buchan to present masters such as Ian Fleming, Len Deighton and John le Carré, while subjects range widely from discussion of the formal characteristics of the genre to the conditions governing modern state surveillance and control of which the spy novel is not only a symptom but also a warning. The book, which combines a comprehensive range of literary approaches is the companion volume to *Nineteenth-Century Suspense: From Poe to Conan Doyle*, *Twentieth-Century Suspense: The Thriller Comes of Age*, *Literature and Imperialism* and *American Crime Fiction: Studies in the Genre*, all available in the Insights Series.

Thanks are due to Sarah Roberts-West who saw the value of such a book, to John Simons, Michael Hayes, Dudley Jones and Bob Lee for stepping into the breech, to Anne Rafique for her work on the manuscript and to Lesley for her patience and support.

C.B.

Notes on the Contributors

Clive Bloom is a member of the Faculty of Humanities at Middlesex Polytechnic. He is the General Editor of the Insights Series and the author of books on literary criticism, Romanticism and popular culture.

Richard Bradbury teaches in the Department of English at the University of Warwick.

Dennis Butts recently retired from the English Department at Bulmershe College of Higher Education and is the Editor of *Stories and Society: Children's Literature in its Social Context* (forthcoming in the Insights Series).

Miles Donald is a novelist and literary critic whose work includes the thriller *Diplomacy*. He currently teaches in the School of English at Middlesex Polytechnic.

Michael J. Hayes teaches at the Lancashire Polytechnic. Besides American Crime Fiction, his research interests include Disraeli's early writings.

Dudley Jones lectures at Reading University. His research interests cover popular fiction and media studies.

A. Robert Lee is a Senior Lecturer in English and American Literature at the University of Kent in Canterbury. He is Editor of the Everyman *Moby Dick* and numerous collections in the Vision Critical Series.

David Seed lectures at Liverpool University, is the author of numerous articles and has recently published books on Thomas Pynchon and Joseph Heller.

John Simons lectures in English Literature at King Alfred's College, Winchester. He is the co-editor with Christopher Mulvey of *New York: City as Text* available as an Insights volume.

Michael Woolf is a Director of the Council for International Educational Exchange in London. He has written numerous articles on cultural matters and regularly contributes to BBC programmes.

1

Introduction: The Spy Thriller: A Genre Under Cover?

CLIVE BLOOM

In many respects the spy genre like the world it depicts is a form attempting to exist in disguise. Of the three main strands in its make-up one attempts to become adventure-romance (John Buchan's *Thirty-Nine Steps* for example, or the James Bond novels), one attempts to become the classic domestic novel (Joseph Conrad's *The Secret Agent*) and one may loosely be described as attempting the level of a state-of-the-nation fable (Robert Harling's *The Enormous Shadow*).[1] In all three cases the form struggles with its origins and aspirations.

The formal origins of the spy genre lay hazily within an amalgamation of the imperial adventure tale and the detective novel. Both forms emerged in their proper state in the last quarter of the nineteenth century and were themselves responses to social pressure. The spy thriller coming early in the twentieth century (in its fully-developed form) was, more than both its predecessors, *the* genre tied to *international* political and social tensions. Indeed, more than any other form the spy thriller responded to a need to represent *covert* activity by state organisations. As Eric Hobsbawm has pointed out, when working people gained the vote the overt political agenda was seen more and more to be subverted by governmental agencies organised to *thwart* given political free-doms.[2] The spy genre records that process in one of the least attenuated forms of fiction. In this sense the spy novel read as a historical record as well as a 'mere' form of entertainment can be highly enlightening.

By the end of the last century the power of the State in all western countries had increased dramatically. The growth of the bourgeois ideology of autonomous individual freedom (including the right to privacy) was accompanied by an equally bourgeois need for *public* control of all private functions. At this moment the bourgeois state came into being, armed with the legislative and cultural power to regulate all forms of expression (including dissent), either through governmental interference (bureaucratised secret police forces at one end) or through cultural control of the mass circulation of printed material (novels, newspapers and journals).

Coincidental with this moment came the high point of western imperial pretensions. This meant that the internationalisation of unrest was, from now on, the consequence of both a heightened class antagonism *and* a heightened yet contradictory cohesive national identity based on xenophobia. These contradictory poles found expression both through international clashes like the Fashoda incident and through the spread of anarcho-socialist activity uniting class antagonisms *across* state boundaries. Nation states, through the development of crude propaganda machines and the ownership of the most widely disseminated literature could play off their own disquiet about class division against the rising fear of foreignness. Hence the anarchic warfare on Edwardian streets culminating in the 'Tottenham Outrage', the Houndsditch incident and the celebrated 'Siege of Sidney Street' in London's East End (where Winston Churchill, then Home Secretary, made a much publicised appearance) could be put at the feet of foreign agitators and criminal elements bent on the destruction of the English way of life.

Such an alarmist period not only allowed the spy novel to thrive as a useful propaganda machine to feed paranoia about foreignness (the waves of immigrants who were looked upon as a sinister lumpenproletariat), but also gave a valuable mechanism for an exploration of the new powers of state control over the *indigenous* people. For paranoia here must be understood as both an obsession with violation by *outside* agencies and as violation of individual autonomy by *internal* agencies who are seemingly behind government and beyond its control – quasi-independent *secret* organisations not answerable directly to any one minister, but dedicated to the abstractions of state power and state authority for their own sake.

The function of these agencies was at one and the same time propagandistic in imperial terms and surveillance-orientated in class terms. Between these functions the actual close regulation of life – from workplace to home – could theoretically be monitored and directed (the ultimate fictional version of this is George Orwell's *1984*). In proportion to the growth of competing international technologies for disseminating information so too have these governmental agencies grown in attempting to control informational flow. As a consequence the nature of change has allowed leakages as to methods and activities to be fed into the writing of spy novels.

Such suggests a correspondent evolution in the focus of the genre and this is indeed the case – from novels about anarchists and agitators among working men, to novels delineating fear of German or Russian aggression, to novels about the enemy being *our own* secret forces working against our own democratic freedom rather than on its behalf. From the 1950s onwards the revelations about the lives of real spies have suggested that the agencies in control are themselves the traitorous elements in society – not merely traitorously working against elected government policy (MI6's involvement with the Wilson government or the FBI's tapping of the Kennedy and Luther King phone lines) but also run by demented or perverse ruling-class élites (the Burgess–Maclean syndrome). In recording such activities spy-thriller writers have followed historical fashion.

Essential to such a recording is the awareness that spying is to do with orthodoxy and heresy played out in a twilight world of *secrecy*. *Centralised* bureaucratically organised state operations are *on all levels* dominated by secrecy and the attainment and classification of knowledges which hitherto were either open or non-categorised. These become the secret and confidential property of the State. Unlike all the religiously orthodox authoritarian states of the past, secrecy belongs, par excellence, as a defining feature of the bourgeois state. Such knowledge is reified into an object of consumption and is fetishised beyond all others. Paradoxically, the State claims that secrecy ensures the defence of open democratic interaction.

Such an attitude to secrecy and the· notion of the secret is something the spy thriller shares with the detective novel, but unlike the detective novel where the original owner of the secret (the criminal) must remain in hiding, a relatively passive onlooker at his undoing, the central question in spy writing is the *ownership* of the secret and this involves a *struggle for power* played out at the level of thrills (adventurous chases, etc). Because of the 'thriller' element often associated with the genre we may speculate that in the well-regulated state autonomous private action can only be appreciated at one remove as an attenuated nostalgia for the individual (wrapped in an interlude of reading leisure and contained within 'cheap' entertainment consumed during that leisure).

Conditional upon the allowance of an escapist nostalgia for individual freedom of action would be the actual denial of such a possibility through state control of private pleasures. As such, not merely the content, but the form of spy thrillers becomes suspect and sinister. Indeed, the only real freedom allowed a 'hero' of a spy novel is the freedom of *fear* and of being hunted, following from an ontological precondition to experience – that of totalised paranoia, for there is no knowing who is the enemy (therefore presume *all* are the enemy). In this way, the enemy are that which the hero is not: *faceless*, soulless, amorphous automata who blindly obey unseen masters and whose autonomy and individuality is absolutely curtailed by obedience to absolutism itself.

> The three faces seemed to change before my eyes and reveal their secrets. The young one was the murderer. Now I saw cruelty and ruthlessness, where before I had only seen good humour. His knife, I made certain, had skewered Scudder to the floor. His kind had put the bullet in Karolides. . . . He hadn't a face, only a hundred masks that he could assume when he pleased. (*The Thirty-Nine Steps*. p. 135)

In later spy novels the hero has become the same soulless creature of bureaucracy as his enemies, an anti-hero devoid of any hope or tragic potential – he is one of us (on *our* side) and one of them, a pawn in a wider game. The confrontation between the individual and the state delineated in spy novels differentiates them from detective novels where the individual is confronted by other individuals and aligns it with science fiction where macro sociological and technological changed superstate systems confront each other through individual 'future' people.

As has been said, we can identify three modes in which the spy thriller exists: the adventure-romance, the domestic novel and the state-of-the-nation novel.

The adventure-romance of John Buchan and Ian Fleming owes much to the imperialist war-as-sport literature of G. A. Henty or Henry Newbolt, and Richard Hannay and James Bond can look back to the faded sepia tones of Allan Quartermain (a hero only by accident). Hannay's exploits in *The Thirty-Nine Steps* are those essentially of the sportsman become the hunted, the hound become the fox. In Geoffrey Household's *Rogue Male* the unnamed hero is a 'wild elephant' and, mixing literary metaphors, goes to 'earth' in a hedgerow.[3] The essential nature of the hero is his amateur status (even Bond is caught off-guard on his arrival in Jamaica in *Dr No* having botched a previous operation) and his ability using innate amateur cunning to defeat 'mad' professionals. In that sense Hannay and Bond are the last individuals of spy novels. In *Dr No* Bond calls himself a type of 'policeman' who essentially is forced on a quest against mythical beasts: a 'dragon' and a giant-tentacled squid.[4] In *Dr No* Bond's world is literally fabulous, borrowed from Haggard and spiced with Sax Rohmer. Dr No himself is surely modelled on Dr Fu Manchu created as long ago as 1913. As a type this mode presents the 'hero' as entrepreneur on behalf of his country, a privateer, 'licensed to kill'.

In a world grown cold and old during the 1950s, the decline of British political prestige amid spy scandals and the debacle of Suez could be halted, at least in imagination, by a Bond-style hero tied to a supposedly stable Edwardian life of class snobbery, imperial ardour and gentlemanly behaviour. The very worst excesses of class snobbery and racism which masqueraded as patriotism from the beginning of the century until the 1930s could be recuperated in the 1950s as the expression of a golden stable age. In such a way Fleming's direct references to Jamaican independence and Cold War Russian activity in *Dr No* become attenuated, through an outdated and therefore static formula borrowed from Buchan. What brutality or casual sexuality there is owes as much to Sapper and Sax Rohmer as it does to Mickey Spillane, Fleming's contemporary. The final result is a casual universe, not a paranoid one, deeply conservative and tied to a nostalgic vision of history as heroic myth.

In Joseph Conrad's *The Secret Agent* the adventurous world of the spy is filtered through the bleak landscape of Slavic realism. Here, instead of adventure and excitement is banality and degradation. Essentially, the story concerns itself with sordid domesticity and, as such, has antecedents in Dickens and Dostoevsky. The

spy thriller, the 'romance' of spying, is itself subverted via this
petty bourgeois interlude. 'From a certain point of view we are
here in the presence of a domestic drama' (p. 213); 'Mr Verloc . . .
was thoroughly domesticated' (p. 244).

This is important, for in *The Secret Agent*, there are no secrets,
nor is there any central mystery, hence the detective nature of
such work is radically curtailed. Indeed, the only concession to the
spy novel format is to pastiche the nature of spy behaviour with
'customers of the little shop' being described in this way: 'men of
a more mature age . . . had the collars of their overcoats turned
right up to their moustaches' (p. 1). Of course, most of the
customers are there to purchase pornographic material. Tracing
this path the novel records the flood of anarchist activity during
the late nineteenth century, but it does this by exposing the subtle
complicity between anarchist organisations and governmental
agencies supposedly set up to monitor and destroy them.

> Chief Inspector Heat . . . could understand the mind of a burglar,
> because, as a matter of fact, the mind and the instincts of a
> burglar are of the same kind as the mind and instincts of a police
> officer. Both recognize the same conventions, and have a working
> knowledge of each others methods and of the routine of their
> respective trades.   (Ibid., p. 88)

In this way a vicious and nonsensical circle is set up between those
who offend against the state and state agencies themselves. It is
not surprising that the central metaphor for the book is Stevie's
endless circular scribblings.

> Stevie, seated very good and quiet at a deal table, drawing
> circles, circles, circles; innumerable circles, concentric, eccentric;
> a coruscating whirl of circles that by their tangled multitude of
> repeated curves, uniformity of form, and confusion of intersec-
> ting lines suggested a rendering of cosmic chaos, the symbolism
> of a mad art attempting the inconceivable.   (Ibid., p. 42)

Conrad's *The Secret Agent* is the first great book, and perhaps
the only one, to tackle the nature of surveillance and the needs of
modern state bureaucracies to maintain terrorist organisations in
order to justify surveillance activity almost for its own sake. And
hence social and 'moral' degeneracy leads from Stevie's simple-

mindedness to the (ill-named) professor's obsessional terrorism for its own sake.

> And the incorruptible Professor walked too, averting his eyes from the odious multitude of mankind. He had no future. He disdained it. He was a force. His thoughts caressed the image of ruin and destruction. He walked frail, insignificant, shabby, miserable – and terrible in the simplicity of his idea calling madness and despair to the regeneration of the world. Nobody looked at him. He passed on unspected and deadly, like a pest in the street full of men.   (Ibid., p. 300)

The Professor is the key figure in this novel – the ultimate product of the police state and later the bourgeois state. (Ibid., p. 26). He is at once totally alienated as an individual and fully integrated as a subject into the 'game' of surveillance, a game played at the level of international class warfare.[5] Ironically, the novel makes clear that if all changes at the rhetorical level, nothing changes at the political level; for the anarchist and the 'central Asian' police state are *accomplices* whose actions on the terrain of the liberal bourgeois nation seem to fall apart on contact leaving British liberal democracy untouched. The Professor finally emerges onto the streets covered in explosives yet impotent to use them, caught as he is in the stasis of an obsessional paranoia.

We have seen so far two of the genre types associated with the spy thriller. The first, associated with Hannay or Bond, replicates the essentially amateurish and nostalgically buccaneering spirit of early spying (both Buchan and Fleming were in the service) in defence of a debilitated imperial mission. Conrad's work reflects the rise of state *machines* (of which the anarchists form part) to carry out surveillance of the general population (Mr Verloc insists that he is 'a natural-born British subject' (*The Secret Agent*, p. 19)). In reflecting current trends these two genre types are both essentially conservative, seeking to preserve the status quo (in Conrad as an ironic complicity of enemies). The third genre-type has its origins in the Cold War years and deals with the conditions governing traitorous behaviour. This type of novel does not reflect actions by the state, it acts as a *direct vehicle of state propaganda*. Whereas the antics of Hannay are attenuated propaganda the works stemming from the Cold War era are constructed *as* state propaganda masquerading as art. The overt message of these books is itself paranoid and designed to create paranoic thinking in readers. The genre type is Robert Harling's *The Enormous Shadow* published in 1955.

Only partially an adventure book, this work attempts to diagnose the state of Britain, a country in a dreadful malaise, caught between American and Russian expansionism (the hero is a Washington correspondent for a British paper). The return of the Washington correspondent in the opening scenes allows for a descriptive analysis of Britain in decline.

> Two days later, therefore, I got to London, to a land I deeply cared for but scarcely ever saw. . . .
> I . . . relaxed, gazing fondly around at the nearer fields, yet not for long. In a matter of minutes the fields had gone and we were moving into one of those approaches to great cities common to so-called civilized lands: a long straight line of metalled road, paralleled by poster hoardings and wasteland dumps. Then, later, rows of sad houses and dingy shops. (*The Enormous Shadow*, pp. 5–6)

The novel continues to document this decline in pseudo-factual terms by recounting the political atmosphere of contemporary international politics and British politics in disarray.

> 'Your Washington stuff has been pretty good, all the same,' he said, almost as an afterthought. 'You made some good guesses about McCarthy'. . . .
> I took a deep breath and said my piece. To me, I said, it looked as if the Tories, mainly under the thoughtful drive of Butler, were trying to live down the legend of the bad old days. . . .
> But they had another, tougher legend to cope with, the Churchill legend. That would cling to them for another twenty or thirty years. . . .
> I couldn't think it was a healthy prospect. 'Truman suffered from much the same kind of process after Roosevelt's death,' I said. . . .
> He nodded. 'And Labour?'
> To me they seem tired. . . .
> Even Bevan must be pretty tired sometimes.   (Ibid., pp. 14–15)

All of this, including a long discussion of Communist infiltration into the Labour party amounts to Harling's analysis of 'Britain's problems in the post-war world' (ibid., p. 39). Through all of this a yearning nostalgia for an older, better, essentially *rural* Britain comes through.

> In a hired Morris I made a slow round of the Cotswolds and the West Country: Oxford, Burford, Stow-on-the-Wold, Chelten-ham, then back to Winchester by way of Marlborough. Turning south, I drove down to Corfe and back by way of Salisbury, the New Forest, Horsham. A quiet and leisurely and strangely moving journey. . . .
> The English landscape was more rewarding.   (Ibid., p. 19)

The rest of the novel documents the investigation of one of the 'new men' of British politics – 'Matthew Chance, the Labour MP' (ibid., p. 31). This 'Man of Peace' (ibid., p. 43) is, in fact, a hard-bitten covert Stalinist, whose background would be strikingly familiar to contemporaries of the Auden generation.

> We began to speak of other things. His early life in Aberdovey. His father's determination to make him a scholar against his own inclinations to swim and sail. His scholarship from a local private school of Winchester. The unrelenting habit of work, fostered by his tutors and his father at more distant range. Then Oxford. Then Spain.   (Ibid., p. 44)

Yet what damns him is not ideology but class jealousy for 'he was a scholarship boy' (ibid., p. 45): let in but socially excluded. Indeed, Chance is effectively a corrupt and insidious monster whose household includes a 'sallow face[d]' and worryingly 'Polish' butler (ibid., p. 64) who brainwashes foolish scientists into defecting. The scenario was all too real in the late 1940s and 1950s, yet the litany of names since repeated ad nauseum, acts here not just as a talisman of realism but also as a rosary of hate of which this quote must stand for more than half a dozen:

> My own belief is that it's a Pontecorvo–Nunn May–Burgess–Maclean story all rolled into one.   (Ibid., p. 163)

In place of narrative and suspense we have a dreary repetition of a catalogue of class traitors, traitors to their *class obligations* (and therefore to their country). This repetition functions almost as an example of Orwell's two minutes of hate, destroying the very 'art' of this 'serious novel'.[6] This propagandistic function in the novel (backed by touches of topographical 'insider' knowledge – so beloved of modern thriller writers) makes the genre a direct intervention by the state at the level of the imagination by one of its unpaid functionaries: the Cold War Artist. Hence the insistence that this novel deals in reality, in facts and has as its hero a journalist. If spying is no longer an adventure it is also, through its presentation, more terrifyingly 'real'. The coolness of the banality during a description of the work of MI5 recorded as 'A desk, dockets, stacks of card indexes, a brief-case and a job as dreary as a pay clerk's in the army' (ibid., p. 210) exists only to heat up the hysterical fervour of the witch-hunt against both the Labour party and the British ruling classes. In the worst sense this book feeds the 'I told you so' fantasies of a generation brought up to accept propaganda. The insidious, near to last lines read 'The dawn was already treacherously pink' (Ibid., p. 270).

If Harling's book comes to acting as vehicle for state attitudes, others have used the 'excuse' of historical research to propagandise on behalf of state organs. The closeness of journalists like Chapman Pincher to sources of 'occult' knowledge in the business of covert operations lends his voice a technical authority which masks a contentious state-sponsored moralism.[7] In *Traitors: The Labyrinths of Treason* he carefully extends the available area for state intervention by widening the boundaries of 'traitorous' activity. Here analysis is propaganda:

> . . . treachery is a growth industry with no shortage of traitors to commit it. In fact, with up-to-date intelligence at such a premium in the nuclear missile age and the ever-urgent Soviet requirement to acquire the West's technological secrets, there has never been treachery on such a scale in the world-wide context, even in wartime. The scope of espionage and the temptation has been expanded due to literally millions of people – in government departments, the armed forces, and the defence industries – now having access to valuable secrets. All major nations – the Soviets in particular – are making unremitting efforts to secure traitor agents among them. In Britain, and in parts of Europe, with the mushrooming of so many left-extremist

organizations intent on revolution, there have never been so many potential subversives.   (pp. xii–xiii)

Politically motivated strikes and sit-ins may be as effective as explosives in wrecking a factory. The main purpose of widening the definition was to legitimize clandestine counter-measures against those planning or taking part in acts to destabilize the government by the means described. When such activities, usually claimed as 'legitimate dissent', are proved to be responses to the requirements of the Soviet Union or any other foreign power intent on promoting disorder, instability and chaos, then subversives qualify as traitors.   (Ibid., p. xvii)

The spy-thriller genre, like spying itself, is a discourse that hovers uneasily on the borders of factuality. It may be no coincidence that so many writers and fictionalists, from Marlowe to Greene, have been involved, given the 'fantastic' nature of the spying project. It remains to be seen if the nature of spying and therefore spy fiction will radically alter in the next century – for spy fiction may be *the* popular genre for the present age.

NOTES

1. All quotations from these novels are from the following editions: John Buchan, *The Thirty-Nine Steps* (London: Pan, 1981); Joseph Conrad, *The Secret Agent: A Simple Tale* (London: Methuen, 1946); Robert Harling *The Enormous Shadow* (London: Reprint Society, 1956).
2. Eric Hobsbawm in a recent television programme.
3. See Michael J. Hayes's essay in this volume.
4. Ian Fleming *Dr No* (London: Coronet, 1988).
5. He is truly called into being as a 'subject' by the state's police, as Louis Althusser has pointed out.
6. Dust-jacket 'blurb' to edition cited.
7. Chapman Pincher, *Traitors: The Labyrinths of Treason* (London: Sidgwick & Jackson, 1987). For a description of the way surveillance operations widened the definition of traitor to include those considered *morally degenerate* see the later chapters of Richard Gid Powers, *Secrecy and Power: The Life of J. Edgar Hoover* (London: Hutchinson, 1987).

2

Cracked Bells and Really Intelligent Detonators: Dislocation in Conrad's *The Secret Agent*

A. ROBERT LEE

Spy thriller: the term, for sure, serves to open the bidding on *The Secret Agent* (1907). Who, at a first glance, would doubt that Conrad gives every indication of having drawn upon the accepted stock of the genre? A dim Foreign Embassy plan to provoke an English government crack-down on political radicalism ends in a fatally botched bomb attack on Greenwich Observatory. Verloc as the agent in question, a hireling to the Russians and the metropolitan police alike, causes the martyrdom of an innocent and ends up dead by the hand of his own wife, herself an eventual suicide. Assorted anarchist types, from pacifist utopians to believers in terror, vie for pride of place – all, by their own word-laden accounts at least, luminaries of a new kingdom on earth. Arrayed against them stand the guardians of public order, a descending hierarchy of the Minister of State, the Assistant Commissioner, Chief Inspector Heat, and even the bobby who patrols Brett Street where the Verlocs have their Soho shop. As basic working terms for this or any other spy thriller, there would seem few grounds for cavil.

But it takes no very long acquaintanceship with *The Secret Agent* to recognise that if Conrad's purpose is thrillerdom, then he has gone about it in ways which we could hardly have anticipated. Everything which plays into the story has been subtly turned inside out, quite perfectly subverted. All the clandestine meetings, the dutiful talk of revolution, the toings and froings between London and that dire place 'The Continent', the calculations of a Mr Vladimir, and even the bomb which takes poor Stevie to his death, amount to an outward show as Conrad projects them, an ever-darkening comedy of errors. Suspense applies, but not as the main aim. In this respect, whatever the 'plot' hatched by Verloc and his mentors, or by Sir Ethelred and his subordinates as a counter-action, or imprecisely dreamed of by the anarchist roster of Karl Yundt, Michaelis, Ossipon or the Professor, each acts as but the shadow of that which engages Conrad overall.

For the plot that truly matters in *The Secret Agent* arises out of Conrad's vision of English society, late Victorian or Edwardian or whichever, as itself one huge collusive dislocation or masquerade. Its endlessly vaunted composure – cool, pragmatic, understated, indelibly Anglo-Saxon, conceals a kind of shared madness or oddity. Surfaces do duty for substance. Inertia, national vanity, imposture of all kinds, hold sway. And to bring off *this* vision, this far more consequential 'plot', Conrad deploys an irony stronger, and at times angrier, than anywhere in his fiction, including the masterpiece which precedes it, *Nostromo* (1904).

It is to this end too that Conrad depicts the English capital as masking behind its daytime face a deeply more sinister and eccentric reality. Beset by fog, mud, general murk and shadow, a 'darkness enough to bury five million lives' as he terms it in his Author's Note of 1920, it offers the very image of the metropolis as conspiracy, a city of the hidden and subterranean.[1] Be it thus in the offices of the state, the bureaucracies, the parks or the Soho sidestreets, plotting of one kind or another abounds, whether expressed as government policy, would-be insurrection or, more to the point, as the construct known all too simply as middle-of-the-road England. The novel seeks nothing less than to encompass each in their different but interlinking turns.

Writing to his friend Cunninghame Graham in October 1907, Conrad himself gave more than a passing indication of his true aims in *The Secret Agent*: 'But I don't think I've been satirizing the revolutionary world. All these people are not revolutionaries – they are shams.'[2]

It hardly surprises, in this light, that he frequently disavowed any real inside knowledge of the likes of Blanqui, Kropotkin and Bakunin or of proponents of 'politics by the deed' such as Sergei Nechaev and Peter Tkachev; or of the figure of Martial Bourdin, the historic actual bomber who blew himself to near smithereens in the Greenwich Observatory outrage of February 1894; or of the different Czarist, Marxian and Fenian groups whose activities ran like a fever through the 1880s and the years immediately following.

For Conrad, the matter went infinitely deeper than the portrait of some mere alarum or sectarian politics. He had in mind, it is clear, a far larger moving target, that of London as a paradigm of the human city.

In this respect his repeated disavowels of Dostoevsky as a factor in the creation of *The Secret Agent* also deserve mention, though to a different purpose. Conrad, as is well enough known, always belittled Dostoevsky, accusing him of guilt by association with the imperial Russia which had so often and brutally subjugated his native Poland. This was unfortunate in two ways. It demeaned Conrad in and of itself. But more importantly, it suggests that he could not fully bring himself to acknowledge how much directly or otherwise he owed to works like *Notes from Underground* (1864), *The Idiot* (1869) and *The Devils* (1871–2). For although one can see why Dickens, say, or Zola, or the Turgenev of *Virgin Soil* (1876), have been advanced as influences on *The Secret Agent*, is not Dostoevsky the true fellow-spirit behind the book – the darkly prophetic Dostoevsky, too, of *Crime and Punishment* (1866) and *The Possessed* (1871–2)? Whatever else, Dostoevsky more than anyone sets up the image of human existence as an 'underground', a destined hell on earth. From this vantage-point, also, *The Secret Agent* has frequently been compared with Henry James's *The Princess Casamassima* (1866), at one reach psychological drama yet at another the portrait once again of the modern city as hive or web or conspiracy. But although Conrad's debts may have been several, including those to a number of Scotland Yard memoirs, they finally will not account for the essential singularity of *The Secret Agent*. For that we need to look at the kind of imagination at work in the book itself, especially for present purposes its resort to 'dislocation' as one of its key modes of operation.

The two items alluded to in my title offer markers, working points of departure, for the pattern of the novel as a whole. Consider first the cracked bell. Conrad begins *The Secret Agent* on a note of seeming impeccable realism. Verloc steps out from his shop, leaving it in the care of his brother-in-law with Mrs Verloc as back-up. The shop appears almost insistently ordinary, familiar. Have we not before us that most English of institutions, the residential small family business? But several anomalies quickly press for attention. Why is Verloc's business done at night for the most part? Why does he care 'but little about his ostensible business' (p. 46)? What else lies within this 'grimy' 'square' house and shop (p. 46)? As the scene builds, Conrad as if effortlessly causes the focus to shift. This is not quite realism, but things caught obliquely, at a slight but deliberate angle or tilt. The result suggests a world to be held up for interrogation, not to be taken at its own self-ranking. A first and necessary dislocation has taken place.

'In the daytime the door remained closed; in the evening it stood discreetly but suspiciously ajar' (p. 45). The Verloc shop may indeed look like a place of respectable commerce. But its traffic has to do with buying and selling by stealth, the surreptitious clink of coins and no questions asked. Here, the emporium's forlorn inventory of goods plays a crucial role. Shoddy in themselves, they also suggest the shoddiness of lives lived on counterfeit terms – those of manufactured sexual fantasy, hopelessly schismatic politics, the substitution of wind-blown polemic for action. So, at least, we might infer from Conrad's list of the soft porn, the French comic-book publications, the 'dingy' (p. 45) casket of charcoal, the inks and stamps and the like, and the obscure and ill-printed journals triumphally called *Torch* and *Gong*. A name like *Gong*, especially, offers an unstated parody of whatever imagined call to arms. And it also points forward to the Verloc bell.

Casting a shadow over all are the gas jets, 'turned low' (p. 45), a kind of sanctioning half-light 'either for economy's sake or for the sake of the customers' (p. 45). As to the latter, a sorrier parade would be hard to imagine. Young men pass in and out bent upon their off-colour purchases often comically caught out by having to buy from Mrs Verloc. Their elder counterparts, usually in threadbare clothes, muddied, their coats tight about them, equally turn desire on its head. They 'dodge' (p. 45) into the stop 'sideways', (p. 45) fidgety and 'one shoulder down' (p. 45). Step for step, this amounts to consummate pastiche, things seen not only through a glass darkly but through a glass which distorts or dislocates in just the right degree.

It is the bell, however, which most completes the picture, a bell Verloc's column of 'customers' are 'afraid to start' (p. 46) lest it draw attention to their shabby sexual plight:

> The bell, hung on the door by means of a curved ribbon of steel, was difficult to circumvent. It was hopelessly cracked; but of an evening, at the slightest provocation, it clattered behind the customer with impudent virulence.   (p. 46)

Aptly as 'hopelessly cracked' reflects on Verloc's commercial clientele, it typically also does still larger service. It speaks to the society as Conrad will imagine it overall. Is Sir Ethelred, for instance, any less 'cracked' than the would-be politicos who troop in and out of Verloc's parlour? Or the Assistant Commissioner with his allusions of playing colonial Big Game Hunter than, say, The Professor, as he threatens mutual destruction by dynamite of anyone who gets too close? Or Verloc himself, who if he indeed purveys 'shady wares', be they sexual, political, or even his dubious displays of marital responsibility, does so in the guise of the upstanding paterfamilias and tradesman? Conrad, further, also invites our recognition of what is implied by the accompanying lexicon of 'clattered' and 'cracked' and 'virulence'. These point to the genuine ineptness and nastiness in play behind all the surface convention. For ahead will lie the bomb and Stevie's fate, scenes like the cab ride to south London, Winnie's spirals of despair, and the double violence of Verloc's and her own death. Thus, as literal as discomfiture by the bell is to ear and nerve, it also sounds for the yet profounder dislocation being explored at the centre of the novel.

The bell 'clatters', accordingly, at frequent intervals, but most of all at key moments of change. It does so the night before Verloc leaves on one of his clandestine missions to the Continent and as he senses a coming change of regime on account of Vladimir's summons to duty and his mother-in-law's removal to the almshouse (p. 172); it does so when Verloc is surprised by the arrival of the anarchist fugitive (p. 189) and Heat arrives shortly afterwards in hopes of questioning him (p. 190); it does so again, and even more portentously, after Heat confers with Verloc on Stevie's death and is overhead by Winnie (p. 148); and, an absolute last time, it does so on Winnie's departure with Ossipon after the murder of Verloc (p. 356). In each case, a major dislocation is signalled, the toll as it might be thought of each successive lurch or descent into the abyss.

In like manner, The Professor's detonator provides the terms for another round of dislocation. 'To deal with a man like me', The Professor tells Ossipon as more than a touch discrepantly they go about the all too ordinary business of supping beer, 'you require sheer, naked, inglorious heroism' (p. 91). He speaks as the ranking anarch, the ex-laboratory assistant who has elevated himself into a human time-bomb. To this end, he carries in his pocket the onanistic 'indiarubber ball' (p. 91) which when squeezed will ignite on a delay of twenty seconds an explosion of magnum force. Conrad, however, resists the temptation to turn him into simple caricature, a cloak-and-dagger or nitroglycerine-carrying figure out of melodrama. Obsessional, absolutist, he may be, but he also operates out of an undeniable if quite unlovely logic. Indeed, Conrad scarcely covers up a certain personal relish of The Professor's adversarial urge to pull down the whole house of English life and society. Nor can it be thought other than a stroke of genius to have The Professor, one of the fraternity's own, berate his fellow anarchists. Karl Yundt he mocks as a 'posturing shadow' (p. 93). Ossipon and the others he thinks self-incriminatingly 'talk, print, and do nothing' (p. 96). Verloc, who has made a fiasco out of the Greenwich bombing, is said in sternest condemnation to require a 'disclaimer' (p. 100).

But however plausible in these aspects, Conrad endows The Professor with others which show him to have tilted off-balance. Born of 'a delicate dark enthusiast' (p. 102) father, an adherent 'of some obscure but rigid Christian sect' (p. 102), he has given way to 'a frenzied puritanism of ambition' (p. 102), the messianic duty of destroying law and institutions in the case of a new justice. That we also learn he is 'lost in the crowd, miserable and undersized' (p. 102), helps explain his compensating resort to the indiarubber ball, and all it portends ('the supreme guarantee of his sinister freedom' (p. 102) as Conrad calls it). The Professor, in other words, represents the idealism which can kill, the Grand Design gone askew.

The details of his appearance give added support. He has eyelids which snap 'nervously' (p. 60), a 'sallow' face (p. 90), spectacles like 'unwinking orbs flashing a cold fire' (p. 90), and 'thin vivid lips' (p. 90). He wears suitably meagre clothes of 'nondescript brown' (p. 91), at once 'threadbare' and 'dusty' (p. 91) and marked by 'ragged' buttonholes (p. 91). The tube, just visible, which connects the rubber ball to the sinister flask suggests 'a slender brown worm' (p. 91). And to complete matters, The Professor discloses with exactly the right, but rather suspect high seriousness the great challenge of his life:

I am trying to invent a detonator that would adjust itself to all conditions of action, and even to unexpected changes of conditions. A variable and yet perfectly precise mechanism. A really intelligent detonator. (p. 92)

Yet if in one way odd, even comic, the likely implications of The Professor's search for his detonator are anything but lost on Ossipon. Especially not when, over a further round of drinks, The Professor boasts that were his bomb to ignite there and then 'nobody in this room could hope to escape' (p. 92). Even Ossipon, the robust philanderer, the ex-medical student who enjoys the sobriquet of 'The Doctor', finds his nerves jangled. He conjures up 'a dreadful black hole belching horrible fumes' (p. 92), 'smashed brickwork' (p. 92) and 'mutilated corpses' (p. 92). Ossipon, viscerally, dislocatedly, has registered the true import of The Professor's ferocious pre-conditions for his new society.

The detonator localises all of this. In the Professor's scheme it recurs like an incantation: not only the 'really intelligent detonator' but the 'perfect detonator' (p. 93), the 'really dependable detonator' (p. 97), and the 'absolutely foolproof detonator' (p. 99). Through its means this 'moral agent' (p. 102) will engage in an authentic terrorism, the final, truly explosive overthrow of 'the immense multitude' (p. 103). That his search for the right detonator, too, links to the one which has obliterated Stevie, or Verloc as he mistakenly thinks, can be of no consequence for The Professor. He honours only his own inner dictates of 'a new concept of life' (p. 107), 'a clean sweep and a clear start' (p. 97). Thus, driven, shabby, a hater of crowds, this would-be usher of the new millenium stalks the streets of London muttering and with the gleam of private revolution in his eye. Dislocated himself, he seeks to dislocate all about him – subject, such is Conrad's sardonic vision, to the appropriate 'sudden hole in time and place' (p. 105) and, lest we forget, 'a really intelligent detonator'.

Bell and detonator, then, typify the dislocation which Conrad portrays as the condition of things in *The Secret Agent*. Other features equally symptomatic recur, all of them made to gather in resonance as the narrative takes its course. One thinks of the circles drawn by Stevie (p. 50), the image in small of an English world turning endlessly on its own provincial axis. Or of Verloc's hat, that of a creature of habit, even apathy, rather than of some likely disturber of the peace. Or of Michaelis's obesity, that of a ticket-of-leave jailbird to be sure but also of an overweight child, a dreamer funded by his lady patron rather than a maker of socialism.

Or of Ethelred's 'Be concise', the catch-phrase of a gloriously out-of-touch Whitehall mandarin more concerned with the fisheries than with political violence. Or, to add to this list, Chief Inspector Heat's search-and-arrest mentality, which equates politics with burglary and anarchism – with everyday law-breaking; Winnie Verloc's style of political as much as sexual acquiescence; the Verloc's fatal carving knife, which Conrad has hover between metaphor (the stab in the back for Verloc by Vladimir) and fact (the literal cutlery used by Verloc for his last meal and as the murder weapon); and even the misnumbering of the London houses so unperturbedly accepted as normal by Verloc as he makes his way from Brett Street to the Embassy. Conrad allows none undue pride of place, but works each into the novel's overall catalogue of things finely off-centre. Nor does such dislocation lie only inside the specific detail of the novel; it permeates each major sequence and relationship. Four instances come to mind most especially.

In stepping out from his shop, Verloc steps out from a domestic set-up not so much eccentric but as mentioned earlier just out of focus with itself. Verloc himself has 'an air of having wallowed, fully dressed, all day on an unmade bed' (p. 46). Mrs Verloc, Winnie, for all the implied sexual energy of her 'youth' (p. 47) and 'full, rounded form' (p. 47) gives off an 'unfathomable reserve' (p. 47). Both Verlocs, indeed, might be said to live at an agreed one emotional remove from the other, partners in the deal struck over Stevie rather than in any authentic marital intimacy or love. Winnie's mother, legs swollen, more heart than head, belongs in their menagerie as part of the 'furniture' (p. 48). And as for Stevie, his dislocation lies in what he is biologically – retarded but benign, one of Nature's Innocents. He registers the world, like William Faulkner's Benjy, only by the evidence of his nerves and senses. His eventual victimry, blown to nothing except for his name-tag, brutally completes all that has gone before: his lack of memory for messages, alarm at stray animals, distraction at 'the comedies of the streets' (p. 49), panic at fallen horses and, above all, frenzy at the sight and sound of fireworks. In the spectrum of London, from Ethelred to The Professor, supposed order to a would-be end to all order, Stevie becomes the almost inevitable casualty.

Certainly it is as a servant more of order than unorder that Verloc makes his way to Vladimir. 'Bloodshot' (p. 51) may be the sun which shines over the capital, yet the aspects which win Verloc's

approval are those of 'opulence and luxury' (p. 51), the 'hygienic'
(p. 52) display of high bourgeois English life. Nor, even more of
note, does Verloc propose the slightest disruption of this state. To
the contrary, he is devoted to it with a sort of 'inert fanaticism'
(p. 52). Or as Conrad inverts matters, with 'a fanatical inertness'
(p. 52). Were we not to know otherwise, and despite his French
mother, Verloc would pass as the exemplary Little Englander, the
model citizen. His mission, however, much against his best instincts
has exactly to do with the end of his *socialiste de salon* posture.
'Inert', 'undemonstrative', 'steady' (p. 52) as Conrad's deflationary
irony terms him, Verloc must do that most un-English thing: take
action.

The signs become ominous. Number 10, Chesham Square, stands
between numbers 9 and 37. 'What is desired', announces Wurmt,
the lugubrious Chancelier d'Ambassade whose trade is words not
action, 'is the occurrence of something definite' (p. 55), 'an alarming
fact' (p. 56) to bring down the arm of English authority in line with
Czarist action against dissidence. Wurmt notes Verloc's corpulence,
hardly the expected weight for an agent in the field. On confronting
Vladimir, Verloc hears from the First Secretary a tirade anything
but in keeping with someone who has 'a drawing-room reputation
as an agreeable and entertaining man' (p. 57). Verloc has bumbled
plots in the past; is now too fat even to fall for some *femme fatale*;
is accused of taking money under false pretences; lacks an education
in Latin; and in the unkindest cut of all is mocked for having been
given star billing since the time of 'the late Baron Stott-Wartenheim'
as 'the celebrated agent Δ' (p. 63). Just as Vladimir can switch
accents and languages at will, so Verloc comes over as a fake, the
counterfeit anarchist out of bed too early and the supplier of
information simply contemptible to his paymaster. His 'confounded
nonsense' (p. 69) completes itself for Vladimir in the fact that he is
married, yet another break with anarchist style. Little wonder that
Conrad directs attention to London's 'rusty sunshine' (p. 62)
and the 'first fly of the year' (p. 62) as sardonically appropriate
harbingers of Spring – and of 'the jolly good scare' (p. 64) which
will be the bomb attack on Greenwich Observatory. Even Verloc's
'providential' (p. 72) marriage to Winnie, as her mother calls it,
takes on a darker implication; this will be providence truly
disastrous. Again dislocation has found its working idiom.

Nor, for a moment, does Conrad depict only the Verloc family
and the anarchists at an angle. Sir Ethelred, The Assistant Commis-

sioner and Heat as the three exemplars of English public officialdom are done in exactly matching idiom, again well to the right side of caricature yet subtly awry. Each, credibly, holds an office of consequence: Cabinet Minister, police second-in-command at the London Met, 'operational' detective. Yet each signifies behaviour once again just off-centre, and off-centre it can be added, in a very English sort of way. For though they hold real power in a real London, they also have given way to a dislocation in their make-up. Conrad invites us to see them, darkly, comically, as being for the most part out of sync, off the essential point. Guardians of the law, institutional stalwarts, they may be, but no less than Verloc, Vladimir, The Professor and the rest, they reflect the whole game or show of society. Their 'dislocation', too, puts us on familiar ground.

Sir Ethelred we meet through his secretary, the Dickensian Toodles. Where Vladimir's Wurmt was all in black, bald and 'with a mincing step' (p. 54), Toodles has 'symmetrically arranged hair' and the look 'of a large and neat schoolboy' (p. 141). That parallel established, so, equally, is that of Vladimir and Ethelred, both men high in their own self-esteem and both political actor-managers. Conrad gives us Sir Ethelred in the following terms:

> Vast in bulk and stature, with a long white face, which, broadened at the base by a big double chin, appeared egg-shaped in the fringe of greyish whisker, the great personage seemed an expanding man. Unfortunate from a tailoring point of view, the crossfolds in the middle of a buttoned black coat added to the impression, as if the fastenings of the garment were tried to the utmost. From the head, set upward on a thick neck, the eyes, with puffy lower lids, stared with a haughty droop on each side of a hooked, aggressive nose, nobly salient in the vast pale circumference of the face. A shiny silk hat and a pair of worn gloves lying ready at the end of a long table looked expanded, too, enormous.   (p. 142)

Rarely can born-to-rule mandarinism have been caught better. Inflated in body and dress, Sir Ethelred personifies upper-class English insouciance. And that, we are left in little doubt, Conrad takes upon himself to confirm in the run of catch-phrases put before the Assistant Commissioner in his interview about the Greenwich explosion. 'Don't go into details. I have no time for

that' (p. 142), Sir Ethelred insists, to be followed up with 'Spare
me the details' (p. 143), 'No need to go into details' (p. 144) and
'Be as concise as you can' (p. 146). He speaks, as it were, a perfect,
upper-echelon jargon quite as mystificatory in its own way as
anything spoken by the anarchists.

As to The Assistant Commissioner, he could well be in the
wrong country altogether, the ex-colonial officer who patrols the
English capital as though set down in some unexpected part of the
Empire. His dislocation has the familiar ring of the servant of the
crown who finds he has no real knowledge of the crown he serves:
the outsider suddenly on the inside and not unlike Virginia Woolf's
Peter Walsh in *Mrs Dalloway*. Back and forth as he journeys,
between Sir Ethelred's office and the Verloc shop, between Heat
and The Professor, he does so as a man oddly out of joint with his
mission, less master than servant of the situation. Equally so Chief
Inspector Heat; even less so than the Assistant Commissioner does
he perceive what has been at stake in the Greenwich affair. For
him, this is all police procedure – a crime committed, suspects to
be arrested, reports to be filed. He grasps nothing of the moral
calamity at the heart of what has happened, nor the different kinds
of sham and ineptitude which have led to Stevie's death. As the
details emerge, Ethelred at least understands that something
'very fantastic' (p. 202) has occurred; The Assistant Commissioner
discerns 'a ferocious joke' (p. 202); but Heat, too close to events,
can only pay Verloc 'a friendly call' (p. 190) – and in a supreme
irony as he goes about his 'regulation' enquiries cause Winnie to
overhear and so bring down the last curtain on the drama. Neither
Sir Ethelred, nor The Assistant Commissioner, nor Heat, in other
words, grasps the whole. Conrad's strength is to allow us to do
that through their mutual and overall dislocation.

If Conrad's 'ironic method' (p. 41) applies to *The Secret Agent* as
a spy or political thriller, it assuredly also does so as 'a domestic
drama' (p. 204) to use the Assistant Commissioner's phrase to Sir
Ethelred. The Verlocs are offered as a counterfeit marriage at one
with the goods they sell. They typify a family who have settled
for less. Winnie has foregone her young butcher, married Verloc
to her mother's uncomprehending approval in order to protect
Stevie, and fondly and mistakenly come to think Verloc and Stevie
an image of father and son. But Conrad shows them actually to be
a family which has become unfamilial, as about-turn and self-
prostituted as the larger London in which they take their place.

The evidence lies in the removal of Winnie's mother to the almshouse south of the river, and then in the final, momentous dislocation of Verloc's death and Winnie's suicide.

First there is the mother-in-law's conception of what she is doing, handing over means and property to both her children and Verloc (a 'sensible union with that excellent husband', p. 156). But the cabbie who comes to fetch her resembles a gargoyle ('His enormous and unwashed countenance flamed red in the muddy stretch of the street' p. 157). The journey itself down Whitehall seems to cause 'time itself . . . to stand still' (p. 157). And for Stevie, it is the whip on the horse which arouses his excitation – the cabbie having dilated into a Devil, with the boy as his spell-bound victim. Yet as they wend their way through London as a City of Dreadful Night ('dirty', 'noisy', 'hopeless', 'rowdy', p. 159), the old lady is moved to tears at the thought of Mr Verloc's 'excellence' (p. 159), his role of family protector. She could not be more adrift, however generous her instincts.

When, finally, the 'night cabby' (p. 165) whose 'decayed clothing' (p. 164) and diatribe on being cold and hungry, without a fare, and beset by drunks, has worked his way on the impressionable Stevie, it is the completion of a journey by 'the Cab of Death' (p. 167). London, literal London, is without a doubt all to hand. But through Stevie we are encouraged to see it as also the Infernal City, whose surfaces hide pain, grief, compromise, and tragedy. It is this dislocation that he registers when the cabman arouses his 'dread' (p. 164) at the thought of the horse's being lame and of what it involves to sit looking for fares until two in the morning. Nor does Stevie fail to note that the cabman touches him with an 'iron hook' which protrudes from 'a ragged, greasy sleeve' (p. 164). The cabman, too, invokes his put-upon wife and four children, summarising his predicament with the phrase 'This ain't an easy world' (p. 165). The journey, the horse, the cabman and his family, and the loss of his own mother understandably all compete for primacy in Stevie's 'sensations' (p. 165). He utters the one gloss – 'Bad! Bad!' (p. 165). It speaks worlds.

Stevie's broken words, his instinctive vocabulary of dislocation, do not stop there however. 'Poor brute' (p. 168) he says of the horse to his sister. 'Poor! Poor!' (p. 168), he repeats as he and Winnie deposit their mother. His staccato utterances so build one upon the other than they resemble a chorus, a set of antistrophes. Whatever may posture as the myth of a benign 'condition of

England', for Stevie its condition lies rather in hurt and poverty. The paradox of his flawed but consummate articulacy adds even greater emphasis to the point:

> The docile Stevie went along; but now he went along without pride, shamblingly, and muttering half words, and even words that would have been whole if they had not been made up of halves that did not belong to each other. It was as though he had been trying to fit all the words he could remember to his sentiments in order to get some sort of corresponding idea. And, as a matter of fact, he got it at last. He hung back to utter it at once. 'Bad world for poor people.'   (p. 168)

'Halves that did not belong to each other' applies in the immediate instance to Stevie's speech habits. But it equally applies to the world at large of *The Secret Agent*. The Verlocs have married only to lead emotionally separate lives. In turn, the politicos, whether establishment or anarchist, as much split one against the other as across the political divide. Sir Ethelred works at a distance from his Assistant Commissioner as does he in his turn from his Chief Inspector. London itself may give the semblance of a hub of empire, of an England for ever unitedly and contentedly England, but it harbours great recesses of human aloneness and alienation. Stevie's words once again indicate a human order more dislocated than joined in any communal purpose.

Winnie's decline and fall stretches across the four final chapters of the novel, beginning from her 'acute pang of loneliness' (p. 173) at her mother's action. She hears the 'lonely' clock tick towards 'the abyss of eternity' (p. 175) and then as she and Verloc lie side by side puts out the light, the perfect accompanying act for the darkness between them. Verloc goes off to the Continent, would-be top spy as ever, returning so Conrad's mock-heroic imagery asks us to believe like an Odysseus to his Penelope (p. 176). The emphasis falls, calculatedly, all upon Verloc's doings, *his* importance, *his* view of his wife as marital property, *his* interview with Heat, and *his* estimate of Vladimir as 'Hypoborean swine' (p. 198). But Conrad, at every turn, has us respond to Winnie's silent reaction – and more than anything to her contemplation of the unspeakable literal destruction of Stevie. She bears witness to the label from the coat, and even more, to the image of Stevie as a body exploded into shreds. Heat's description appals:

'Blown to small bits: limbs, gravel, clothing, bones, splinters –
all mixed up together. I tell you they had to fetch a shovel to
gather him up with.'   (p. 196)

She reacts as one made catatonic, 'immobile' (p. 198). And as if to
stress even more her retreat from Verloc, from Brett Street, from
all thought of past marriage, from life, she is left only with the
mock-glimmer of her wedding ring (p. 198). She has become the
very figure of dislocation, a woman who has both sold herself
short and been sold short by those about her.

Verloc, meantime, continues in his own sublime egoism. 'I didn't
mean any harm to come to the boy' (p. 211), he tells her as if Stevie
had been merely injured or exposed to some passing ailment. His
ever more expressing 'apology' in not taking better care contrasts
magnificently with her refusal to use words. The imagery offers
its own ironic commentary: the carving knife and fork which Verloc
uses to eat the cold beef and bread; the 'prison' which Verloc
thinks will be his home for a while; the Brett Street parlour as a
'cage'; and Winnie's swelling perception that 'freedom' lies in
plunging the knife into her husband's body. The more her grim,
lost and infinitely sad recognition grows, the more Verloc talks
on – of his pride in being a part of 'every murdering plot for the
last eleven years' (p. 217), of his own outrage at the inconvenience
of Stevie's death, of his own powers to woo and bed Winnie. The
gap becomes grotesque, black. And in knifing Verloc she becomes
not only a widow, but a parody of the solicitous wife gazing upon
her beloved.

As she flees, the bell clattering a last fateful time, she encounters
Ossipon. Conrad's description again stresses dislocation, a world
turned from feeling into unfeeling:

Winnie Verloc turning about held him by both arms, facing him
under the falling mist in the darkness and solitude of Brett Place,
in which all sounds of life seemed lost as if in a triangular
well of asphalt and bricks, of blind houses and unfeeling
stones.   (p. 244)

No more than Verloc can Ossipon grasp what has passed through
Winnie, her sheer trauma both as Stevie's sister and unexpected
avenger. It falls to him, too, to offer a last dislocated picture of
Verloc, the fallen prince of spies:

Night, the inevitable reward of men's faithful labours on this earth, night had fallen on Mr. Verloc, the tried revolutionist – 'one of the old lot' – the humble guardian of society; the invaluable secret agent Δ of Baron Stott-Wartenheim's dispatches; a servant of law and order, faithful, trusted, accurate, admirable, with perhaps one single amiable weakness: the idealistic belief in being loved for himself. (p. 252)

Winnie knows better. But her fear of the fourteen-foot drop in being hanged, her hysteria, unmans even the robust Ossipon. In a supreme parody of the lover's leap, he jumps from the train as it leaves the station, a womaniser mocked and the inheritor, as may be, of Verloc's cash but not of his wife. Only the waters of the English Channel await Winnie, her last night-time dislocation completed. Our parting shot in *The Secret Agent* almost inevitably has to be of The Professor, his thoughts turned to 'images of ruin and destruction' (p. 269), in all 'like a pest' (p. 269). Conrad so bequeaths one final turn of the screw, one final and enduring image of a dislocated world.

'Spy thriller', then, offers a point of departure, a starting-place. But no reading of *The Secret Agent* can comfortably rest there. For Conrad's purposes throughout are indubitably darker, more full of indictment. If 'espionage' really applies, it is as a metaphor for Conrad himself: that of the author-exile spying upon the society which at once so beckoned and infuriated him. In its own way, it might best be thought a parody of 'England, Their England'. Who, after all, and with a subtler animus, more subverts the myth of a one-nation England, an England content in its own workings? Conrad's novel offers a dissenting view, and such is the greatness of its art, to no one's easy contentment.

NOTES

1. Joseph Conrad: *The Secret Agent* (Harmondsworth: Penguin, 1963). Reprinted as a Penguin Classic, 1986, 1987, 1988. p. 41. All page references are to this edition.

   I am indebted to a number of major studies of Conrad in writing this article, but the following more so than others: F. R. Leavis, *The Great Tradition* (London: Chatto & Windus, 1948); Irving Howe, *Politics and the Novel* (Cleveland, Ohio: Meridian Books, 1957); E. M. Tillyard, 'The Secret Agent Reconsidered', *Essays in Criticism*, vol. XI, no. 3, July 1961, pp. 309–18; Leo Gurko, *Joseph Conrad: Giant in Exile* (New York: Macmillan, 1962); H. M. Daleski, *Joseph Conrad: The Way of Dispossession* (London: Faber and Faber, 1977); Jacques Berthoud, *Joseph Conrad: The Major Phase* (Cambridge University Press, 1978); and Daniel R. Schwarz; *Conrad: Almayer's Folly to Under Western Eyes* (London: Macmillan, 1980).

2. Frederick R. Karl and Laurence Davies (Eds): *The Collected Letters of Joseph Conrad*, vol. 3, 1903–1907 (Cambridge University Press, 1988). Conrad to R. B. Cunninghame Graham, 7 October 1907, p.491.

3

The Adventure of Spying : Erskine Childers's *The Riddle of the Sands*

DAVID SEED

In 1903 Smith, Elder & Company issued a novel which immediately caught the reviewers' attention as a strikingly unusual narrative. It recounted the experience of two young Englishmen cruising in a yacht around the East Frisian Islands who stumble on a secret rehearsal of an invasion of Britain. The *Daily Telegraph* proclaimed that 'the special merit of the book lies in the graphic presentation of the little yacht's adventures among the dangerous shallows'.[1] 'Adventures' is a key term for understanding the nature of this novel for *The Riddle of the Sands* draws extensively on its author's earlier reading and experiences. One of Erskine Childers's first attempts at narrative concerns a bicycle tour which he made of Ireland in 1889. Childers's exhilarated evocation of 'vigorous physical exercise' leads to a Keatsian withdrawal from the mundane present : 'then may a man drink deep of a sparkling, giddying Lethe, then may he leave the grosser things of earth, and mingle his being with etherial elements'.[2] Slight as it is, Childers's description established two contrasting poles to his sensitivity : the enjoyment of physical action, and his romantic fascination with the historical and mythical associations of the landscape. Action did not necessarily come easily to Childers for when the Boer War broke out he wrote to his sister : 'normally alas, I am an idle man on the whole . . . and I feel this is a chance of useful action'.[3] He subsequently recorded his experiences (*In the Ranks of the C.I.V.*, 1900) in a diary-narrative which concentrates on the day-by-day movements of Childers's section rather than on broad political analysis.[4] His detailed recording of engagements with the enemy and traversing the South African interior represented necessary apprentice-work before Childers came to compose his novel which also briefly adopts a diary method.

The world of this novel is essentially one of male physical endeavour (as we shall see, the one female character represents an irrelevant distraction from the central plot) and male camaraderie implicity supported by such institutions as Oxford University (the two protagonists are old college friends), the navy – whether British or German, and London clubland. Even the fact that a yacht is used in the novel's action has its institutional dimension. In 1909 and 1910 Childers contributed a series of articles on yachting to *The Times* where he praised the Royal Cruising Club for organising and encouraging a desire for adventure at sea, a desire further encouraged by popular narratives of sea travel some of which appear in the library of the yacht *Dulcibella*.[5] Childers himself was a keen sailor and *The Riddle of the Sands* draws constantly on voyages he made during the 1890s in his yacht *Vixen*.[6] In the letters he wrote home while on holiday in France and Italy Childers generalised the desire for physical exertion into a national characteristic, one which might be pursued to the point of eccentricity, and a British reputation for wilful imprudence serves Childers's two protagonists well as a mask against the prying eyes of German officialdom when they are exploring the north-west Frisian coast. Around the beginning of the century Childers became a member of a rambling club called the Sunday Tramps which included among its members John Buchan. There is no direct evidence that the two writers knew each other but Buchan's own beginnings as a writer are suggestively similar to those of Childers. In the title essay to a collection of pieces published in 1896, *Scholar-Gypsies*, Buchan sketches out an opposition between town life and rural hiking. The countryside is presented as a place of mental and physical renewal which puts the man abroad in touch with a literary or mythical past : 'he begins to feel the . . . joy of living that the old Greeks felt . . . he goes on his way with a healthy clarity of mind'.[7] For Buchan, the visible token of hiking's literary associations is the pocket edition of his favourite writer which is an essential part of every hiker's equipment.

Buchan's essay makes an excellent gloss on the first section of Childers's novel but before this can be demonstrated we need to consider the contrast between the novel's two protagonists. Childers presents himself as the editor of *The Riddle of the Sands*, simply mediating between the reader and the protagonists' own accounts. The narrator proper is Carruthers, an employee of the Foreign Office, a landsman, a 'peevish dandy' (as he later describes himself) and a worldly-wise aesthete.[8] The owner and sailor of the *Dulcibella* (named after Childers's sister and modelled on Childers's own yacht) is Davies, a failed candidate for the navy. The two characters are established in the opening chapters as extreme opposites. Where Carruthers is finicky and hesitant, Davies is straightforward and direct; where the one prides himself on a certain sophistication, the other is so simple that his naïveté seems childlike. In the manuscript of the novel Childers went to considerable lengths to stress these contrasts, so that when Davies starts expounding his theories of maritime strategy the narrator patronisingly reflects : 'the boy was dominant : but I had had fugitive glimpses of the man : I seemed to listening to the hot-headed vagaries of youth: his very manner of talking on his pet subject of navies and naval war reminded me of a school-boy enlarging on his stamps . . . '[9] Carruthers's reaction is premature because one of the main developments in the first section of the novel (Chapters 1–9) is that he (and therefore the reader) comes to take Davies seriously. In a variation of the autobiographical fallacy it has been suggested that Davies rather than Carruthers is based on Childers himself, but this naïve search for correspondence ignores the possibility of fictional characters being the projections of different facets of an author's personality.[10] Childers's most sophisticated biographer Andrew Boyle has demonstrated that the former was not only a politician but also a 'thwarted poet with a romantic vision', concluding that his protagonists represent the 'two contradictory halves of his own complex self'.[11] Davies represents the man of action, in brief; Carruthers the observer, commentator, and therefore becomes a particularly self-conscious narrator. It is he accordingly who draws literary parallels, seasoning his narrative with quotation (from 'Dover Beach', for instance).

The opening chapter of *The Riddle of the Sands* not only introduces the character of the narrator but functions as a springboard to the main action. Carruthers like Ishmael at the beginning of *Moby Dick* is stagnating (in the doldrums of London out of season) ineffectually searching for anything which might vary the monotony of his routine. The external agent turns out to be a letter from Davies inviting him to his yacht. Departure thus characterises this chapter, departure for a new place, and departure from the humdrum. In this respect Childers is working within the generic pattern of the adventure which regularly detaches itself from the normal run of experience with a preliminary section where the hero sets off from home or at least from the familiar. At the beginning of *Treasure Island* Jim Hawkins's home life is irreversibly disturbed by the arrival of alien figures who ultimately lead him to undertake a sea journey; Kipling's Kim must leave his father and Lahore behind before he can experience the adventures of the Grand Trunk Road; and Huckleberry Finn similarly must light out from the Widow Douglas's oppressive piety before he can risk a journey down the Mississippi. Similarly John Buchan uses country houses in *Greenmantle* and *The Three Hostages* and the small town of Kirkcaple in *Prester John* as points of departure for his main narratives. In all these cases it is implied, however briefly, that the adventures to come are qualitatively different from the routine operating at the beginning of these narratives. The difference might be underlined by sheer geographical distance, by transporting the hero to the South Seas for instance, or variations might be woven on the pattern. Carruthers tries to realise Stevenson's *New Arabian Nights* which transposes romantic adventure onto the London scene, but finds that he is no Prince Florizel and that a muggy East End music-hall completely fails to live up to his literary expectations. It seems that Carruthers's experiences confirm Clennell Wilkinson's generalisation that 'any adventure in Cochin-China is grist for our mill, but one in the Old Kent Road is not'.[12] In fact Childers steers between these extremes of the exotically remote and the familiarly prosaic by locating his novel in an unfamiliar area of the North Sea coast which is nevertheless comparatively close to England. Unfamiliarity and proximity combine to produce a narrative of adventures which have repeated relevance to the domestic politics of Britain.

Carruthers's unsuccessful foray into Soho implicitly warns the reader not to expect romantic glamour in the ensuing narrative but ironically leaves him totally unprepared for his experiences on board the *Dulcibella*. The establishing of the novel's central subject – the discovery of Germany's secret military plans – can only be achieved through the erosion of Carruthers's dandyish assumptions about yachting. The comedy of these early chapters thus revolves around collisions between his preconceived images and the actuality. The following lines are typical (Davies has just suggested lunch): 'a vision of iced drinks, tempting salads, white

napery, and an attentive steward mocked me with past recollections'.[13] A set of references to Cowes, the Broads, Boulter's Lock,
etc. and a series of images similar to that quoted distance the kind
of yachting pursued by Davies from a fair-weather sailing associated
with holidays and full crews. The local humour of Carruthers's
recollections falling flat as he grovels in the bilge of the *Dulcibella* for
beer grows out of the chronological gap between his retrospective
recollections and his behaviour at the time in these chapters; quite
literally he has no role on the yacht beyond that of passenger.
Bracing plunges into the Baltic physically refresh him but – much
more importantly – wash away the hostile moods associated with
urban monotony. As exercise improves Carruthers's fitness these
moods are externalised into absurd self-images which he casts off
and at the same time his respect for Davies's seamanship grows.
The latter is crucial to the novel. If the reader doubts Davies's
sailing skills he will also doubt the facts of the narrative since the
former become evidence in the hypotheses of espionage.

 The Riddle of the Sands is a layered novel with narrators within
narrators. Childers functions as the editor of Carruthers's account
and Carruthers in turn channels the story told him by Davies of
an earlier cruise. The dimension of palimpsest now becomes quite
complex, including Childers's own log-books from the *Vixen*, and
E. F. Knight's *The 'Falcon' on the Baltic* (1889). Childers explicitly
writes over the latter text (which appears in the *Dulcibella's* library)
which describes a yachting cruise to Copenhagen. Knight, like
Davies after him, explores the canals of Holland and the East
Frisian Islands, noting: 'the indications on my chart were entirely
misleading . . . for the sands on this coast are constantly shifting'.[14]
The inadequacy of British charts is no mere detail in Childers's novel
but is woven into the central political and narrative implications of
the work. Once Davies reached the Frisian islands an encounter
with one Captain Dollman, as it transpires a former member of
the British navy and now a German agent, almost leads to his
death. Carruthers's essential function at this point is to assess
Davies's story, to perform the role of a sceptical reader. In
informational terms this section of the novel thus anticipates the
subsequent sequence of action in progressing from partial details
delivered reluctantly by Davies through his log-book (another of
the texts which proliferate in this work) which has a crucial page
missing, to his final total explanation.

 It should be obvious by now that the novel shares another

characteristic of adventure narratives, namely their firm structural demarcation. In contrast with Carruthers's previous life in London which is a mere continuity, the voyage of the *Dulcibella* and therefore the structure of the novel breaks into four main phases, each with a clear beginning and end: the first concludes with Carruthers's decision to follow Davies in his quest to ascertain the true identity of Dollman; the second section (Chapters 10–13) is transitional and takes the protagonists from the Baltic coast to Frisia via the Kiel Canal; the third (Chapters 14–20) opens their engagement with German antagonists; the final section focuses on the mystery of Memmert Island, the confrontation with Dollman and the solution of the riddle. Within these broad sections Childers exploits very firm chapter breaks so that each chapter more or less corresponds with an episode or extended passage of analysis. Childers constantly reminds us of a structure taking place through Carruthers's realisations of new beginnings (with the arrival of Davies's letter; or with their passage through the Kiel Canal which opens a 'new act'), with increasing references to the denouement or crises as the narrative tempo increases, or through the separation of the voyage into separate sections introduced by the necessity of taking on fresh supplies.

The shift from the first to the second section in the novel is the most radical since it alters both the terrain to be traversed and the means of examining it. Take, for instance, the following description of Ekken Sound on the east coast of Schleswig: 'cottages bordered either side, some overhanging the very water, some connecting with it by a rickety wooden staircase or a miniature landing-stage. Creepers and roses rioted over the walls and tiny porches' (p. 54). In general the descriptions of sights on the Baltic coast (where the voyage proper begins) stress the picturesque which Carruthers appreciates at leisure. By contrast the Frisian coast has literally to be read with the help of maps. Childers originally planned to include a whole series of maps with the novel but in the event only two maps and two charts were printed. Partly this confirms E. F. Knight's impression that British (that is Admiralty) charts were inadequate; partly it is necessitated by the unfamiliarity of the location. Like Carruthers the reader has to *read* the landscape with the help of these charts (Carruthers travels armed with a Bradshaw, Baedeker and later an ordnance map of the district). The change comes with the Kiel Canal: 'for two days we travelled slowly up the mighty waterway that is the strategic link between the two seas of Germany. Broad and straight, massively embanked, lit by electricity at night till it is lighter than many a great London street; . . . it is a symbol of the new and mighty force which, controlled by the genius of statesmen and engineers, is thrusting the empire irresistibly forward to the goal of maritime greatness' (p. 117). From roughly this point onwards Carruthers and Davies are constantly examining the Frisian coastline for channels which might serve as waterways to vessels with a shallow draught. They are looking for potential means of communication and the Kiel Canal performs a symbolic role in the novel as the main strategic (and therefore military) waterway between the Baltic and the North Sea. The comparison with a street is not decorative but rather an analogy which alerts the reader to potential functions within the landscape.

Two main areas are covered in this novel which draw on the respective skills of Carruthers and Davies: the Frisian coast and its hinterland. Once the narrator's resistance to the discomforts of yachting has been disposed of Childers no longer plays one protagonist off against the other, but instead has the skills of one complement the skills of the other. The Frisian coast has the physical peculiarity of seeming featureless to the ignorant eye while the falling tide actually exposes range upon range of sand-flats. Davies's sailing skills are drawn on to impose a geography on the area between the islands and the mainland. Apart from its obvious visual difference from the Baltic this area even seems to possess its own harsh climate, rendered all the more dangerous by the smallness of the *Dulcibella*. In his essay 'On Desert Islands' Walter de la Mare complains that the modern means of travelling have really removed the possibility of physical risk and therefore of adventure: 'we stay at home . . . and dabble in physical extremes at second hand. . . . Our adventures are less . . . of the body than of the mind and imagination. . . .'[15] *The Riddle of the Sands* juxtaposes these modern means of transport (train, steamboat, etc.) with the vulnerability of the yacht before the North Sea storms which confront the two Englishmen before political opponents. And yet although Childers dramatises the danger of the North Sea he never allows it to remain a purely physical one. In Chapter 12 particularly the coast becomes the locus for a struggle between rival forces which again and again take on political undertones. The wind becomes a predator; the sea an 'insolent invader' of the 'strongholds' of sand; the flapping of sails against a mast is like the 'rattle of a Maxim gun'. These analogies perform an agile tactical function in relating the coast to the German war effort, confirming its strategic importance which is made explicit elsewhere in the novel.

If Davies is the sailor, Carruthers is the landsman of the novel. In the final section he explores the Frisian hinterland alone looking for signs of expansion in the canal system and interconnections between those canals, the railway and channels leading to the coast. He himself is conscious of the change that Davies has wrought in him: 'yesterday I paid no heed to the landscape; today I neglected nothing that could conceivably supply a hint' (p. 281). Accordingly he notes that appearance of a torpedo boat in the Emden canal without spelling out its military significance. This is unnecessary because by now in the novel the reader has grown accustomed to spotting details which have an actual or potential strategic meaning. The group of officials with whom Dollman is collaborating have given out for public consumption the story that they are engaged in salvage work off the island of Memmert in the Ems estuary and the two Englishmen row some twelve miles through thick fog to ascertain the truth. This journey involves a race against time since they must return before the fog lifts, and totally dislocates Carruthers's sense of reality:

> Once we were both of us out in the slime tugging at the dinghy's sides; then in again, blundering on. I found the fog bemusing, lost all idea of time and space, and felt like a senseless marionette kicking and jerking to mad music without tune or time' (p. 229).[16]

In the novel's storm sequences we have already seen the two characters pitting themselves against the elements. Now the urgency of their journey makes their slow progress through the fog seem interminable and Childers brilliantly captures their moment-by-moment need to improvise and adjust their movements to changing circumstances, confirming Clennell Wilkinson's assertion that a true adventure must include 'physical danger; some pitting of oneself alone against the fates'.[17] Similarly in an article which appeared in the Christmas 1926 issue of *John O'London's Weekly* John Buchan defined the genre of the adventure story as a 'rapid, close-textured narrative in which the bulk of the incidents involve physical violence and peril'.[18]

The episode in the fog dramatises the two protagonists' need to rely on their own physical resources and, even more important for the suspense of the novel, also their willingness to take risks. The journey is a calculated gamble which only just pays off. Similarly during a dinner with Dollman and his associates (in a chapter appropriately entitled 'Finesse') Carruthers exploits the analogy with bridge by telling the Germans directly that he wants to see Memmert. This deliberate provocation, a way of bringing their story under pressure, pays off but Carruthers is well aware of how precariously he is riding good fortune. As long as the two men are in German waters they cannot be safe.

One particular example of risk-taking sheds a general light on the actions of the two Englishmen. When Carruthers conceals himself aboard a German tug he reflects that there was no 'empty apple-barrel' (p. 299). This allusion to romantic fiction appears to contrast romance with actuality but Childers has ingeniously woven elements of Stevenson's novel into his own narrative. Buried treaure, for instance, is the ostensible goal of the Memmert salvage works.[19] The references to Stevenson (to *Kidnapped* as well as *Treasure Island*) suggest that Carruthers is haunted by the possibility of romance in the pursuit of what he calls their 'perilous quest'. In the 1926 article quoted earlier Buchan divides the modern adventure-genre into two broad categories: romances which exploit the extraordinary and those works which are 'at immense pains to give verisimilitude by a multitude of concrete details.' Into the first class he places *Treasure Island*, and in the second *The Riddle of the Sands* which he describes as the 'best story of adventure published in the last quarter of a century'.[20] Childers has in effect combined two different modes within the same work but although Carruthers repeatedly applies the epithet 'quixotic' to their undertaking this does not serve as a means of mocking romance out of existence so much as a wry recognition of how their quest might strike a more level-headed reader. Their decision to hazard all in the pursuit of Dollman is explained as follows: 'if it imparted into our adventure a strain of crazy chivalry more suited to knights-errant of the Middle Ages than to sober modern youths – well, thank Heaven, I was not too sober, and still young enough to snatch at that fancy with an ardour of imagination, if not of character' (p. 215). By describing them as latter-day Galahads Carruthers is making explicit that they are gentlemen adventurers pursuing their course of action, with a firm set of values (honour, generosity to one's opponent, etc.) and its own codified and severely dated vocabulary of 'blackguard' and 'lilylivered cur'. Simultaneously pursuing and undermining romantic postures Carruthers and Davies identify themselves as what John G. Cawelti calls 'one of us' heroes, whose flaws and unglamorous style encourage the reader's identification with them.[21] This identification involves not only the success of the narrative but also the creation of an implicit feeling of national solidarity against potential German foes.

Childers's evocation of adventure is thus cautious but it also matches every characteristic identified by George Simmel who argues that the adventure is a 'form of experiencing'. Simmel stresses that the adventure takes place outside the normal run of experience, possessing a sharp beginning and end. The adventurer is an ahistorical individual (almost an existentialist *avant la lettre*) living in the present (for example the immediacy of the storm-sequences or fog journey in *The Riddle of the Sands*) and drawing on his youth to take risks. In fact the gambler is for Simmel one type of the adventurer (e.g. Carruthers's finesse). Self-reliance is crucial : 'the adventurer relies to some extent on his own strength, but above all on his own luck; more properly, on a peculiarly undifferentiated unity of the two. Strength, of which he is certain, and luck, of which he is uncertain, subjectively combine into a sense of certainty'.[22] The other sequence which for Simmel typically exemplifies the adventure is the love affair and here we must mention the least successful area of Childers's novel: a supposed romantic involvement between Davies and Dollman's daughter. The requirement of a love-interest was imposed by Childers's publisher Reginald Smith and Childers made a virtue of necessity by using the daughter to help confirm Dollman's identity. Essentially, though, she had no role to play in the book and creates the difficulty of reducing the two Englishmen to embarrassed silence when much of the novel consists of a free exchange of information and opinion between the two. Some of the reviewers were equally embarrassed and the *Times Literary Supplement* complained that the presence of the daughter outraged our sense of plausibility: 'the Germans . . . are a practical people, and would not permit a professional traitor to drag a pretty daughter about through his muddy courses'.[23]

A throw-away reference to Sherlock Holmes by Childers's narrator suggests that his novel is actually straddling two genres – the tale of adventure and the story of detection. This fact would help to explain the amateur status of the two protagonists who work for Britain but independently of any official British organisation. As with yachting Childers is careful to distinguish his own protagonists from a ludicrously stylised image of the spy as 'one of those romantic gentlemen that one reads of in sixpenny magazines, with a Kodak in his tie-pin, a sketch-book in the lining of his coat, and a selection of disguises in his hand luggage' (p. 103). One way in which Childers establishes such a distinction is by concentrating the reader's attention on the terrain (from Chapter 10 onwards) rather than on individuals. Just as Davies explains its importance to Carruthers so Carruthers in turn addresses the reader directly inviting him or her to draw analogies : 'follow the parallel of a war on land . . . See, too, how the strong invader can only conquer his elusive antagonists by learning their methods . . . ' (p. 144). This injunction to engage in analysis ushers in the sections of the novel dealing with espionage which alternate periods of action with passages of commentary where provisional hypotheses are put forward, revised and revised again. Attention focuses constantly on what the protagonists experience or suspect, i.e. grows *from* them, and is regularly reinforced by the vocabulary of 'clues', 'links' and of course the riddle in the novel's title. The mystery generated transforms the shifting sands of the Frisian coast into a metaphor of the novel's central but elusive subject. Accordingly the actions of following a course and of resisting distracting cross-currents, while retaining their physical status, also enact the protagonists' search for truth.

The last passage quoted above exemplifies a self-consciousness in the novel's narrative which proves to consist of a running dialogue with the inferred scepticism of the reader. Partly this involves Childers's narrator in making his effects explicit. It is not enough for adventures to happen; they must be named as such. Equally it is not enough for Carruthers to describe an unusual effect of lights falling on Dollman's face to distort it towards the demonic; he must assume a reader's resistance to the effect: 'accuse me, if you will, of stooping to melodramatic embroidery' (p. 249). To a certain extent such narrative gestures enable Carruthers to smuggle elements of melodrama or romance into his account without compromising its realism. At the same time his ingratiating references to the 'indulgent reader' anticipate the impressions which his narrative might make. The most important area where this scepticism is incorporated is the developing analysis of the facts relating to Dollman. Here dialogue becomes positively constructive, as for instance in the possibility that the salvage work at Memmert was genuine and therefore Dollman's efforts to lure Davies to his death false:

> . . . to accept the suggestions we must declare the whole quest a mare's nest from beginning to end; the attempt on Davies a delusion of his own fancy, the whole structure we had built on it, baseless.
>
> 'Well', I can hear the reader saying, 'why not? You, at any rate, were always a little sceptical.'
>
> Granted: yet I can truthfully say I scarcely faltered for a moment.   (p. 250)

This projected reader is no more than the externalised voice of Carruthers's own scepticism which never quite disappears until the mystery is finally solved. The thrust of a tale of detection is regularly to make a pattern manifest and, as we shall see, it is not until very late in the novel that the pieces fall into place.

Before this happens Carruthers and Davies have to deal with fragments and hints, glimpses of what might be happening on the Frisian islands. Even the smallest discrepancies (a sailor wearing shoes, for instance) become charged with possible meaning. A gap widens between things seen and their significance and between the surface and latent meaning of dialogue. When the two protagonists meet von Bruning, the commander of the gunboat patrolling that coast, polite questions about their movements mask what is in effect an interrogation. That is countered by a different mask of naïveté worn by Carruthers and Davies who promote the fiction that they are simply looking for good duck-shooting. The element of theatre reaches its peak when the two men go for dinner at Dollman's house. The guests grouped around the table all wear their different disguises: 'roughly divided though we were into separate camps, no two of us were wholly at one. Each wore a mask in the grand imposture' (p. 270). The novel as a whole deals increasingly in masks since it starts out with a description of tourism. The tourism in turn is transformed into a means of disguise long before Carruthers physically dons the clothes of a sailor. The language of covert military combat ('weapons', 'sapper', etc.) at times shades into the composition of political miniatures. So when the two protagonists return from Memmert they find German 'invaders' on 'English soil' (the

Dulcibella) and Carruthers's opponents at Dollman's dinner-table become the 'triple alliance'. These implicit analogies remind the reader of the political status involved in such an apparently slight action, broadening signification away from mere individuals. The same function is performed by the identification of antagonists in a 'war of wits' which glances at Sherlock Holmes's struggles with Moriarty but which also looks forward to le Carré's opposition between Smiley and Karla where contrasting political systems stand behind each figure. Davies's personal opponent is Dollman, repeatedly associated (as befits a traitor) with Satan and 'devil's work'. Carruthers, however, takes the engineer Bohme as his antagonist: 'Bohme was *my* abstraction, the fortress whose foundations we were sapping, the embodiment of that systematized force which is congenital to the German people' (p. 271). Just as the Kiel Canal functions as a topographical synecdoche so Bohme personifies the organised engineering which is central to Germany's war effort. Germany as a whole is figured as a huge machine whose sheer scale and efficiency induces respect but which must be resisted at all costs.

When *The Riddle of the Sands* was published the *Courier* complained: 'it is difficult to say how much of Mr. Childers's present work is fiction and how much fact'.[24] Childers himself seemed to clear up this uncertainty when he wrote to his friend Basil William : 'as a fact I invented the whole thing, building it, though on careful observations of my own on the German coast, but I have since had the most remarkable confirmation of the ideas in it'.[25] Two issues blur together here: the specific plausibility of a German plan to invade Britain from the Frisian coast and the general historical dimension to the novel. Essentially the novel is predictive, building on the evidence of Germany's economic and military expansion since the Franco-Prussian War to hypothesise a possible invasion. In fact the First Lord of the Admiralty was so impressed by the details of the novel that he immediately ordered a secret study of the plan's feasibility; and recent research in the German military archives has shown that, unbeknown to Childers, just such a plan was indeed under consideration at the time.[26]

Childers's sharpest divergence from the adventure formula was to incorporate countless details into his novel which define a specific historical moment in the expansion of the German canal system and the growth of the Imperial navy. Childers sidesteps the contradiction of condemning German imperialism while condoning that of Britain by passing no judgement on the wider moral issue.

It was only later in the decade that he began to examine the ethics of colonisation, declaring himself a supporter of Irish home rule in 1908. In the novel Germany has to be opposed for reasons of practical necessity, so that neither Britain's naval supremacy nor her home counties are threatened. The pivotal moment of realis-ation comes when Carruthers identifies the course being followed by the tug and lighter as heading for England: 'I was assisting at an experimental rehearsal of a great scene, to be enacted, perhaps, in the near future – a scene when multitudes of sea-going lighters, carrying full loads of soldiers, not half loads of coals, should issue simultaneously, in seven ordered fleets, from seven shallow outlets, and, under escort of the Imperial Navy, traverse the North Sea and throw themselves bodily upon English shores' (p. 304). This recognition involves a rapid revision of his theory's premise from defence to offence. The narrative tactic which Childers uses again and again throughout the novel is to direct the reader from the fiction to a strategic possibility within the landscape itself so that acceptance of a codified, mapped out terrain leads easily to the acceptance of the hypothesis of invasion.

The Riddle of the Sands belongs among the invasion fantasies of *The Battle of Dorking* (1871), Saki's *When William Came* (1913), and *The War of the Worlds* (1898) with the difference that its point of view is physically located within Germany looking towards England.[27] When Carruthers overhears the conspirators talking on Memmert he can only catch fragments of information, which summarised in miniature the partial nature of the novel's narrative. Once the picture is completed the reviewer in the *Guardian* noted that 'Mr. Childers throws aside the veil of fiction', but in fact the narrative recedes abruptly into a framing fiction introduced in the preface that the 'facts' discovered by Carruthers and Davies have been communicated to the proper authorities without effect.[28] Publication thus becomes a means of warning the British public at large, as in *The Battle of Dorking*, of the inadequacy of their civil defence. The narrative's completion demonstrates its expendability. Carruthers and Davies quite simply cease to exist as the text revises itself from realistic narrative to the 'transcription' of a secret memorandum to the German government summarising the exact procedure to be followed in the invasion. From being one kind of document the novel attempts to place itself within a context of official reports and memos so as to open up an avenue for its own political consequences.

NOTES

1. 'Notes and Reviews', *Daily Telegraph* (5 June 1903) p. 11.
2. 'Ride Across Ireland', in Maldwin Drummond, *The Riddle* (London: Nautical Books, 1985) pp. 204–5. This study gives an invaluable account of the novel's historical context.
3. MS letter of 2 January 1900. Trinity College, Dublin, MSS. I am grateful for financial assistance from the British Academy which made it possible to consult these manuscripts.
4. Childers also wrote (with Basil Williams) an account of the Honourable Artillery Company in South Africa which was published in 1903.
5. The three books named in the text are Edward Frederick Knight's *The 'Falcon' on the Baltic* (1889), Frank Cooper's *Sailing Tours* (1892–6), and Richard Turrell Macmullen's *Down Channel* (1869, revised 1893). Childers also acknowledges a debt to Kipling and to C. J. Cutcliffe Hyne, author of the Captain Kettle novels.
6. V. Hugh and Robin Popham, *A Thirst for the Sea: The Sailing Adventures of Erskine Childers* (London: Stanford Maritime, 1979). Chapter 4 documents in detail how *The Riddle of the Sands* draws on the log of the *Vixen*.
7. John Buchan, *Scholar-Gipsies* (London: Bodley Head, 1927) pp. 16–17.
8. The narrator is probably modelled partly on Rudolf Rassendyll, the narrator-protagonist of Anthony Hope's *The Prisoner of Zenda* which Childers read during his Baltic voyage in the *Vixen*.
9. 'The Riddle of the Sands', p. 193. Trinity College, Dublin, MSS.
10. Drummond p. 147.
11. Andrew Boyle, *The Riddle of Erskine Childers* (London: Hutchinson, 1977) pp. 61, 110.
12. Clennell Wilkinson, *The English Adventurers* (London: Longmans, Green, 1931) p. 3.
13. *The Riddle of the Sands*, forwd. by Geoffrey Household (Harmondsworth: Penguin, 1978) p. 55. Subsequent page-references incorporated into text.
14. E. F. Knight, *The 'Falcon' on the Baltic* (London: W. H. Allen, 1889) p. 146. The development of the German canal system and of Wilhelmshaven as a naval base only receives brief glances from Knight but assumes major importance in Childers's novel.
15. Walter de la Mare, *Stories, Essays and Poems* (London: J. M. Dent (Everyman's Library), 1938) p. 357.
16. In *The Adventures of Huckleberry Finn* fog becomes a crucial complicating factor in the river journey and in the relationship between Huck and Jim.
17. Wilkinson, p. 4.
18. John Buchan, 'Adventure Stories', *John O'London's Weekly* (4 December 1926) p. 274.
19. Similarly the position of Long John Silver, the cunning antagonist, might be compared with that of Dollman in so far as the former changes sides. The reference to *Treasure Island* could even implicitly 'revise' the mutiny of the *Hispaniola's* crew into a betrayal of the ship

    of state, i.e. into a reversal with political implications.
20. Buchan 'Adventure Stories', pp. 274–6.
21. John G. Cawelti, *Adventure, Mystery, and Suspense* (Chicago: University of Chicago Press, 1976) p. 40.
22. Georg Simmel, 'The Adventure', in Kurt H. Wolff, ed., *Essays on Sociology, Philosopy and Aesthetics* (New York: Harper, 1965) p. 250.
23. 'Fiction', *Times Literary Supplement* (14 August 1903) p. 242.
24. Drummond, p. 144.
25. Boyle, p. 113.
26. V. Drummond and also Paul Kennedy, 'The Riddle of the Sands', *The Times* (3 January 1981) p. 7.
27. This context is examined in detail by I. F. Clarke, *Voices Prophesying War 1763–1984* (Oxford University Press, 1966) and Bernard Bergonzi, 'Before 1914: Writers and the Threat of War', *Critical Quarterly* 6. ii (1964) pp. 126–34.
28. 'Will Germany Invade Us?' *Guardian* (21 October 1903) p. 1577.

4

The Hunter and the Hunted: The Suspense Novels of John Buchan

DENNIS BUTTS

All of us in the last War had moments when we felt the stable universe dissolving about us. We were like pilgrims who, journeying on a road to an assured and desirable goal, suddenly found themselves on the edge of a precipice with nothing beyond but a great void. The common way of describing such moods was to say that our civilisation had become insecure and was in danger of perishing.

(John Buchan, *Memory-Hold-the-Door*, p. 279)[1]

'By God!' he whispered, drawing his breath in sharply, 'it is all pure Rider Haggard and Conan Doyle.'

(John Buchan, *The Thirty-Nine Steps*, p. 51)[2]

Whatever claims can be made for the influence of his fellow-countrymen Scott and Stevenson upon Buchan's literary work, there can be no doubt that the immediate influence on his earliest suspense stories, especially *The Thirty-Nine Steps* (1915) and *The Power-House* (1916), are those of Erskine Childers, William Le Queux and E. P. Oppenheim. Indeed, while on a cruise to the Azores in June 1913, Buchan himself described how he was proposing to amuse himself by 'writing a real shocker – a tribute at the shrine of my master in fiction – E. Phillips Oppenheim – the greatest Jewish writer since Isaiah.'[3] The resulting story, *The Power-House*, was first published in *Blackwood's* magazine in December 1913, a date which suggests that Buchan's early work at any rate shared to some degree in that unease verging on paranoia about the fear of foreign invasion and of civilisation's overthrow which swept through Britain in the last decades of the nineteenth century, stimulated initially by the Franco-Prussian War of 1870–1.

The first and clearest expression of Britain's anxiety about invasion by some foreign power was the pamphlet *The Battle of Dorking*, published in 1871, where the narrator describes to his grandchildren at some date in an imaginary future how England was attacked by Prussians who swept aside Britain's unprepared forces and forced her to surrender. The pamphlet caused a sensation and was republished many times, inspiring what Brian Aldiss has called the 'Dreadful Warnings' novel.[4] William Le Queux (1864–1927) was one of the most prolific exponents of the genre, specialising in stories which prophesied foreign invasion, such as *The Great War in England in 1897*, which was first published in 1894, and reached a ninth edition by 1895. But this account of the way French and Russian armies invaded Britain is barely a novel, however, for most of the book is taken up with lengthy and detailed descriptions of military tactics as Birmingham, Manchester and Edinburgh are captured in rapid succession before the tide is eventually turned. A more recognisable novel, *England's Peril*, of 1899, is a romantic spy story in which Irma, the beautiful heroine, is blackmailed into revealing England's defence secrets by an unscrupulous French spy. Fortunately her lover, who is himself accused of being the spy at one point, is able to rescue Irma and, with the assistance of the British Secret Service, saves the plans and defeats the French spy.[5]

E. P. Oppenheim (1866–1946) was as passionately concerned about the state of Britain as Le Queux was, and in the years before the Great War began, in his own words, 'what was almost a crusade against the menace of German militarism.'[6] In his novel *The Secret* of 1907, for example, the hero, Hardcourt Courage, a gentleman and county cricketer, is approached for help by a stranger who reveals that he is a famous British spy, and entrusts a secret involving British security to him before dying. Gradually, and with the help of disguise, the hero uncovers a German conspiracy to invade Britain while the fleet is away on a courtesy visit overseas. But the plot is foiled by the amateur agent, and so the crisis is averted and Britain saved.

By far the best and best-known example of this genre before Buchan is, of course, *The Riddle of the Sands* (1903) by Erskine Childers. The story of how two young Englishmen stumble across German exercises for the invasion of Britain, while they are on a boating holiday among the Frisian Islands, contains a vivid account of sailing a small boat in the North Sea, and the relationship between the two heroes, the grumpy Carruthers and the more romantic Davies, is particularly well observed. By beginning slowly and lingering over so much apparently unnecessary detail, the story achieves a hard-won authenticity which makes the discovery of the German invasion-plans, the riddle of the sands, all the more powerful as the story reaches its climax. By now we are able to identify some recurring features of the rapidly-growing genre, the use of an amateur agent, the accidental discovery of a mystery, the gradual discovery of the mystery's serious implications, and the hero's ultimate defeat of the conspiracy.

John Buchan's professional career, quite apart from his literary taste, would seem to have destined him to write this kind of fiction. Born in Perth in 1875 into a Calvinist household, the eldest son of a Free Church minister, he was educated at Glasgow University and Oxford, where he had a distinguished academic career as well as publishing several books while still a student. He was called to the bar in 1901 but Lord Milner, the High Commissioner, invited him to join his staff in South Africa, and he soon became deeply involved in administrative duties following the Boer War. On his return to England, Buchan joined the publishing firm of Nelson, but continued to write and was also adopted as a parliamentary candidate for the Unionist Party, but his health began to suffer, and when the war started in 1914 he was actually unfit for active service. (It was while he was ill in bed in fact that he wrote *The Thirty-Nine Steps* during the first months of the war.) *The Times* newspaper invited Buchan to visit the Western Front as its special correspondent early in 1915, and in October he returned to France as a lieutenant in the Intelligence Corps to report the battle of Loos. While working for the War Office and often visiting the Front, he continued to write, and when Lloyd George became Prime Minister in 1917, Buchan was appointed Director of Information, responsible directly to the Prime Minister. The Department's work presented Buchan with many problems, but it also gave him the opportunity to see the war at very close quarters, and he met a great variety of people from ordinary soldiers to top generals, and from secret service agents to members of the War Cabinet.[7] When the war ended, he bought a manor house at Elsfield, near Oxford, and continued to write and work in publishing as well as holding many important public offices. He was Member of Parliament for the Scottish Universities from 1927–35, when he was invited to become Governor-General of Canada and made Lord Tweedsmuir. He helped to organise King George VI's successful visit to Canada in 1939, and later in the year signed Canada's Declaration of War against Nazi Germany. But his health, never very good, continued to decline, and he died after a stroke in February 1940.[8]

Altogether John Buchan wrote over sixty books, including historical romances, biographies, a history of the Great War, and collections of essays and short stories. But well regarded though some of the other works were, it is the suspense stories in general, and the Hannay books in particular, which have commanded the greatest interest. The combined sales of the Hannay books published by Hodder and Stoughton, and by Nelson, up to 1960 averaged 258,000 copies in Britain alone, with *Greenmantle* the most popular, selling 368,000 copies. In paperbacks published by Pan and Penguin Books from 1952 onwards *The Thirty-Nine Steps* sold 670,000 copies and *Greenmantle* 330,000 copies up to 1965 only. (By comparison Buchan's well-received biography of *Sir Walter Scott* had sold 47,000 copies by 1960.)[9]

There are five full-length books about Richard Hannay – *The Thirty-Nine Steps* (1915), *Greenmantle* (1916), *Mr Standfast* (1919), *The Three Hostages* (1924), and *The Island of Sheep* (1936); and Hannay also makes brief appearances in *The Runagates Club* (1928) and *The Courts of the Morning* (1929).

Hannay makes his first appearance in *The Thirty-Nine Steps*. He is a wealthy Scot from Bulawayo, bored with his London holiday, until Scudder, an American journalist, asks for his help, and reveals that he has discovered an international plot to assassinate the visiting Greek Prime Minister. When Scudder is then murdered, Hannay, believing that he will be accused of the crime by the police but also that the murderers will hunt him as well, escapes to Scotland. There he manages to decipher the journalist's notebook and discovers that, though there is a plan to assassinate the visiting Prime Minister, that is only part of an international plot to steal the secrets about the disposition of the British Home Fleet and then to attack Britain. Evading the pursuits of the police and the murderers by a series of disguises and improvisations, Hannay succeeds in having the conspirators arrested as they leave England from a house near Broadstairs, which is identified because it has thirty-nine steps down to the sea.

Greenmantle finds Hannay now a Major convalescing during the Great War. Sir Walter Bullivant of the Foreign Office tells him that the Islamic peoples of the Middle East are preparing a holy war against the Allies. Hannay decodes a note left by a dying British agent, and then with the help of Sandy Arbuthnot, an aristocratic adventurer, an elderly American Blenkiron, and an old African big-game hunter Peter Pienaar, travels across Germany in a variety of disguises. The group enter Turkey, where they foil the German plot to ferment the holy war, and help the Russian cavalry to crush the Turkish army at the battle of Erzerum.

Mr Standfast shows Hannay, now a General, summoned from his brigade in France to do more intelligence work in Britain. Working with Blenkiron and Peter Pienaar again, Hannay gradually uncovers a German spy-ring masterminded by Moxon Ivery, ostensibly an academic pacifist, but really the German agent von Schwabing. Hannay pursues him through France, Italy and Switzerland to his final capture and the defeat of the German army's advance.

The Three Hostages finds Hannay after the war. Now over forty and married with a small son, he is living the life of a country gentleman until he is approached with a request to help find three recently-kidnapped hostages. By brilliantly deciphering a piece of verse, Hannay's suspicions fall on Dominick Medina, a well-known MP and public figure. Gradually, with the help of his old friend Sandy Arbuthnot, Hannay uncovers Medina's conspiracy to use the kidnappings as part of an attempt to destabilise society generally. The hostages are rescued, and Medina falls to his death when attempting to kill Hannay high up in the Scottish mountains.

Hannay's final appearance is in *The Island of Sheep*, when he responds to an urgent plea for help from Valdemar Haraldsen, the son of an old Danish friend, who is being pursued by a gang of criminals in search of his father's fortune. In a final desperate battle, on Haraldsen's Island of Sheep in the far north, the conspirators led by D'Ingraville almost overcome Haraldsen and his protectors before Hannay's fourteen-year-old son Peter John comes to the rescue with the help of a host of islanders who are out on a gigantic whale-hunt.

The broad characteristics of Buchan's stories about Hannay are clear, and have been well discussed by such critics as J. Randolph Cox, David Daniell, Graham Greene and Richard Usborne.[10] We are in the world of the modern romance, the kind of suspense story which Buchan himself called the 'shocker'. Here, as he said in the Dedicatory Letter to *The Thirty-Nine Steps*, 'the incidents defy the probabilities, and march just inside the borders of the possible'. (p. 9)[11] But whatever he found in the novels of Scott and Stevenson, Oppenheim and Le Queux, Buchan took them and made them his own, through his unique combination of plot and characters, and his imaginative creation of an apparently authentic world.

The plots of John Buchan's novels depend to an enormous degree upon the intrusion into the apparently safe and familiar world, usually of upper middle-class England, of an unexpected event which disturbs and threatens its security. The Russian critic Yu. K. Scheglov has pointed to the manner in which Conan Doyle's stories about Sherlock Holmes brilliantly and often simultaneously combine the two opposite principles of adventure and security, in the way, for example, such crimes as those associated with the Hound of the Baskervilles penetrate the domestic comforts of 221B Baker Street.[12] Buchan's story-telling works in a very similar fashion. Who can forget the way a bored Hannay, returning from an evening at the music hall to his flat behind Langham Place is approached by an American journalist with his tale of an assassination-plot? Who can forget that moment when the hunted victim appeals for help to an elderly gentleman with a face like Mr Pickwick's, and suddenly realises that he has walked straight into the enemy's headquarters? It is the nature of the genre that coincidences should be possible, and Buchan does not fail to exploit the opportunity.

There are two other characteristics of Buchan's plots which are worth mentioning at this point. The first is the way he introduces a coded message or mystery of some kind early on in the story, the solution to which has an important bearing on the subsequent main plot, and which Hannay usually manages to solve. Thus in *The Thirty-Nine Steps* he manages to decipher Scudder's notebook and even eventually to solve the meaning of the enigmatic reference to 'Thirty-nine steps, I counted them – high tide 10.17 p.m.,' (p. 58)[13] and in *Greenmantle* to explain the puzzling references to 'Kasredin,' 'cancer' and v.I.' (p. 11).[14] Of course, the device of introducing three apparently unrelated phrases, and then telling a story which shows how they are all closely connected, could be artificial. Buchan himself pokes fun at his use of the device, through Dr Greenslade's ironical explanation of how it works in *The Three Hostages*:

'Let us take three things a long way apart – ' He paused for a second to consider – 'say, an old blind woman spinning in the Western Highlands, a barn in a Norwegian *saeter*, and a little curiosity shop in North London kept by a Jew with a dyed beard. Not much connection between the three? You invent a connection – simple enough if you have any imagination, and you weave all three into the yarn. The reader, who knows nothing about them at the start, is puzzled and intrigued and, if the story is well arranged, finally satisfied. He is pleased with the ingenuity of the solution, for he doesn't realise that the author fixed upon the solution first, and then invented a problem to suit it.'   (p. 19)[15]

This is actually the most brilliant double-bluff on Buchan's part, for though he seems to be telling us that his use of three apparently unrelated objects is factitious, he then goes on a few pages later to show that Dr Greenslade's examples were far from arbitrary but sprang from his unconscious memory of a conversation with the villain which Hannay can then investigate further.

Indeed the way the search for an explanation of some apparently minor crime or mystery gradually widens into the discovery of a much greater danger is one of the most important aspects of Buchan's plots. Behind the irritating activities of a group of pacifists in *Mr Standfast* lies a German spy-ring working to destroy Britain's war effort; behind the projected assassination in *The Thirty-Nine Steps* is the plan to destroy the British fleet; and behind the kidnap-plot in *The Three Hostages* is the greater conspiracy to destabilise society and to threaten civilisation itself:

I think he wanted to win everything that civilisation would give him, and then wreck it, for his hatred of Britain was only a part of his hatred of all that men hold in love and repute. The common anarchist was a fool to him, for the cities and temples of the whole earth were not sufficient sacrifice to appease his vanity. I knew now what a Goth and a Hun meant, and what had been the temper of scourges like Attila and Timour.   (p. 351)[16]

Thus Buchan's plots in the end often turn on the discovery that the minor mystery, which Hannay is called upon to cope with, is actually the key to a much greater problem, involving much greater dangers. And though Buchan, like all his generation, was deeply affected by the suffering caused by the Great War, the evil he was most profoundly worried about went beyond even that to the horror and anarchy he felt was always beneath our civilisation, however secure we feel ourselves to be. As early as *The Power-House*, written in 1913, before the war, Buchan said, 'You think that a wall as solid as the earth separates civilisation from barbarism. I tell you the division is a thread, a pane of glass. A touch here, a push there, and you bring back the reign of Saturn.' (pp. 211–12)[17]

Fortunately Hannay and his companions are well able to cope. Hannay, the mining engineer from Rhodesia, as narrator has to be suitably modest, but, while making no pretensions to being an intellectual, he is in fact brilliant at solving indecipherable codes, and, though always stressing how afraid he is, a superb master of improvisations in moments of crisis, and well able to carry off the occasional disguise as milkman or barge-engineer. Though apparently largely based upon a genuine military hero, Lieutenant (later General) Edmund Ironside, whom Buchan first met in Africa, Hannay is in fact essentially an amateur, not a professional agent, who, almost against his will, gets caught up in a world of intrigue and bizarre circumstances.[18] It is, of course, Hannay's suggestion of normal, almost banal, pipe-smoking decency which helps to heighten the sense of danger which lies lurking beneath the surface of familiar surrounding.

In *The Thirty-Nine Steps* Hannay is pretty well on his own, but in *Greenmantle* his other companions gradually come together – Sandy Arbuthnot, the aristocratic Scottish adventurer, Blenkiron, the elderly American businessman, and Peter Pienaar, an old big-game hunter friend from Africa. The character of Blenkiron, the least obviously heroic because least athletic of protagonists, enables Buchan to pay tribute to the importance of stamina as well as intelligence in his heroes, for Blenkiron keeps going somehow despite suffering from the duodenal ulcer that plagued Buchan most of his life. Peter Pienaar demonstrates the rough, resourceful, disreputable kind of virtue Buchan always admired. Though his drunkenness almost gives the game away to the Germans in *Greenmantle*, he dies a self-sacrificial death in *Mr Standfast*, when Hannay actually compares him with Bunyan's Mr Valiant-for-Truth. Sandy Arbuthnot is, however, Hannay's most memorable companion. Younger son of an ancient house, skilled in many languages and an absolute master of disguise, he is an inveterate traveller and explorer, who has wandered far and wide through the Middle East and Central Asia. When Greenmantle, the Arab prophet of the holy war, dies, it is Sandy whom the Germans plan to use as his most convincing substitute, and when Hannay is outwitted at the end of *The Three Hostages*, it is Sandy who, disguised as the Indian guru Kharama, comes to his rescue with characteristic, Bertie-Woosterish insouciance. Yet readers who find him completely preposterous have to be reminded that much, if not all, of Sandy's character and adventures are based upon Buchan's Oxford contemporary, Aubrey Herbert, who before the war had travelled extensively in Albania, Greece and Turkey – he was actually offered the throne of Albania twice! During the war, as well as helping to negotiate a truce between the Turks and the Allies in 1915, he travelled with Lawrence of Arabia to Mesopotamia to try to negotiate the release of a besieged garrison in 1916. It was he, almost certainly, who told Buchan of the rumours foretelling a general rising of Islam against the Allies, which is the inspiration behind the plot of *Greenmantle*, and when Herbert died in 1923, Buchan said he mourned 'the possessor of the most powerful combination of tenderness and daring that he had ever known'.[19]

Helped as he was then by his education and social opportunities, Buchan realised the world of his novels with remarkable completeness. 'The backgrounds to many of us may not be sympathetic, but they are elaborately worked in', as Graham Greene reminds us.[20] Buchan etches in each character with a few details about his school, his club, what his regiment did in the war; and each scene carries with it authenticating details, whether Buchan is describing a dinner-party, a meeting of the Defence Committee, a journey through wartime France, or an account of deer-stalking in Scotland, for all are the fruits of real experience.

And yet, as Graham Greene hints, the values and the assumptions apparently underlying Buchan's world are not altogether comfortable ones, and his work has been criticised for its snobbery, its worship of success and its racism. It is certainly true that Buchan's characters usually, if not always, come from the upper classes. A dinner-party in a Buchan novel is always likely to contain a leading financier, an outstanding sportsman, a legal expert, an explorer just back from South America, and one or two cabinet ministers. But such characters are not obsessed by success; they have already achieved a certain status in society and that gives them access to the kinds of adventures Buchan was interested in. And though Buchan perhaps refers a little too frequently to regimental associations, he is also sympathetic to such unexpected 'outsiders' as a Scottish road-mender or a German railway-engineer.

Many readers find Buchan's references to Negroes and Jews offensive, and the books are indeed sprinkled with such words as 'niggers' or such phrases as Scudder's contemptuous remark about 'a little white-faced Jew' (p. 17).[21] Though it is possible to argue that some of these references are dramatically appropriate – it is Scudder speaking in the last example, not Buchan – one surely has to accept what Gertrude Himmelfarb has said on the topic:

> The familiar racist sentiments of Buchan, Kipling, even Conrad, were a reflection of a common attitude. They were descriptive, not prescriptive; not an incitement to novel political action, but an attempt to express differences of culture and colour in terms that had been unquestioned for generations.[22]

We have, in other words, to adopt a historical perspective when considering Buchan's attitude to race, and one can always point to Buchan's admiration for such Jews as Chaim Weizmann, his sympathy for the suffering German families in *Greenmantle*, and his recognition of the negro Laputa's heroism in *Prester John* (1910).[23]

As with Buchan's treatment of Laputa, however, there is nearly always a marked ambivalence in Buchan's treatment of his villains, and an investigation of this, together with an examination of the formal structure of his plots, suggests that Buchan's work possesses a greater complexity than it has sometimes been given credit for.

In most of the Richard Hannay novels, Buchan fuses many of the elements of the adventure story, with its use of the initial catastrophe, the journey, and the combat, with the suspense novel, with its emphasis on a mystery and its solution. But whereas the whodunit, following Todorov's suggestive essay on 'The Typology of Detective Fiction', concentrates on the crime and its investigation, the suspense story retains that element but refuses to reduce the investigation to simple detection. 'The reader is interested not only by what has happened but also by what will happen next; he wonders as much about the future as the past . . . there is the curiosity to learn how past events are to be explained, and there is also the suspense: what will happen to the main characters?'[24]

Thus, in Buchan's stories the reader is impelled to ask not only what the reference to the thirty-nine steps means, or why the three

hostages have been kidnapped, but also to ask what will happen
to Hannay and his companions as they pursue their dangerous
investigations. And Buchan turns the screw of his suspense stories
still further by his use of what can be called the double-journey
structure. For as Hannay sets out on his journey to investigate the
mystery as a kind of amateur detective, so he in turn is followed
by pursuers who try to prevent him. As Hannay sets out to find
out just what Moxon Ivery is up to in *Mr Standfast*, so forces are at
work to obstruct and kill him. In *The Thirty-Nine Steps* Hannay is
actually believed to be a murderer himself, and so he is pursued
by the police as well as by the villains, as he sets about his
investigations, and this may be what gives that book its particular
force. But in every book, with the possible exception of *The Island
of Sheep*, the structure of the plot places the hero in between two
journeys, his own to solve a mystery, and the villains' to prevent
his success. Richard Hannay is thus usually in the dual role of an
investigating detective and a pursued victim, both hunter and
hunted.

Now when we examine the nature of the villains in Buchan's
novels, we find a similar kind of dualism present. They are villains,
of course, and must be fought at every turn – the Black Stone
in *The Thirty-Nine Steps*, von Stumm and Hilda von Einem in
Greenmantle, von Schwabing (alias Moxon Ivery) in *Mr Standfast*,
Medina in *The Three Hostages*, and D'Ingraville in *The Island of Sheep*.
They are scheming, ruthless, murderous fanatics, who would, in
their different ways, not only defeat England and its assumed
values of democracy and decency, but in many cases are actually
trying to bring down the whole edifice of civilisation. They are all,
in Alan Sandison's words, 'deeply hostile to established society
and all have plans for its overthrow'.[25] The Black Stone may be
intent on destroying the British fleet, but Hilda von Einem has 'the
simplicity of the madman that grinds down all the contrivances of
civilisation', (p. 207) and Medina 'wanted to win everything that
civilisation would give him and then wreck it, for his hatred of
England was only a part of his hatred of all that most men hold in
love and repute' (p. 351).[26]

Yet all, or almost all, Buchan's villains are people of immense
gifts, not only subtle organisers and skilful plotters, but dedicated,
heroic, often charismatic personalities. Hilda von Einem may be 'a
devil incarnate, but she has the soul of a Napoleon,' says Sandy
(p. 205).[27] Medina is not only a wicked conspirator but also a

politician, first-class sportsman, fine classical scholar and poet with gifts of genius. Even Black Stone, for all his attempted treachery, finally wins Hannay's grudging admiration – 'This man was more than a spy; in his foul way he had been a patriot' (p. 170).[28]

Buchan's villains are then 'false Lucifers,' to borrow David Daniell's phrase; people with immense gifts who have lost their way. Both Daniell and Coleman O. Parsons attribute Buchan's awareness of this combination of heavenly and diabolic elements in the human soul to his Calvinist upbringing, but whatever the origins, Buchan's development of the theme in his suspense stories gives them rather more complexity than those of his predecessors with their more stereotyped villains.[29]

And though many of Buchan's enemies are not British – Laputa is African and von Einem German – it is not too fanciful to suggest that Buchan became increasingly aware that these villains, far from simply being external threats, represent dangers in the very middle of our society, and that they share many of the qualities of his heroes. Thus the arch-plotters in *Prester John* and *Greenmantle* are foreigners, but the threat is much nearer home in *The Power-House* and *The Thirty-Nine Steps*, while the dangers in *Mr Standfast* come not only from the pseudo-Englishman Moxon Ivery, but also from his genuinely British associates.

This sense that evil is not only present in the very heart of society, but that villainy and virtue are often very close to each other, is a theme that recurs in Buchan's work. There is an extremely interesting analysis of a genius who is lost but then reclaimed by humanity in the portrait of Castor, the political leader, in *The Courts of the Morning* of 1929. But the most powerful expression of the theme is found in *The Three Hostages*, where Sir Richard Hannay, war hero, country gentleman, patriot supreme, finds himself instantly drawn to Dominick Medina, the brilliant and fascinating villain. Though Hannay never falls under Medina's spell completely, he almost succumbs to it, and in the closing chapters of the novel they come very close to each other indeed. For Hannay realises that Medina intends to take revenge for his defeat by hunting Hannay down and murdering him on the Scottish mountains, and his response is very confused. 'I don't think that I wanted to kill him,' he says, 'but indeed I never tried to analyse my feelings' (p. 417). Clambering up the rocks, Medina manages to wound Hannay, but finds himself in acute danger as the cliff-face begins to crumble around him. Then Hannay realises that 'I seemed only to be watching a fellow-mountaineer in a quandary' (p. 444). At once he offers help and throws a rope down to Medina, and to his delight Medina accepts it. Tragedy soon follows, however, when the rope frays and Medina falls to his death, but for a moment he and Hannay were united both physically and in trust, hero and villain together.[30]

It is an impressive moment, and though Buchan's work is not always at this level, there is enough evidence here and elsewhere to suggest that he possessed a more complex moral vision than the Manichean ideology of good and evil that is found in the James Bond novels, for example.[31] His narrative structure's use of situations where the hero is both hunter and hunted reinforces the dualism he evidently felt to be somewhere near the heart of human nature, particularly in his treatment of heroes and villains.

Buchan's literary craftsmanship unfortunately did not always live up to the subtlety of that vision. The initial crisis in his novels is usually intriguing, and the suggestion of anarchic forces lying just below the surface of humdrum things is nearly always telling. But the organisation of those forces, even in the hands of the 'fallen Lucifers', frequently suffers from being couched in vague melodrama. It is not the imaginative force of von Schwabing or Medina as symbols that one questions but the unconvincing nature of their organisations. Are the pacifist intellectuals of *Mr Standfast* quite the threat Buchan imagines? Would not an alert police force be able to cope with the petty thieves of *The Island of Sheep*? And would the kidnapping of three citizens, however, eminent their relations, quite bring down civilisation as we know it?

For, in the end, despite all his narrative gifts and attempt at a moral vision, Buchan gives the impression that it is all a game. It is a Great Game, of course, with all kinds of references to Patriotism and Honour and Evil, but a game nonetheless. Buchan had decided quite early on that literature 'should be my hobby, not my profession',[32] and it is a tribute to his undeniable gifts that he should have been able to create so individual a fictitious world that it should lend itself so readily to parody:

'Yes, but what is coincidence? There are forces outside the world of which we know next to nothing. Why did I meet Eric –' he pointed his pipe-stem at Sir Eric Chalmers Troope – 'Why did I meet Eric in Zerka when we were both supposed to be in Bigadich? Or what made Philip' (indicating Admiral Sir Philip

Delmode) 'suspect our Dutch friend Joos Vuyterswaelt?' We all laughed at the memory of the neat way in which the Admiral had outwitted the Roumanian Secret Service. And while we were still laughing, the squat little figure of Sandy Argyll, that astounding baker from Forfar, who had become a merchant adventurer and had helped to save the Queen of Holland from the Red Hand Society – that squat figure moved in a chair by the fire. 'Coincidence,' he said. 'Hm! Ask Graham to tell you about the hat that didn't fit'.[33]

NOTES

1. John Buchan, *Memory-Hold-the-Door* (London: Hodder & Stoughton, 1940) p. 279.
2. John Buchan, *The Thirty-Nine Steps and The Power-House* (London: Nelson, 1947) p. 51.
3. Quoted by Janet Adam Smith, *John Buchan: a Biography* (London: Hart-Davis, 1965) pp. 177–8.
4. Brian Aldiss, *Billion Year Spree: The History of Science Fiction* (London: Weidenfeld & Nicolson, 1973) pp. 100–2.
5. William Le Queux, *England's Peril: a Novel* (London: White, 1893).
6. E. Phillips Oppenheim, *The Pool of Memory: Memoirs of E. Phillips Oppenheim* (London: Hodder & Stoughton, 1941) pp. 27–8.
7. For a discussion of Buchan's possible involvement with the Secret Service, see Anthony Masters, *Literary Agents: The Novelist as Spy* (Oxford: Blackwell, 1987) pp. 15ff.
8. For much of this, see Janet Adam Smith, op. cit., but see also Janet Adam Smith, *John Buchan and his World* (London: Thames & Hudson, 1979); John Buchan, *Memory-Hold-the-Door*, op. cit.; William Buchan, *John Buchan: a Memoir*, (London: Buchan & Enright, 1982); and *John Buchan by his Wife and Friends*, with a preface by G. M. Trevelyan (London: Hodder & Stoughton, 1947).
9. These figures were taken from Smith, *John Buchan: a Biography*, op. cit., pp. 295–7.
10. See J. Randolph Cox, 'The Genie and his Pen: The Fiction of John Buchan,' *English Literature in Transition*, vol. 9, 1966; David Daniell, *The Interpreter's House: A Critical Assessment of the Work of John Buchan* (London: Nelson, 1975); Graham Greene, 'The Last Buchan,' *The Lost Childhood and other Essays* (London: Eyre & Spottiswoode, 1951); Gertrude Himmelfarb, 'John Buchan: An Untimely Appreciation', *Encounter*, London, September 1960; A. C. Turner, *Mr Buchan, Writer* (London: SCM Press, 1949); and Richard Usborne, *Clubland Heroes: a nostalgic study of some recurrent characters in the romantic fiction of Dornford Yates, John Buchan and Sapper* (London: Constable, 1953).
11. Buchan, *The Thirty-Nine Steps and The Power-House*, op. cit., p. 9.

12. Yu. K. Scheglov, 'Towards a Description of Detective Story Structure', *Russian Poetics in Translation*, translated by L. M. O'Toole (unpublished manuscript, 1975).

13. Buchan, *The Thirty-Nine Steps and The Power-House*, op. cit., p. 58.

14. John Buchan, *Greenmantle* (London: Hodder & Stoughton, 1947) p. 11.

15. John Buchan, *The Three Hostages* (London: Nelson, 1945) p. 19.

16. Buchan, *The Three Hostages*, op. cit., p. 351.

17. Buchan, *The Thirty-Nine Steps and The Power-House*, op. cit., pp. 211–12.

18. For Hannay's identification with General Ironside, see *inter alia*, Usborne, op. cit., pp. 90–1.

19. Masters, op. cit., pp. 25–7; see also Aubrey Herbert, *Ben Kedim; a record of Eastern Travel*, edited by D. MacCarthy (London: Hutchinson, 1924); Aubrey Herbert, *Mons, Anzac and Kut*, introduced by D. MacCarthy (London: Hutchinson, 1919); and Liddell Hart, *'T. E. Lawrence' in Arabia and After* (London: Cape, 1934).

20. Greene, op. cit., p. 104.

21. Buchan, *The Thirty-Nine Steps and The Power-House*, op. cit., p. 17.

22. Himmelfarb, op. cit., p. 49.

23. See Smith, op. cit., pp. 156–7; Buchan, *Greenmantle*, op. cit., pp. 108–9; Buchan, *Prester John* (London: Nelson, 1949) pp. 112–13.

24. T. Todorov, *The Poetics of Prose*, translated by Richard Howard, with a new foreword by Jonathan Culler (Oxford: Blackwell, 1977) pp. 50–1.

25. Alan Sandison, *The Wheel of Empire: A Study of the Imperial Idea in Some Late Nineteenth and Early Twentieth-Century Fiction* (London: Macmillan, 1967) p. 159.

26. Buchan, *Greenmantle*, op. cit., p. 207; Buchan, *The Three Hostages*, op. cit., p. 351.

27. Buchan, *Greenmantle*, op. cit., p. 205.

28. Buchan, *The Thirty-Nine Steps and The Power-House*, op. cit., p. 170.

29. Daniell, op. cit., pp. 123–31; Coleman O. Parsons, *Witchcraft and Demonology in Scott's Fiction with Chapters on the Supernatural in Scottish Literature* (London: Oliver & Boyd, 1964) pp. 316–18.

30. Buchan, *The Three Hostages*, op. cit., pp. 417 and 444.

31. See Umberto Eco, 'The Narrative Structure in Fleming', *The Bond Affair*, edited by Oreste del Buono and Umberto Eco, translated by R. A. Downie (London: MacDonald, 1966) pp. 59–62.

32. Smith, op. cit., p. 105.

33. 'The Queen of Minikoi,' by Jxhn Bxchxn, *Beachcomber: the Works of J. B. Morton*, edited by Richard Ingrams (London: Muller, 1974) pp. 261–2.

5

John Buchan: The Reader's Trap

MILES DONALD

John Buchan's fiction is, in a sense, a bundle of leanings. The comforting solidity of his fictional world – a world of moral certainties and a high degree of reader-security – paradoxically thrives on a combination of inconsistency, underdevelopment and contradiction. Examined closely Buchan's fiction is full of surprises. I shall attempt to show that one of the greatest of these is the manipulation of the reader. Put simply, Buchan develops a rhetoric of escape which persuades the reader to embrace and approve what would otherwise be rejected.

In order to clarify the context, a few preliminary words are necessary about Buchan both as a man and as an author. Brilliant classical student at Glasgow and then Oxford universities, Buchan went on to pursue enough careers for four or five men – and to pursue them all successfully. A colonial civil servant in South Africa (he had some harrowing experiences in the Boer War refugee camps), a journalist, a barrister, a publisher, a Member of Parliament, a soldier, a Director of Information during the First World War, High Commissioner to the General Assembly of the Church of Scotland, and finally Governor General of Canada – it is remarkable that he ever found time to write. Yet here too his energy was prodigious. He published five books while still at Oxford; although better known as a writer of fiction he wrote history, biography, autobiography and even (in 1905) an authoritative legal work *The Law Relating to the Taxation of Foreign Income*.[1] This was very useful. He earned a lot of foreign currency.

The range of Buchan's fiction is too wide to consider here. We shall draw only on a limited number of works which are representative of Buchan's fame as a writer of adventure stories or, as he deprecatingly called them, 'shockers'. These – *Prester John, Greenmantle, Mr Standfast, The Three Hostages* and *The Dancing*

Floor – address themselves to violence on a relatively major scale.[2] *Prester John* deals with colonial rebellion, *Greenmantle* and *Mr Standfast* with the First World War, *The Dancing Floor* with mob violence and ritual murder. Only *The Three Hostages* restricts itself to a less intense species of violence – that conspiracy of international master malefactors so generally beloved of the run of the mill thriller writer (although *The Three Hostages* does, via the thematic use of hypnosis, venture into the area of psychic violence). It is important to stress that these works are by their very settings less able to slip into the romantic cosiness with which Buchan elsewhere eludes the responsibilities of violence. For example, in the series beginning with *Huntingtower*, Dickson McCunn the romantic grocer (and as the description implies one of Buchan's more original characters) manages to dispense a quasi-parental, quasi-episcopal glow over everything from Bolshevism to Ruritania.[3] McCunn's youth pack of gutter sleuths, the Gorbals Die Hards, quickly and cleanly translates into sober middle class citizenship. The natural violence of the boys' upbringing is either quickly discarded or reworked into a socially acceptable outlet; thus at the opening of *Castle Gay* an ex-Die Hard, Jakie Gault, appears representing Scotland at rugby; he is permitted to cleanly knock down Antipodean tourists.[4] War and mob murder cannot be so easily tidied away.

A further point should be made about the representative choice of works. They are among those novels of Buchan recently republished in paperback; despite their chronological remoteness (published between 1910 and 1926) they plainly must offer the *modern* reader something. Yet, as we shall see there are a number of areas – race and sex are only two – which might very well cause the modern reader to anathematise Buchan. For that very reason *Prester John* et al. pose a particularly interesting critical problem. How does Buchan get away with it? Assuming that utter idleness can be discounted as an explanation, what is it that readers find in Buchan's writing which prevents them from attacking an author who, for example, richly praises the values of white South Africa? Why is the republication of his 'shockers' so unshocking? It is significant that in his recent extensive study *British Writers of the Thirties* Valentine Cunningham delivered an incisive and otherwise comprehensive account of popular fiction without a single mention of John Buchan. This is surprising.[5] Buchan's last novel *Sick Heart River* was published as late as 1941.[6] Also Cunningham frequently discusses works which, since they were published before the decade, affect its development. One would certainly expect Buchan's treatment of race to be of particular relevance. Perhaps though the omission suggests something else; that he is not as obvious as he seems, that he is difficult to pin down, that he does not quite fit in. In short that Buchan does somehow get away with it.

Let us be clear. Buchan's works are a social and psychological treasure trove. Here, as elsewhere, popular fiction frequently provides more cultural raw material than its 'literary' counterpart. However, this essay doesn't attempt a specific study of such material *per se* but rather uses it as a focus for Buchan's characteristic rhetorical approach, beginning with the vexed issue of racial prejudice in general and anti-semitism in particular.

> John Buchan has quite often been accused of anti-semitism. Such accusations have referred to certain slighting remarks about Jews which are to be found in his novels . . . there are only about half a dozen disobliging references to Jews in all of JB's many works of fiction. . . . And here, I think, JB has been the victim of his own style, and of a radical change in attitude to racial difference which he was never to live to know. He was guilty, for once, of thoughtlessness, of using a commonplace of his time without considering its implications.[7]

The language used there is hedging towards euphemism. 'Slighting' and 'disobliging' suggest a little local difficulty, a minor irritation, something over which sensible people would not make a fuss. Moreover the total of six such remarks in all Buchan's fiction is absurd; wherever the subject matter permits half a dozen instances *per novel* would be likelier, if a conservative, figure. Nevertheless the thrust of the argument is no weaker for being familiar. Things were different then; the Holocaust hadn't happened. And after all (the argument continues), Buchan had many Jewish friends including Chaim Weizmann, and his name was inscribed in Israel's Golden Book for his work for the Jewish National Fund. Well nobody is denying that John Buchan was to all intents and purposes a good man, nor suggesting that he was anti-semitic in life. But good men have written odd things before now. The conduct of a life and the conduct of a book are different matters. The features of a book cannot be told to go away, nor can they be seen differently simply because they do not fit what is apparently known about the author's life. At the same time Buchan is intentionally a decidedly moral novelist who values kindness, human decency and a sometimes surprising tolerance. An accusation of anti-semitism sits oddly with these qualities. It needs closer examination.

In truth the operation of anti-semitism is of greater *structural* interest in some of its less obvious manifestations; where a case can be made for its thorough placement in the texture of Buchan's fiction, its continual presence, its unavoidability. Even *Greenmantle*, a novel first published in 1916 and with consequently large racial fish to fry (the German and the Turkish enemies for a start) needs to employ the *automatic* assumption of Jewish inferiority. Here Sir Walter Bullivant, the British Secret Service Supremo delivers his Boy's Own version of Turkey's recent political development to the narrator/protagonist Richard Hannay: ' "You are an intelligent fellow, and you will ask how a Polish adventurer . . . and a collection of Jews and gypsies should have got control of a proud race" ' (p. 13).

Well Hannay isn't an intelligent fellow. There are no intelligent fellows in Buchan. If there were they would follow intelligent courses of action and begin to ask really searching questions about the author's plots, which would then disappear. Nevertheless Hannay is *supposed* to possess the authorial seal of approval indicating straight thinking and common sense. And clearly, therefore, one sign of intelligence, as the term is to be understood in Buchan-speak, is to recognise immediately the inferiority of Jews. Hannay knows their place and, as far as *Greenmantle* is concerned they have no fictional opportunity to alter it. Buchan, who is prepared to take the human risk of showing 'good' Germans during an actual World War, has no picture at all of the non-inferior Jew. It is moreover no argument to suggest that the presence of a favourable characterisation in one novel necessarily compensates for, or even cancels out, an unfavourable characterisation in another. Even if we wrongly assume that the portrayal of Jewish characters is plausibly positive in *A Prince of the Captivity* or *The Dancing Floor*, that does not mean that the negative comments – the *automatically* negative comments – of other novels are disposed of.[8]

The oddity is more marked when, in *The Three Hostages*, we encounter an abusively-described crowd of low grade criminal Jews who simply fictionally co-exist with a sensitive Jewish millionaire of impeccable breeding and philanthropic bent. The assimilation of the latter into the gentile upper class is not discussed but is surely signified by his daughter's engagement to the genial aristocratic war twerp, the Marquis de la Tour du Pin. The Marquis carries one of Buchan's ultimate guarantees of clean limbed honesty – he can box – and he is quick to use the Queensbury Rules on the (sometimes Jewish) criminal underworld. Yet there is no comment whatsoever on the racial or religious obstacles which his engagement must have faced. Nor is there any awareness that the author has two competing views of Jewry to resolve. Instead of a balanced portrayal we are simply offered positive and negative aspects which exist independently, without connection. If they were brought together, if an attempt to forge a connection was made, the reader might begin to be uneasily aware of problems that are too complex for Buchan's world and its characters to accommodate. As matters stand the division of Jewishness offers the reader the weird moral dubiety of being pro- and anti-semitic at different times in the same book.

The issue becomes more interesting when one senses Buchan's own uneasiness. This is especially evident in *The Dancing Floor* where the supposedly prosaic lawyer Leithen finds his imagination stretched by a succession of events of a decidedly mystical bent. He also makes friends with a Jew.

> 'There was nothing romantic about Ertzberger. I dare say he had the imaginative quickness of his race, but the dominant impression was of solid good sense. He looked at the thing from a business man's point of view, and the cold facts made him shudder.' (p. 87)

The implications of that statement are contrary. We might naturally think that imaginative quickness was a good thing; however it is to be ranked below phlegmatic British good sense. Ertzberger is a better Jew for being less Jewish. Also, when one realises that the cold facts in question involve a family curse, unspeakable sexual vilenesses (one wishes they were spoken) and the ritual sacrifice on an Aegean island of a prominent Virgin of the characters' joint acquaintance, it might reasonably be supposed that Ertzberger's imaginative quickness would constitute an appreciating fictional asset.

A few pages later and the situation is more acute for Leithen.

'If anyone had told me that I would one day go out of my way
to cultivate a little Jew financier, I would have given him the lie,
yet the truth is that . . . . . I hungered for Ertzberger's company.
He alone understood what was in my mind, and shared my
anxieties.'   (p. 107)

Note that Leithen's self-congratulation derives not from having
overcome or even understood his own anti-semitism but rather for
having condescendingly realised that an exception should be made
for Ertzberger. And of course making an exception is one way of
reinforcing the established type. Also, the very quality which
would have explained how Ertzberger could understand Leithen –
namely his imaginative quickness – has already been denied. A
not dissimilar denial is to be found in Ertzberger's marriage.

His wife was another matter. She was a large flamboyant
Belgian Jewess, a determined social climber and a patron of art
and music, who ran a salon and whose portraits were to be found
in every exhibition of the young school of painters.   (p. 83)

That does for her. Buchan's is a world of genial philistinism, where
no poet must be tainted by the 'modern' (as in Medina's case in
The Three Hostages). His idea of composition is a girl/boy figure
silhouetted against a nice wet grouse moor. Madame Ertzberger is
guilty of what Evie Wilcox called 'artistic beastliness'. More directly
to the point she has nothing in common with her husband
except for a marriage certificate. Leithen almost appears sorry for
Ertzberger because he is married to such a typically Jewish Jew!
As I suggested earlier, though anti-semitism remains an important subject in the consideration of Buchan's fiction, anti-semitism
is not *itself* the main point here. Critically speaking the main
issue is non-connection. Buchan sees no reason to face up to
contradictions or complexities when they can be evaded. In
ignoring, in not connecting the different aspects of Jewishness, he
absolves the reader from thinking something through, from making
a choice, from thinking. In fact he offers the reader an escape to
which he/she is not entitled. Furthermore, if that escape route is
not taken the very structure of Buchan's fiction is seriously
threatened. Like many exponents of popular fiction he relies

heavily on suppression – too much release, too many connections and audience gratification won't come half as easily.

Let us expand the discussion a little further into other aspects of race where, it has been argued, Buchan shows a breadth of humanity and vision – a surprisingly mature tolerance.

In this regard it is certainly true that *Greenmantle* ought to be remarkable. It appears to eschew propaganda and to sympathise in human terms with the enemy. This is true only to a limited and qualified extent, and is nowhere near as humanly generous as is sometimes suggested. Gaudian, the engineer first encountered in *Greenmantle* (he becomes Hannay's post-war friend and ally in *The Three Hostages*), is mostly seen as a clean and simple patriot, morally speaking the German equivalent of Hannay (a point which Hannay himself makes in *The Three Hostages*). Yet, even in the case of the good Gaudian we still have to encounter an element not of human weakness but rather of *inhumanity*: 'Then I realised something of the might of Germany. She produced good and bad, cads and gentlemen, but she could put a bit of the fanatic into them all'. (p. 68) Fanaticism is, of course, a very un-Hannaylike, un-British trait. Under the guise of sympathetic even-handedness the Germans are revealed as inferior in humanity. The reader is able both to congratulate him/herself on compassion for Germans and to enjoy taking a step on the road to dehumanising them.

No discussion of this kind can proceed without Hannay's famous fictional encounter with the Kaiser.

'I felt' [says Hannay] 'that I was looking on at a far bigger tragedy than any I had seen in action. Here was one that had loosed Hell, and the furies of Hell had got hold of him. He was no common man, for in his presence I felt an attraction which was not merely the mastery of one used to command. That would not have impressed me, for I had never owned a master. But here was a human being' (p. 75).

Yes, one sees that he is. That description is certainly superior Buchan. His imagination is genuinely fired and the result is at the very minimum a remarkable picture of the Chief Wartime Enemy of his country. Nevertheless all is not quite what it seems. Perhaps we may set aside as unduly cynical the fact that it is impolite to vilify a ruler who might well have played an important part in the post-war settlement of Europe, who was in any case first cousin to Britain's King (the Kaiser was, of course, Queen Victoria's grandchild) and therefore potentially less thoroughly and unfavourably *echt Deutsch*. Still it is worth pointing out that Hannay's reaction manages to employ the phrase 'no common man' without apparent irony. On the one hand Buchan/Hannay is impressed by the Kaiser's condescending majesty. On the other hand that same quality has led to the war and, if we are to take the references to hell at face value, to the Kaiser's damnation. Add it all up and the reader gets a thrill out of meeting a Royal together with the moral satisfaction of finding that he's damned. Once again (whether consciously or unconsciously this is very skilful on Buchan's part) the reader enjoys both experiences at a superficial level and *without connecting them*. After all once the grounds for the Kaiser's damnation have seriously sunk in (the responsibility for horrendous slaughter) it would be shameful to let him give you a snobbish thrill.

Before we leave the treatment of Germans we might notice how it illustrates a further curious feature of Buchan's narrative method. Less than thirty pages before his meeting with the Kaiser, Hannay (impersonating a Boer) is addressed thus by a German officer, one Captain Zorn:

> 'You must bow your stiff necks to discipline first. Discipline has been the weak point of you Boers, and you have suffered for it. You are no more a nation. In Germany we put discipline first and last, and therefore we will conquer the world. Off with you now.' . . . That fellow [Hannay says] gave me the best 'feel' of any German I had yet met. He was a white man and I could have worked with him. I liked his stiff chin and steady blue eyes. (pp. 46–7)

Whatever his taste in eyes and chins it isn't sufficient to explain how Hannay, who has never acknowledged a master in one part of the book, apparently derives such enthusiasm from overbearing masterliness in another. Yet the contradiction is ignored. Why? Perhaps so that the reader can enjoy a combination which can only be offered in fiction, which in life would be self-cancelling – the pleasure of both resisting a master and acquiescing to him.

Clearly then once inside Buchan's work the reader is manipulated in some surprising directions. It is interesting to consider how this process manifests itself in situations where Buchan does not wish to split up experiences which can be undergone separately but must, perforce, go for a resolution. *Prester John* provides a striking instance.

In it Buchan has created the epic black character, the Reverend John Laputa, who speedily metamorphoses into the great revolutionary leader who almost succeeds in uniting the various tribes of Southern Africa, assuming the monarchical inheritance of the fabled Prester John, and driving the white man into the sea. He is foiled by the narrator, the young Scots storekeeper Davy Crawfurd, an early example of what later develops into the Richard Hannay prototype – namely the ordinary man called forth by the author to perform extraordinary feats. Crawfurd admires Laputa and sees much in him that is great and admirable. (Otherwise it would be hard to see how he could make much headway in the substantial task of tribe uniting and Empire dismemberment.) Laputa's death is therefore described in a scene of considerable power and not a little beauty and is deliberately couched in high epic terms.

On the point of suicide Laputa first adapts the epitaph of the Emperor Charlemagne to the immediate needs of his own name and of his desire to achieve pan-Africanism. 'Under this stone is laid the body of John, the great and orthodox Emperor, who nobly enlarged the African realm, and for many years happily ruled the world' (p. 181).

Having raised the epic stakes he keeps them high by placing himself on a level with Shakespeare's Antony.

> 'No one will come after me and in a little while they will have forgotten my name. I alone could have saved them. Now they go the way of the rest, and the warriors of John become drudges and slaves.' . . . 'Unarm, Eros' he cried. 'The long day's task is done.' With the strange powers of a dying man he tore off his leopard skin and belt till he stood stark as the night when he had been crowned.   (p. 181)

There can be no doubt that Buchan wants the reader to record and respond to the grandeur of man and situation together. Laputa has chosen to die in terms of the two great epic figures of Western civilisation, and it might reasonably be thought that this process, if it does not exactly grant Laputa equal status with either Antony or Charlemagne, at least places him on their heroic epic scale. Yet considered more closely Laputa's mythic expropriations are decidedly inappropriate. Charlemagne's was a long and successful reign – Laputa's was abrupt and a failure. Charlemagne successfully defended Europe against African invasion – Laputa, confronted with the reverse problem, fails; he sees his people's future as slavery. And to touch on the ridiculous, Charlemagne was actually buried in a tomb, hence under a stone, while Laputa drowns himself. It begins to look as if Laputa's claim for epic company is presumptuous.

A slightly different form of inappropriateness applies to the use of *Antony and Cleopatra*. Antony is about to bungle his suicide – Laputa is not. Antony's downfall involved a woman (and a dusky one at that) – Laputa, who flaunts his physique often enough to make him seem like a denizen of some early colonial Muscle Beach, appears satisfied (and subsequently destroyed) by narcissism. David Crawfurd has absolutely nothing in common with Shakespeare's Eros. The only correspondence between the two scenes lies in the fact that they are both removing something dramatically – Antony his armour, Laputa the sacred collar of Prester John. Yet even here the comparison is a trifle forced; the verb 'unarm' must be artificially stretched to apply to the removal of a collar, no matter how sacred. Increasingly it seems as if the mythic comparisons actually *diminish* Laputa's epic grandeur; his use of Charlemagne and Antony is vainglorious, crude, barbaric, and for all Laputa's Westernised schooling, half-educated.

All of this is, I would suggest, a means to an end; a preparation for the absorption of Laputa into the controlled ideological resolution with which Buchan attempts to end the novel. The profits from a diamond mine discovered during the rebellion have now been used to establish 'A great native training college. It was no factory for making missionaries and black teachers but an institution of giving the Kaffirs the kind of training which fits them to be good citizens of the State' (p. 202). Well, one can be immediately certain that this is neither the sort of state nor the kind of citizen that Laputa had in mind! Yet, amazingly, he is to be incorporated into its mythopoeic framework.

> In front of the great hall of the college a statue stands, the figure of a black man shielding his eyes and looking out over the plains to the Rooirand. On the pedestal it is lettered 'Prester John' but the face is the face of Laputa. So the last of the kings of Africa does not lack his monument.   (p. 202)

Evidently not, but he would hardly want it. The white colonists have imposed the solution they desired and forced Laputa to look on in symbolic agreement – neutered into a purely ceremonial and conveniently post-mortem role. Yet the reader is supposed to have been lulled by Buchan into believing that everything is for the best. White society wins but sportingly acknowledges black grandeur just as long as it keeps out of the way and stands still on a plinth.

This is the resolution that does not resolve. It is, in fact, a victory disguised as an agreement – a rhetorically managed means by which the reader escapes from the bitterness, bloodshed and racial intractability which the life of Laputa actually stirred up.

One cannot leave this question of reader manipulation and false resolution without a brief consideration of perhaps the most awkward aspect of Buchan's fiction – the treatment of women. Relative brevity is possible because there is little dispute about their unsatisfactorily typical presentation. There are no points for recognising the obvious – Buchan's is a man's world and that fact is merely underscored by supplying a restricted number of restrictedly drawn women with pivotal plot roles (this is especially true if the plots themselves become subject to accusations of thinness). Females between puberty and the menopause are either evil sirens like Hilda von Einem in *Greenmantle*, the possessor of a thoroughly and therefore destructive sexuality – or squeaky-clean boy/girls, later permitted a mutation into motherhood, such as Hannay's Mary. This, at any rate, seems at first to be Buchan's actual intention. It would probably confirm the prejudices of his original readership; also his bifurcation of the female sex prevents his readership (once again) from having to encounter any odd or contradictory elements inside any one given woman.

Obviously to any extensive reader of Buchan there is considerable truth in that statement. At the same time it is not, as a statement, wholly true. Let me give a few examples, bearing in mind that they are narrated by Richard Hannay, who has somehow managed to anaesthetise himself against women.

'Women had never come much my way, and I know about as much of their ways as I know about the Chinese language. All my life I had lived with men only, and a rather rough crowd at that.' (p. 167)

All his life? Men *only*? Who, for example, had given birth to all the men? However, the exaggeration contained in that quotation is, nevertheless, very useful. While it doesn't in the least challenge Hannay's moral infallibility (he may make practical mistakes but he is never morally in the wrong), it does suggest that the portrayal of women will be clumsy, perhaps even rough and ready. At any rate the depiction of Hilda von Einem is interesting indeed.

> Her cool eyes searched me, but not in suspicion. I could see she wasn't troubling with the question whether I was telling the truth. She was sizing me up as a man. I cannot describe that calm appraising look. There was no sex in it. . . .
> I see I have written that I knew nothing about women. But every man has in his bones a consciousness of sex. I was shy and perturbed, but horribly fascinated. . . . I hated her instinctively, hated her intensely, but I longed to arouse her interest. To be valued coldly by those eyes was an offence to my manhood, and I felt antagonism rising within me.   (p. 168–9)

And perhaps not antagonism only. There is a complex of feelings here quite beyond Hannay's experience. He wishes to both attract and repel Hilda's sexual interest yet, as always in Buchan, life must be kept as simple as possible – contradictory impulses lead in dangerous directions. So the erotic must undergo a shift, must be made safe and secure for the reader. It turns out that Hilda von Einem is attempting to hypnotise Hannay. Once aware of this Hannay has to resist. He does this successfully with the following result: 'for a second her eyes drooped. I seemed to read in them failure, and yet a kind of satisfaction, too, as if they had found more in me than they expected.' (p. 169)

And clearly what she has now found, presumably through Hannay's manly resistance, is a degree of sexual interest. '"You have fought with men in battles?" "I have fought in battles." Her bosom rose and fell in a kind of sigh.' (p. 169)

Since the erotic causes trouble it has been given back to the trouble maker. It has been transferred from Our Hero to the Naughty Lady, to whom it more properly (or improperly!) belongs. The scene still remains, of course, erotic but because of Buchan's uneasiness eroticism must be *displaced* – moved from one character to the other so it can never be shared, never go causing problems.

One finds something similar in the character of Mary Lamington, who is courted by Hannay in *Mr Standfast* and has married him and become the mother of his child by the opening of *The Three*

Hostages. Despite the demands placed upon her by the plots of these novels – in the former, to quote Hannay's narrative, she must behave 'like a shameless minx' to entrap the spy Moxon Ivery; in the latter she has to pose as a dance hall hostess – she is not customarily thought of in erotic terms. Indeed one could argue that the more she is forced into situations such as those already described, which possess sexual implications, the less erotic and the less plausible she becomes. For example Buchan is quick to express Mary's virtuous shame at her dance-hall shenanigans, but never *explains how she learned the tricks of the trade*. Of course, up to *his* old rhetorical tricks, Buchan wants the reader to feel the illicit excitement of the good girl required to play at being bad while being assured that she couldn't possibly enjoy the same. Thus, while in William Buchan's phrase Mary cannot be 'explicitly sexual', she can be used as a species of sexual receiver for erotic impulses which are quite literally otherwise displaced; no character in these novels is ever given either a constant or a detailed sexual drive. Here Mary is finally confronted with the physical attentions of Moxon Ivery.

They walked together in the Bois de Boulogne, and once, with a beating heart, she motored with him to Auteuil for luncheon. He spoke of his home in Picardy, and there were moments, I gather, when he became the declared lover, to be rebuffed with a hoydenish shyness.   (p. 215)

I think it may be fairly submitted that while no international mastermind is going to be *rebuffed* by a spot of hoydenish shyness, it might well keep him interested and the reader titillated without the least moral blame attaching to the virginal hoyden in question.

Early on I asked how Buchan gets away with it (and as we have continued that 'it' has expanded). Of course the issue is wider than the scope of this essay. Doubtless much of his success derives from the reader's acceptance of, and indeed acquiescence in, the moral authority and moral reliability of his narrator/protagonists. Yet, closely considered in the light of the inconsistencies and contradictions and limitations with which the narrator makes contact, such a position looks dubious.

Baldly speaking it goes like this:

Since the narrator is tolerant he cannot be prejudiced.
Since he likes a Jew/German/African he cannot really be racist.
Since he is fair he cannot be unfair.
Since he is right he cannot be wrong.
And since he is a Buchan hero the reader must not challenge him in any of the above.

The last sentence of that litany is vital. Buchan's fiction rests ultimately on the reader's rhetorical re-direction, deflection from a challenge to the author, and the finding of a safe untroubled haven; it relies in fact on the careful authorial provision of a rhetoric of escape.

NOTES

1. John Buchan, *The Law Relating to the Taxation of Foreign Income* (London, 1905).
2. All quotations from John Buchan are from the Penguin editions unless otherwise stated.
3. John Buchan, *Huntingtower* (London, 1922).
4. John Buchan, *Castle Gay* (London, 1930).
5. Valentine Cunningham, *British Writers of the Thirties* (Oxford University Press, 1988).
6. John Buchan, *Sick Heart River* (London, 1941).
7. William Buchan, *John Buchan, A Memoir* (London: Harrap, 1985) p. 250.
8. John Buchan, *A Prince of the Captivity* (London, 1933).

6

The Story of an Encounter: Geoffrey Household's *Rogue Male*

MICHAEL J. HAYES

Rogue Male opens with the hero stalking the leader of a foreign power at his country retreat near the Polish border.[1] The assumption is usually made that the figure in question is Hitler. Perhaps it is, but Household never states that it is, and one asks, did Hitler wear waistcoats? The figure in the sights of the hunting rifle certainly does (p. 18). One might dismiss the point as fairly trivial, fictionists' licence, and given the date of publication, just before the war in 1939, courtesy might demand circumspection.

But the point is important because for all its paraphernalia of 'real' places, times and action the created world is fictional and Household is aware of his manipulations. He is clear that the reality is himself struggling, not to kill a cruel other, but to write a story, and in writing it to discover some of his own inner self.

> I am not content with myself. With this pencil and exercise book, I hope to find some clarity. I create a second self, a man of the past by whom the man of the present may be measured. (p. 14)

Of course the process referred to is a part of the story itself, but that self-discovery is so self-consciously wedded to the narrating of the story that the line between the real author and the writing hero dissolves.

The strategy of blurring the distinction between the hero (even at times the villain) and the teller of the tale is familiar. It invests the story with the authenticity of the human being who tells the tale. What is of particular interest here is that the physical circumstance, the 'pencil and exercise book', are brought before us. We are reminded both of the immediacy of the teller, and of the distance – the act of writing clearly places us at a distance – from the authentic voice. Even as Household draws us into his story he accentuates his isolation from us.

Is Household 'not content' with himself because the invocation of himself as part of a community, that community he speaks to through his story, is at odds with his individuality? An individuality which will not be confined in either the role of storyteller or of user of a common language. Is the sense of isolation at the heart of the book not merely the result of the story's circumstances but the shadow of the missing 'second self' whom the author is trying to delineate?

Before joining that arch-critic, Quive-Smith, in pursuit of our quarry, the author/narrator, it is important to look at the tradition from which the book derives. It is important not simply so that we know how to read the book, but so that we have some sense of what is appropriate to draw from the book. In distinguishing the two I am differentiating narrative expectations from the meaning of their particular realisation. So when the narrator gets to the coast we expect him to achieve a passage to England. What is interesting is why there is so much talk of class involved in the accomplishment of our legitimate narrative expectations.

An obvious forerunner is Buchan's Richard Hannay who, like the narrator, is a gentleman, hunter and patriot. The tracking across the Highlands in *The Thirty-Nine Steps* reminds us of the opening of *Rogue Male*. Moreover, the Highland association echoes Alan Breck and David Balfour in *Kidnapped* particularly as they lie on the hilltop watching the redcoats beating through the opposite hillsides. In some ways Household's book is closer in spirit to Rider Haggard's strange adventures, the landscape of England proving, in its way, to be every bit as strange as Africa. The rather odd intensity of the Haggard books is shown to have its emotional counterpart in life in England.

This reference to a context of fiction within which *Rogue Male* exists is by no means scholarly pretension. It is rather a general observation as to the reverberances created in myself on reading the book. The tradition is of resourceful heroes, moral and capable, struggling with larger and sinister forces. The heroes are moreover outsiders: David Balfour is dispossessed and Hannay is back from South Africa. The adventures they undergo are tests of their qualities, physical and moral, and the outcomes show us their qualities triumphant. We are justified in seeing Household's hero in this light, hence the book's easy popularity. What is more interesting though is the journey of self-discovery that the hero undertakes more through the reflectiveness that attaches to *the act of writing* about the adventures than to the adventures themselves.

The heroes of the books that I see as forerunners of *Rogue Male* frequently retell their own stories either through letters, journals or some imagined storytelling context. They recall events and describe their own parts with a becoming modesty. Generally they are removed from the initial events, so what self-discovery there may be has already been accomplished before the tale begins. In Household's book the writing is commenced during a lull in the crises. Having escaped from the foreign secret service, who have tracked him to England, killing in the process one of his pursuers, the hero is 'holed-up', literally, in the Dorset earth. He is still sought both by the foreign power, in the person of Quive-Smith, and by the English police.

Outwardly he feels secure but inwardly 'I am uncertain of myself' (p. 87). He writes 'I start on this exercise book again, for I dare not leave my thoughts uncontrolled' (p. 88). So writing is seen, at this point, as a means of putting his state of mind into order: readers are not being told anything new, anything of which they might be unaware. But from the opening of the book some odd rationalisations have been going on.

The hero claims that his stalking of the foreign leader was just sport, that the hunt was 'purely formal' (p. 8). He holds to this account even under horrific torture, a torture which takes him beyond thinking to the barest level of animal response. But as he reflects in order to write he has doubts about his behaviour. Why, for example, did he pack a telescopic sight?

Another question that troubles him is his 'strong resistance to coming to this lane?' (p. 89). He apparently concealed even from himself the location of his destination, until 'within twenty miles of it' (p. 89). At this point in the book a whole new layer of meanings and possibilities emerges. The sentimental attachment that has been hinted at earlier in the book, 'the business that had taken me to Dorset was so precious that I kept it to myself' (p. 68), can be seen as altogether of greater intensity. While he is not yet prepared to admit to himself the power of his feelings 'I begin to think that I have never known truly passionate love' (p. 88), he does admit their significance. The subterranean is a necessary part of the way to the real inner self.

In the countryside above his hideaway, without any pressures, he expresses his relationships within the conventions of the heroic figures he derives from. With women he is, like Richard Hannay, upright, tender, gentlemanly and discreet. Now below the selfsame surface of that remembered space he begins to realise the true force of his feelings. He still proclaims, 'I was never in love' (p. 89), but he has to admit, 'Besides all my other incoherent dissatisfactions, questions of sex were worrying me!' (p. 88). The story played out within the conventions of the novel has as its counterpart his own story. His flight is not just from Quive-Smith but from his own real self; as the writer of the tale he is spying on himself.

The 'second self' that he is painfully constructing is the self that lies below the surface of his past life. 'There are times', he writes, 'when I am no more self-conscious than a chimpanzee' (p. 68); the task he has set himself is to raise to consciousness his true self. It is to be accomplished by a combination of writing and loneliness.

Throughout the book there are several references to the potential of writing for ordering and elucidating ideas. The act of writing as I have already argued is presented by the author as a means to understanding. Similarly, loneliness is seen as a means of heightening awareness. 'The essence of safety is that a hunted man should feel lonely. . . . He becomes swift to imagine, sensitive as an animal to danger' (p. 88).

The legendary self-sufficiency of the hero of adventure stories may be effective within the narrative but it does not lead to any deeper understanding. As the hero writes his way to self-awareness under the impact of realising his loneliness now his beloved is dead, so the author might be seen as writing his way to significance in the face of the death of the conventional hero. That's got a nice ring to it, balanced and convincing! The first part obviously arises from the novel, but just how substantial is the second point, the bit about the author? What I have done is juxtapose the individual fictional world of the hero with the social world of the author. Fictions exist within a tradition and the tradition is located in historical time; in other words in a world that exists beyond fictions. If I want to suggest something about Household's relation to the fictions of his time the obvious source is autobiography, letters, etc. Can we though arrive at a justification through the book itself? Are there signs in the book that the author is aware of a failure of the tradition within which he is writing? There are dangers in the genre of course, chiefly that within a few years one ends up on the bookshelves of adolescent boys of all ages.

So far the hero has written about his position from within his own psychological state. He has a sense of being born into a certain class, at a specific time, with the estates and wealth appropriate to that class. But it has been essentially incidental background, at times useful, but nothing more. In fact he is at great pains to distance himself from the significance his social position automatically bestows on him. He worries for example when he is thought to be the agent of his country as opposed to a private citizen. However, through the essential self-scrutiny, through the journey into the unconscious the hero emerges into a life that has 'significance'. Significance I take to be the expression of the self within the context of its implications for society.

Since the point seems to me of crucial importance I will try to express it in another way. The conventional hero is self-sufficient; the parallel with Robinson Crusoe is made by Household himself. The Rogue Male is not only self-sufficient but he is also irrelevant. Irrelevant because by his own admission his hunt was purely theoretical: it was not real. Adventure stories are self-contained but inconsequential because they are not real. They are, as Frederick Forsyth says of his own books, 'pool-side literature', the diversions of a lazy day. If the hero and the books in which he figures so prominently are to become significant, they must be able to be located within the flow of life, recognisable and vital in the flow of either domestic or national history.

I have purposely used the words 'located within the flow of life' to distinguish between a quality I am trying to define – and claim for Household (at least in some of his books) – and a simple 'about the life of the time' which is fairly common in thrillers. John Buchan in *The Thirty-Nine Steps* is well aware of the First World War; Jack Higgins is well aware of the strife in Northern Ireland. What I am claiming is that this awareness does not have implications for their books in the way the awareness does for Household.

In Buchan and Jack Higgins the time and place of the story act as an impetus to the narrative. Prior to the First World War it is plausible that enemy agents should want to steal plans for the British naval dispositions should hostilities break out. At the present time it is legitimate to propose terrorist murders as a trigger to the plot. What these writers, as distinct from Household, are not concerned to do is create narratives which are consonant with the hero's development, derived from the interaction of character and socio-political context.

My claim for closer attention to Household's book is based on the twin features invoked earlier; namely the conscious blurring of the hero with the narrator/writer, and the consequent merging of the tale with the reality of the writer. When the hero kills Quive-Smith he emerges from underground confirmed in his real purpose. In his final letter to Saul he writes of the three parts of the journal 'two written accidentally and the last deliberately' (p. 191). The accidental part is the psychological investigation, the deliberate part is the emergence of the hero into the social reality of the immediate pre-war period. 'My escape was over; my purpose decided; my conscience limpid. I was at war' (p. 190). The hero discovers deeply felt realities in himself which he was not aware of, essentially his capacity to love and the passion of its definition for his individuality. As a consequence of his love's murder by totalitarian forces he is compelled to undertake arms both to revenge her death and to preserve his own personal beliefs. The adventure story is validated because the creative expression, the free play of imagination, has matched the story both to the time and to the context of the struggle to write. The hero discovers himself, the writer creates a satisfying story, in which one '[penetrates] with each reading a little further into what the author meant rather than what he said' (p. 89).

Having suggested that the first two parts of the novel are self-concerned while the last part is outward-looking it is necessary to justify and explore the usefulness of this generalisation in terms of the events of the novel.

There is a readily recognisable and generally agreed tension between the social self and the personal self.[2] In Freudian terms the ego has to mediate between the super ego and the id. It moderates between the peremptory demands of a conventional social existence and the relentless, insistent demands of the lawless, anarchic self. The very description of the process is embedded in a colourful, metaphorical language which is needed in order to get close to describing complex inner states. This metaphorical language relates closely to literature. Freud himself claims that whatever explanations he produced poets had been there before him. Use of the term 'Oedipus complex' is borrowed from the Greek Tragedy, and the complex in its turn can contribute to extending the scope of reference of the play. Unfortunately the metaphorical nature of psychoanalytic language renders it so general that it can be easily adapted to any book, as Graham Greene demonstrated in writing about Beatrix Potter. Where the real usefulness of psychoanalytic language in criticism lies is in the consideration of books where either society or the self is seen to be in crisis, and there is an attempt to resolve the crisis.

Rogue Male is particularly interesting because there is a compounding of crises. At the naive level the hero is in crisis because he is sought both by his own police and by the agents of a foreign power. At a deeper level he is in crisis because he has acted without being aware of his true motives and in ignorance of what he really expected to achieve. At another level the story itself represents a crisis; the individual creative act is struggling to achieve a social existence through being turned into a publicly accessible artefact, a book. The aim of the first part of this study has been to justify the plausibility of this account. The second part aims to explore its implications for a reading of the book. (Just as Household seems all-of-a-piece with his creation so, perhaps, the aim of criticism is to demonstrate readings which make a book all-of-a-piece with a community.)

It was pointed out at the beginning of this essay that *Rogue Male* opens with the hero playing at stalking the leader of a foreign power at his country retreat near the Polish border. The figure in question is usually assumed to be Hitler. That may or may not be the case; what is definite is the outcome. The hero is captured and tortured, he is reduced to 'a pulped substance . . . in the midst of which I carried on my absurd consciousness'(p. 9). He manages to escape but his identity as a human being is severely reduced. As he crawls through the marsh he is 'a creature of mud' (p. 9), his method of getting around has him 'face . . . only six inches above the ground' (p. 11).

What he supposed was a game, a sporting stalk, causes him to be reduced to a primitive being. His task is to escape from this regression of being in order to be reborn at a new level of understanding. The pattern of this reduction to essentials, escape, healing and rebirth is repeated throughout the book, at each stage furthering his level of consciousness. As he says 'I had a preference for hiding, travelling, throwing off pursuit by water' (p. 115).

The explicit, denotative meaning of the first escape is the hero's need to return to his own country, England, in defiance of the forces of law of the foreign country, Germany, where he perpetrated the 'pretend' assassination. He escapes down river by boat, is stowed away on a boat for England and home. But is there a connotative meaning, can we elicit anything of significance from the specific manner in which he escapes? Is there a metaphorical layer of meaning to be unravelled from the circumstances of his flight?

Two things seem to emerge. First the alienated and isolated self, second the hostility of the state that pursues him. His escape is effected by pretending to be, by taking on, the guise of a member of that state. As he begins his flight to the coast he first steals the clothes of an indigenous citizen. Later he pretends to be a schoolmaster on sick leave in order to purchase the boat. His one helper in this is similarly an outcast, someone like himself alienated from the monolith of the state.

Again, when he approaches the English sailors to help him get aboard a ship that will take him to England, it is their acceptance of his membership of the establishment, (two of them even mistake him for a parson), that first prompts them to help him. While his status as a landowner, with all the right connections, (he is even a friend of the German ambassador to England), makes him an establishment figure, he is, throughout the book, ambivalent in his feelings about class. He does not actually feel settled in the position bestowed by birth and possessions. But it is this appearance of belonging to the right groups which facilitates his escape from Germany to his homeland. (I have, I must admit toyed with another level of interpretation for this first part. A concept. A plausible, but I suspect intellectual extravaganza, of an interpretation. If we take the initial violence as orgasmic, a connection Household himself makes later in the book, then the journey down river is the sperm seeking the womb. The womb in this instance is the metal water tank on the ship in which he gestates, then to be born in England. Of couse the metallic artificiality of the womb means the resultant being is artificial – the adventure goes on. What would it mean if one could make such an interpretation stick? That mythic structures emerge from basic human functions, and that Household writes to explore man's basic being?)

Having returned to England he realises that he cannot simply resume his old social life without implicating his friends. He refers to his 'conscience' in contemplating his actions, but then queries its usage, 'I may be wrong in talking of conscience; my trouble was, perhaps, merely a vision of the social effects of what I had done' (p. 51). This distinction is crucial to the first part of the book; it is a product of his developing self-awareness. Although his trips to out-of-the-way places suggest he has not been wholly comfortable with his establishment position, it is only the recent trauma that makes him consider it more seriously. The distinction between morality and social form is the product of this enhanced depth of reflection.

He visits his solicitor, himself a less than totally conventional figure, to equip himself for the next stage of his adventure. Leaving he is pursued by enemy agents into the London Underground. The scene is rich in interpretative possibilities. Having secured for his dependants, namely his tenants, a measure of security he is, like Theseus, able to enter the labyrinth to do battle with the Minotaur. In exploring his relationship with society he descends, as it were, into the hidden world below the surface. As regards himself, having fulfilled his social obligations, he is free to delve into his own subconscious mind.

The narrative outcome is that he escapes his pursuers at the cost of killing one of them. Where previously he chose not to implicate his society in his troubles now his society is in pursuit of him. Underneath the city is 'A queer place for a soul to find itself adrift' (p. 62). He is adrift because he finally cuts himself off from his friends and from the city and sets out for open country. He is of course still pursued by demons; the enemy secret service, the British police and his own burgeoning self-awareness.

He next goes to ground in the Dorset countryside. Led by instinct rather than any rational decision he comes to the very site where formerly he had a love affair. His plan is to 'go to ground', literally, by burrowing into the earth to make a den. As with his descent into the underground so his descent into the Dorset earth is full of possible levels of extrapolation. One is that, like the primitive being he has become, he seeks to make and mark his own territory in which to exist. The form the marking takes consists of strengthening the natural hedge defences of his location and reinforcing the camouflage of weeds and fallen leaves. At another level he might be seen as retreating into a contemplation of the nature of his love affair, supported by the place of its original expression. It can also be seen as a return to the womb of mother earth in order to be reborn by a further delving into the subconscious self.

The real strength of these propositions lies not in their individual plausibility but in their interrelatedness. The fact that each reading can be defended from the rich texture of the book is not so important as their initial relatedness. So, harried by two packs of enemies, the hostile secret agents and his own society, he is forced to reassess his relationships both in himself and to society. He does this in some sense by striving to be reborn. This search for an authentic self, for real values, is both a psychological and sociological task.

As I have already argued the central method of self-scrutiny is the writing itself. The occasion for the examination is the alienation from all society and the key incident for reflection is his love affair. Not only is love a key to individuality but 'In love one becomes a child again' (p. 80). Childhood is a period of intense socialisation, it is a commonplace that it holds the key to much of our adult lives. Love on the other hand is both socialising and individualising in its force. It connects us to another person, but the subtlety and strength of that connection is a critique of our own inner natures, Jung's 'animus' and 'anima' express it.

The clue to the hero's failure as regards society, the key to his rogue male quality, can come from understanding his own nature, not as a social construct but as an individual, loving being. It is from an understanding of his capacity to relate deeply to another being, a relationship that goes beyond social convention, that will help him define his true nature and purpose.

It is at this stage that the real challenge to his identity is personified in the figure of Quive-Smith, the enemy agent. His earlier appearances in the book have been shadowy, now in their game of hide-and-seek he emerges with a personality of his own. He is almost the alter ego of the hero, evenly matched in duel, with comparable qualities as hunter. Indeed the hero several times underestimates Quive-Smith's ability, only extricating himself by fleeing back to his den, or by good luck, as when the bullet meant for his heart hits his whisky flask.

But the real nature of Quive-Smith's sinister presence is not as hunter seeking to kill the hero, but rather as an apologist for fascism trying to persuade the hero into the fold. When he tracks the hero to his den he does not just kill him, he offers him a way out.

Quive-Smith's view of the hero, voiced in one of their discussions, is that he is a complete individualist, 'You won't obey. You are able to deal with our own conscience' (p. 145). The hero understands what Quive-Smith is saying, but he denies that it is a real assessment of his position. 'I hated the philosophy he was ascribing to me' (p. 145). He has, he objects, a respect for other individuals. What he can agree about is that he has no respect for the state, run as it is by self-serving politicians. At this point Quive-Smith offers him a confession to sign; if he signs he will go free. The paper amounts to a confession that he did intend to kill the leader, and the British government knew of the attempt.

He refuses to sign, but as the verbal sparring goes on he is drawn to admit, 'Of course I had intended to shoot' (p. 148). To confess this to himself is to open the gate to a proper self-knowledge. The differences between them are not necessarily great, but they are of fundamental importance. He argues 'from the standpoint of individuals' but Quive-Smith argues 'about a mythical mass', between which there is no common ground' (p. 148). This is the source of his objection to Quive-Smith's definition of his individualism. It is not individualism without reference to the good of the community, but rather the free individual as the cornerstone of the good society that he supports. Respect and mutual obligation are the social framework for man, 'with his insolence, his irony, his ingenuity' (p. 119) being given their proper expression.

In a certain sense Quive-Smith is the super-ego, struggling with the hero who is striving to realise and balance his id and his ego. At the same time Quive-Smith can be seen as a father figure. It may at first sight seem outlandish to think of Quive-Smith as a father, but there is a certain suggestive power in the book which promotes such an interpretation. He is the state's representative, the ultimate patriarchal figure. That same state that possessed and finally denied the hero his beloved; a relationship set in the archetypal oedipal pattern. In a more personal sense Quive-Smith basically has the better of him all along, until the hero 'grows up', and kills him.

The mode of the killing of Quive-Smith, more than anything else, implies his paternal status. His death is the death of the oppressive forces of the state which have continued to constrain and obscure the hero's nature from himself, and have prevented him from seeing clearly what course of action he must take. But why should the killing in particular point to a metaphorical

fatherhood? Having decided to kill Quive-Smith the hero constructs
a primitive hand-drawn ballista. When Quive-Smith looks down
the ventilation shaft at him, his face filling the aperture, the hero
shoots him full in the head. How does this make him the father?

A frequent dream among creative and disturbed people is that
of a tunnel which is filled by a menacing face. As one writer reports
from an informant '[The] face changed and . . . looked horrible,
like a monster'.[3] 'The face became larger and larger. I didn't know
who it was; I screamed'. In literature we have examples other than
the present one from Household, for example when Mowgli is in
the cave with his Wolf Mother, Raksha, the entrance to the cave is
filled with the menacing face of Shere Khan. It is not until Shere
Khan is dead that Mowgli develops from helplessness to autonomy
and mastery – the death being a triumph of intelligence over
power. Hartmann's explanation for this particular phenomenon
lies in childhood. The tunnel is the recognisable optical field of the
young baby, six to nine months. In the normal way the space is
filled with the familiar image of the mother, an image that only
gradually becomes distinguishable from the child's own sense of
self. But every so often into the circle of the perceived a hostile,
frightening, face appears – that of the father. In other words to
the small baby the intermittent image of the father appears as a
threat. The alienness diminishes over time, but the figure remains
one of authority, and even fear, demanding obedience.

In killing Quive-Smith the hero finally emancipates himself from
the conventions inculcated by his father, the representative of
society and he discovers his own true nature. At the same time he
throws off the restrictions of the state and the limitations of his
own social position. He realises his authentic self, 'I am ruled by
my emotions, though I murder them at birth' (p. 153). Paradoxically
the murder of Quive-Smith releases this basic knowledge and
allows him to go on 'to a spiritual offensive' (p. 154).

The ending of the book again reiterates the motif of 'hiding,
travelling, throwing off, pursuit by water', as quoted previously.
The difference this time is that the hero manifestly knows what he
is about. His journeys and his disguise, incidentally taken over
from Quive-Smith, are all activated by his central mission; he 'was
at war' (p. 190). He throws off his establishment persona, he
accepts his crusade to wage a lone war against totalitarianism, not
for itself, but to revenge the murder of his loved one. At the end
of the day the only true object of society, politics or religion, as

Household sees it is 'to produce such a woman – or man, if you will' (p. 153). And what characterises such people? That they should be 'impulsive, spiritual, intelligent, all at such energy that [they seem] to glow'.

NOTES

1. Geoffrey Household, *Rogue Male* (Harmondsworth: Penguin, 1978). All quotations are from this edition.
2. A major influence on the second half of this essay has been my colleague George Campbell, both in discussion and *Kipling and Conrad, Precursors of Modernity* (particularly Chapter 3) an unpublished M.Phil. (Liverpool University, 1989). Other influential works have been Bakhtin, particularly *The Dialogic Imagination*, ed. Michael Holquist (Austin: University of Texas Press, 1986), and Mary Louise Pratt's *Toward A Speech Act Theory of Literary Discourse* (Bloomington: Indiana University Press, 1977).
3. Ernest Hartmann, as quoted in George Campbell (unpublished M.Phil.). See note 2.

7

Ian Fleming's Enigmas and Variations

MICHAEL WOOLF

The combination of sex, violence and alcohol and – at intervals – good food is, to one who lives such a circumscribed life as I do, irresistible.[1]

Hugh Gaitskell

James Bond kills everywhere but that is not considered a crime. He has a licence to kill; as if violence attains the status of psychopathy. Bond's women are never chaste, and matrimony rarely figures in the plans of the secret agent. Moreover, Bond threatens to upset road safety by his mania for pursuing women in cars at preposterous speed, a mania which the immature reader is quick to imitate.[2]

Lieutenant-Colonel Bernard Watson of the Salvation Army

Ian Fleming's novels, and their central creation James Bond, are rarely met with indifference. Instead, they provoke an enormously broad spectrum of approach ranging through the Gaitskell (and incidentally Kingsley Amis) view of the attraction of the novels as vicarious excitement to the outraged moral antagonism to Fleming's hero exemplified by the contributor to the Salvation Army's journal *War Cry*. Further, there is surprisingly no consensus concerning the basic meaning of the novels. These ostensibly simple narratives have provoked responses which range from the assertion that the novels are simply exciting tales to a theological reading which sees Bond as 'a modern knight of faith whose adventures involve a gallery of modern demons which have been attacking contemporary mankind.'[3]

The problem is, of course, that there are many Bonds and that the figure has become both created by the novels and clearly independent of them. In an obvious sense the film character is an

86

alternative figure to the Fleming invention and, further, the Bond figure has become independent of both book and film: an evolving construct within contemporary culture taking many shapes and engendering many contrasting models. In addition to Bond-type figures, the figure of the secret agent has been reconstructed, by John le Carré for example, in a form that is clearly a counterversion of the Fleming model. The basic characteristics of Bond are inverted: glamour, and masculine power and courage become their reverse.

The figure of the secret agent has also had an ambiguous history. Some of Bond's characteristics are found, for example, in John Buchan's Richard Hannay. Like Bond, Hannay has had a military career of some distinction and he shares Bond's patriotic commitment to Britain. A crucial difference is between Hannay's amateurism and Bond's professionalism and, above all, the historical location of Hannay in the dramatic struggles of British imperialism in the 1914–18 war contrasted with Bond's historical location within the period of post-imperial decline. However, the two figures share an essential experience which governs the structures of both Buchan and Fleming's work. They go through successive ordeals as through rites of passage. In a sense, the novels become ordeals of validation through which the central characters assert and re-assert their status. In Bond's case, this often involves justifying the status implied in the 007 designation. In each adventure, Bond and Hannay are called upon to re-establish their credentials in terms of public status and self-esteem by passing, almost ritualistically, through a major trial of courage and ingenuity. Hannay reluctantly accepts the challenge of another adventure from Sir Walter in a manner which prefigures both the nature of Bond's relationship with M, and the obligation to accept the task that derives out of a sense of national duty. In that respect, Hannay and Bond are not free agents: they act and react in accordance with patriotic imperatives. The task that the agent is called upon to perform is both a public responsibility and a necessary act of re-affirmation and re-commitment:

> I knew in my soul that if I declined I should never be quite at peace in the world again. And yet Sir Walter had called the scheme madness, and said that he himself would never have accepted.
>
> How does one make a great decision? I swear that when I turned round to speak I meant to refuse. But my answer was

Yes, and I had crossed the rubicon. My voice sounded cracked and far away.[4]

The alternative model of the secret agent is found in an extreme manifestation in the figure of Mr Verloc from Conrad's *The Secret Agent* (1907):

> Undemonstrative and burly in a fat-pig style, Mr. Verloc, without either rubbing his hands with satisfaction or winking sceptically at his thoughts, proceeded on his way. He trod the pavement heavily with his shiny boots, and his general get-up was that of a well-to-do mechanic in business for himself. He might have been anything from a picture-frame maker to a locksmith; an employer of labour in a small way. But there was also about him an indescribable air which no mechanic could have acquired in the practice of his handicraft however dishonestly exercised: the air common to men who live on the vices, the follies, or the baser fears of mankind.[5]

The contrasting figures of the secret agent, Fleming's Bond and le Carré's Smiley for example, have clear literary antecedents and they both belong within a tradition marked by ambiguity, marked perhaps by the very ambiguity implicit in the notion of secrecy: an act double-edged, both dark and noble. Buchan's Hannay is untroubled by that ambiguity but Bond, the more complex figure by far, has in moments of self doubt a consciousness of the doubleness implicit in the very notion of secrecy itself.

Another problematic variation and enigma in a debate of Fleming's Bond is the degree to which the figure is now inevitably filtered through, and confused by, the films. The Bond of the films is a radically different figure in a number of well-documented ways but the crucial distinction is in the character's attitude to the present and future and its concrete manifestation in objects produced by modernist technology. The film Bond is at home with, and identified by, his association with technological accoutrements. His relationship with modern gadgetry is that of the competent technocrat. He exhibits in fact an amused sense of supremacy over these symbols of the present and future. Indeed, in some respects the technology represents the most potent force in the films. In that sense, the real hero is precisely modernity and its technological symbols.

In complete contrast, the Bond of Fleming's novels belongs to the present lived through the past: the location wherein the primary mode of perceiving the present is through a sense of nostalgia for the past and a correlated sense of loss in the present. A constant thread running through the novels is the notion that the modern world is essentially barbaric teetering uneasily on the edge of apocalypse. Thus, Fleming defines the Queen's Club in Jamaica in *Dr No* (1958) as an institution threatened by the onset of a new barbarism:

> Such stubborn retreats will not long survive in modern Jamaica. One day Queen's Club will have its windows smashed and perhaps be burned to the ground, but for the time being it is a useful place to find in a sub-tropical island – well run, well staffed and with the finest cuisine and cellar in the Caribbean. (*Dr No*, pp. 5–6)

This uneasy anticipation of a less acceptable future is apparent also in Bond's attitudes to objects. Thus, the value of Bond's Bentley in *Casino Royale* (1953) derives precisely from the fact of its age and the qualities it possesses are those of the past and these are increased in worth by the fact that it represents 'one of the last'; it belongs to a lost world of securer, more certain values than those apparent in the present:

> Bond's car was his only personal hobby. One of the last of the 4½-litre Bentleys with the supercharger by Amherst Villiers, he had bought it almost new in 1933 and had kept it in careful storage through the war. It was still serviced every year and, in London, a former Bentley mechanic, who worked in a garage near Bond's Chelsea flat, tended it with jealous care. (*Casino Royale*, p. 36)

Bond frequently resists change both in relatively minor details, as in his resistance to having to change his gun in *Dr No*, and in a more profound sense, Bond of Fleming's novels is to a large degree an unreconstructed conservative confronting, as he sees it, the gross corruptions and distortions of the present with the ethics of an envisaged past that are less ambiguous than those of the troubled present. The trauma of betrayal by Vesper Lynd in *Casino Royale* leads Bond not toward doubt but toward the simple certainties of patriotism. He takes on, in the subsequent novels, the role of defender of the faith: defender of the values of national integrity:

> He saw her now only as a spy. Their love and his grief were relegated to the boxroom of his mind. Later, perhaps they would be dragged out, dispassionately examined, and then bitterly thrust back with other sentimental baggage he would rather forget. Now he could only think of her treachery to the Service and to her country and of the damage it had done. (*Casino Royale*, p. 187)

Faced with complex emotional motivations, Bond holds on to the simplicities and identifies himself as an ideological brother to Hannay: 'Well, it was not too late. Here was a target for him, right to hand. He would take on SMERSH and hunt it down.' (Ibid., p. 188)

Bond of the films reflects the social attitudes of Britain in the 1960s and 1970s whereas Fleming's Bond has his ethical roots in an earlier age and he embodies a sense of existing at the end of a great tradition. Nostalgia for a more heroic and potent past is part of the nature of M and Bond's psychology. The values that Kingsley Amis identifies in the Bond novels point precisely to the degree to which that Bond is a reflection of an older tradition closer to that of imperial Britain than to the ethical world of the Sean Connery or Roger Moore embodiment of James Bond:

> Some things are regarded as good: loyalty, fortitude, a sense of responsibility, a readiness to regard one's safety, even one's life, as less important than the major interests of one's organization and one's country. Other things are regarded as bad: tyranny, readiness to inflict pain on the weak or helpless, the unscrupulous pursuit of money or power.[6]

In ideological terms, Bond is also a profoundly conservative figure in that his role in the novels is to symbolise the persistence of Britain as a great world power not on the surface of events but where, by implication, it really matters. Bond, thus, frequently acts to repair the errors of the CIA or, indeed, to restore world order behind the scenes. In that respect, Bond's relationship with Felix Leiter, the CIA agent, is instructive. Leiter is, for the most part, a kind of junior assistant or younger brother to Bond. His function is a secondary one: to be supportive to the dynamic and effective agency for real action. In the post-war world this is, of course, an idealisation of Britain's political role in international affairs, particularly in comparison with that of the Americans. Fleming creates a province for Bond that reflects a kind of nostalgia for a lost political potency.

There are then many approaches to the Bond figure. There are the direct parodies, the most bizarre example of which must be that by Cyril Connolly, *Bond Strikes Camp*, in which M reveals his homosexuality and Bond, in a plot that combines absurdity with tedium, is forced to become a transvestite.[7] There are also the numerous television versions of Bond-type drama. 'The Man from Uncle' exemplifies the form. Additionally, the Bond of the films is a complicating factor. Indeed, within the films the character of Bond undergoes several transformations even as played by the same actor. Later Bonds increasingly become self-referential, quasi-comic parodies of their earlier forms.

The object of the rest of this discussion is to simplify these complexities by considering the Fleming Bond and to go beyond the figure to consider the novels themselves rather than the mythic shapes into which Bond has been moulded. *Casino Royale, From Russia With Love* (1957), *Dr No* and *You Only Live Twice* (1964) will be taken as symptomatic of Fleming's ideologies and representative of his fictional strategies. They will be considered as dramatisations of cultural and political tensions and as fictions with strategies of construction that are rather more sophisticated and artful than Ian Fleming would have us believe:

> I am not an angry young man, or even middle-aged man. I am not 'involved'. My books are not 'engaged'. I have no message for suffering humanity. My opuscula do not aim at changing people or making them go out and do something. They are not designed to find favour with the Comintern. They are written for warm-blooded heterosexuals in railway trains, airplanes or beds.[8]

That disingenuous statement does not, in the end, fully obscure
the enigmas and variations wrought by Ian Fleming.

Umberto Eco manages to identify 14 conflict points or oppositions
in the Bond novels without quite seeing arguably the most crucial
ones. The betrayal of Bond by Vesper Lynd in *Casino Royale*
establishes the nature of the enemy with absolute clarity.[9] It is
institutionally SMERSH: the representative, appropriately enough
during the Cold War, of what is envisaged as Russian imperial
ambition. By 1961, in *Thunderball*, Fleming re-defines the enemy
as SPECTRE: an agency for international terrorism. While that shift
reflects the changing nature of Fleming's perception of global
politics, SMERSH and SPECTRE share a number of crucial
characteristics. They share cosmic ambitions and trans-national
organisational structures. In effect, Bond's enemies are generally
internationalist in structure and in personnel. Le Chiffre's origins
are, for example, 'unknown': 'First encountered as a displaced
person, inmate of Dachau DP camp in the US Zone of Germany,
June 1945' (*Casino Royale*, p. 19). His ethnic background is, like that
of Goldfinger and Dr No, shadowy:

> Ears small, with large lobes, indicating some Jewish blood.
> Hands small, well-tended, hirsute. Feet small. Racially, subject
> is probably a mixture of Mediterranean with Prussian or Polish
> strains.   (Ibid., p. 20)

Though an agent of the USSR, Le Chiffre is, in fact, a stateless
representative of post-war rootlessness. His murderous assistants
are described as 'stateless Czechs apparently – but one of our men
says the language they talk in their room is Bulgarian'. (Ibid.,
p. 32.)

Le Chiffre may be taken as exemplifying many of the traits
that characterise Fleming's villains: sexual ambiguity, grotesque
physical characteristics and, above all, international rather than
national origins. Exactly the same characteristics are to be found
in Auric Goldfinger. Bond muses upon his elusive background:

> What could his history be? Today he might be an Englishman.
> What had he been born? Not a Jew – though there might be
> Jewish blood in him. Not a Latin or anything farther south. Not

a Slav. Perhaps a German – no, a Balt! That's where he would have come from. One of the old Baltic provinces. Probably got away to escape the Russians.   (*Goldfinger*, p. 28)

Dr No's origins are equally murky: '"I was the only son of a German Methodist missionary and a Chinese girl of good family. I was born in Pekin, but on what is known as the wrong side of the blanket"' (*Dr No*, p. 113). His assistants are Chinese–Negroes, as racially ambiguous as the vast majority of Fleming's villains.

In contrast to these figures, Honeychile Rider's background gives her a moral validity in Fleming's ethical structure:

You see the Riders were one of the old Jamaican families. The first one had been given the Beau Desert lands by Cromwell for having been one of the people who signed King Charles's death warrant. He built the Great House and my family lived in it on and off ever since.   (*Dr No*, p. 93)

Rider thus represents continuity and a sense of national location in direct contrast to the international flux represented by Dr No, Goldfinger and le Chiffre. In one respect, this is a fictional strategy that, as Kingsley Amis argues, has a long history: 'To use foreigners as villains is a convention older than our literature'.[10]

Rider's place within a historically continuous line also contrasts with the ethnic ambiguity of the villains. They reflect Fleming's mistrust of the stateless refugees of post-war Europe and the quasi-conventional anti-semitism that is found throughout the genre. Above all though, Fleming sets up an ethical opposition between the national and the international. The international equates with the enemy while British nationalism is an affirmative counterforce. Fleming's view of the world derives from a combination of traditional xenophobia with an essentially nationalistic view of the post-war world. Fleming's ideology is shaped both by a theory of cosmic-scale conspiracy and by a conventional attitude to Cold War antagonisms.

Fleming was anxious to invent a figure who would not enact many of the clichés of the genre. In a letter to Mary Wickham Bond, the wife of the ornithologist James Bond, Fleming explained his motive in purloining her husband's name:

> I was determined that my secret agent should be as anonymous
> a personality as possible. Even his name should be the very
> reverse of the kind of 'Peregrine Carruthers' whom one meets
> in this type of fiction.[11]

That ambition is, however, undermined to a degree by the elements
of confrontation between nationalism and internationalism that
precisely re-enact many of the shapes associated with the more
traditional forms of secret agent fiction. James Bond's name may
distance himself from those forms but his ethical perception of the
world certainly does not.

Bond's villains, however, are more than merely representatives
of international rootlessness. They are, in many respects, figures
of myth and embodiments of dread. Le Chiffre's torture of Bond
is conducted in tones that grotesquely parody and nightmarishly
invert the roles of doctor and father: 'He might have been a doctor
summoning the next patient from the waiting room.' (*Casino Royale*,
p. 114), and 'Le Chiffre spoke like a father' (Ibid., p. 120). He is
the nightmarish father to co-exist with the nightmarish parody of
maternalism that is accumulated around Rosa Kleb in *From Russia
with Love*. Dr No is, similarly, a grotesque who is reptilian and
dangerous:

> The bizarre, gliding figure looked like a giant venomous worm
> wrapped in grey tin-foil, and Bond would not have been
> surprised to see the rest of it trailing slimily along the carpet
> behind.   (*Dr No*, p. 127)

No's grotesque description is enforced by the absence of eyelashes,
a mouth which is like a 'wound', and steel pincers instead of
hands.

Fleming's villains virtually always combine grotesque physical
distortions with some sense of animalism. The animal metaphor
or simile is, indeed, one of Fleming's primary, and recurrent,
strategies in the presentation of these figures. He thus employs
strategies of characterisation with antecedents as far back as
Chaucer. Animal-like physical characteristics represent the objective correlative of moral corruption.

The twin villains of *From Russia with Love* also belong primarily
to the world of nightmare and myth. The executioner Grant is an
amalgam of a zombie, the living dead, and, like Dr No, a reptilian

horror: 'The naked man who lay splayed out on his face beside the swimming pool might have been dead' (*From Russia with Love*, p. 7). The novel describes Grant initially through the perceptions of a girl giving him a massage. She perceives him as both a reptile and 'like a lump of inanimate meat' (Ibid., p. 10). As with other Fleming villains, the colours red and orange are associated with Grant as a means of heightening the grotesque dimensions of the figure suggesting, in this case, burnt meat. Goldfinger's red hair and Le Chiffre's 'wet red mouth' are further examples of the use of colour symbolism to characterise the villains.

The other villain figure in *From Russia with Love* comes quite clearly out of the myth of the witch. Rosa Kleb is a sexual neuter, an intensely dangerous, half-human puppet:

> The thinning orange hair scraped back to the tight, obscene bun; the shiny yellow-brown eyes that stared so coldly at General G. through the sharp-edged squares of glass, the wedge of thickly-powdered, large-pored nose; the wet trap of a mouth, that went on opening and shutting as if it were operated by wires under the chin.   (*From Russia with Love*, p. 55)

In *You Only Live Twice* Ernst Stavro Bloefeld and Irma Bunt reappear in a chapter appropriately called 'Something Evil Comes This Way':

> Bloefeld, in his gleaming chain armour and grotesquely spiked and winged helmet of steel, its visor closed, was something out of Wagner, or, because of his armour, a Japanese *Kabuki* play. His armoured right hand rested easily on a long naked *samurai* sword while his left was hooked into the arm of his companion, a stumpy woman with the body and stride of a wardress. Her face was totally obscured by a hideous bee-keeper's hat of dark-green straw with a heavy pendent black veil reaching down over her shoulders. But there could be no doubt! Bond had seen that dumpy silhouette, now clothed in a plastic rainproof above tall rubber boots, too often in his dreams. That was her! That was Irma Bunt!   (pp. 150–1)

The references to Wagner and nightmare precisely fix the origin of Fleming's villains. They are figures out of myth and fairy-tale, embodiments of childhood horrors rather than characters constructed to reflect any perceived criminal or political reality. They represent one end of a spectrum that ranges from the mythic to the realist in all of Fleming's novels. In each case, figures drawn out of recognisable human experience (M and, for the most part, Bond) confront diabolic and demonic figures. This, rather than Umberto Eco's list of oppositions, reflects the crucial tension in Fleming's work. This modern version of a classical confrontation may be seen as a primary reason for the popularity of the Bond novels. Fleming presents to the reader an archetypal struggle between recognisably human figures and shapes and forms drawn from mythic horror and profound cultural nightmare.

Fleming's analysis of his own fictional strategies in writing *Casino Royale* reflects the movement in the fiction from the fantastic to the real:

> I realised that the plot was fantastic and I wondered how I could anchor it to the ground so that it wouldn't take off completely. I did so by piling on the verisimilitude of the background and of the individual situations, and the combination seemed to work.[12]

This also helps to explain the concern with the naming of objects in the novels. They serve to root one end of the fictional experience within the known world. In short, the character of Bond is located in the real world through the accumulation of known objects even if he transcends that reality, at times becoming a quasi-Byronic Romantic hero. In direct contrast, the villains glow with the reddish tinge of hell.

This can be precisely illustrated through the issue of psychological motivation. Dr No mocks the idea of a rational, sociologically credible explanation for his evil: '"No love, you see, Mister Bond. Lack of parental care"' (*Dr No*, p. 133). Bond, in contrast, is frequently given fairly complex psychological motivations. He sees M, for example, as a father-figure to whom he owes a responsibility. In the crisis that Bond goes through in *You Only Live Twice*, he suffers a sense of guilt deriving from his failure to live up to M's expectations:

> Suddenly he felt really bad about everything – about letting M down, letting the Service down, letting himself down. This empty desk, the empty chair, were the final accusation. We have nothing for you, they seemed to say. You're no use to us any

more. Sorry. It's been nice knowing you, but there it is. (*You Only Live Twice*, p. 28)

There are a number of psychological motivations established for Bond's activities. The betrayal by Vesper Lynd, the murder of his wife by Bloefeld, his relationship to M, his love of country and so on.

Additionally, Bond goes through a number of crises of conscience as in the opening of *Goldfinger*:

James Bond with two double bourbons inside him, sat in the final departure lounge of Miami airport and thought about life and death.

It was part of his profession to kill people. He had never liked doing it and when he had to kill he did it as well as he knew how and forgot about it. (p. 7)

That, however, is Bond's idealised psychological condition. In fact, the killing of a Mexican bandit leads toward a state of potentially dangerous sensitivity:

What an extraordinary difference there was between a body full of person and a body that was empty! Now there is someone, now there is no one. This had been a Mexican with a name and address, an employment card and perhaps a driving licence. Then something had gone out of him, out of the envelope of flesh and cheap clothes, and had left him an empty paper bag waiting for the dustcart. And the difference, the thing that had gone out of the stinking Mexican bandit, was greater than all Mexico. (*Goldfinger*, p. 7)

From such thoughts, Bond is protected for the most part by a mixture of professionalism and cynicism but that protection is by no means total as in the technically unnecessary, and disastrous, attempt to rescue Vesper Lynd in *Casino Royale*. In the case of Bond, Fleming creates an iceberg theory of emotional complexity. Though showing little, Bond's emotions are implicitly profound though restrained.

Arguably Bond reflects Fleming's own emotional restraint which reportedly obscured a recurrent morbidity. One of Fleming's biographers, John Pearson, quotes Fleming's friend the Turkish shipowner, Nazim Kelkavan. Fleming copied down these words and, according to Pearson, they came to represent Fleming's perception of his own life, and the metaphor through which he perceived death:

> I have always smoked and drank and loved too much. In fact I have lived not too long but too much. One day the Iron Crab will get me. Then I shall have died of living too much.[13]

That ethic of lived experience and consciousness of the ever-present menace of death runs through Bond's perceptions of experience. In its various forms, the dark presence of sudden death permeates the novels and becomes characteristic of Fleming's constructed cosmos.

Bond's actions are seen to derive then from clearly human emotions. In contrast, the villains have motives which are inhuman or psychotic. Thus Grant is a psychotic murderer possessed by a quasi-supernatural evil: 'It was about this time that his body began to feel strange and violent compulsions around the time of the full moon' (*From Russia with Love*, p. 17). Motives of world domination co-exist with diabolical sadism in many of the figures. They are repeatedly characterised by association with animals rather than humans. Fleming's fictional universe thus broadly encompasses the real and the dreamed, the human and the inhuman, the known world and the diabolic universe and sets them in conflict with each other. There is, as Umberto Eco suggests something of 'the purity of the primitive epic' in such a confrontation.[14] Bond's victories save the known world both from earthly enemies and from diabolic nightmares.

NOTES

1. Tony Bennett and Janet Woollacott, *Bond and Beyond: The Political Career of a Popular Hero* (London: Macmillan, 1987) p. 15. All quotations from the works of Ian Fleming are taken from the Panther edition with the exceptions of *Casino Royale* (London: Grafton Books, 1986).
2. Oreste Del Buono and Umberto Eco, *The Bond Affair* (London: Macmillan, 1966) pp. 15–16.
3. Ann S. Boyd, *The Devil with James Bond* (London: Fontana, 1967) p. 25.
4. John Buchan, 'The Second Adventure of "Greenmantle"' in *The Four Adventures of Richard Hannay* (London: Hodder & Stoughton, 1931) pp. 142–3.

5. Joseph Conrad, *The Secret Agent: A Simple Tale* (London: J. M. Dent, 1961) p. 13.
6. Kingsley Amis, *The James Bond Dossier* (London: Jonathan Cape, 1965) p. 85.
7. Cyril Connolly, *Bond Strikes Camp* (London: Shenval Press, 1963).
8. Ian Fleming, 'How to Write Thrillers' in *Books and Bookmen*, May 1963, vol. 8, no. 8, pp. 14–19.
9. Umberto Eco, 'The Narrative Structure in Fleming' in *The Bond Affair*.
10. Amis, p. 86.
11. Letter to Mary Wickham Bond, 20 June 1961, in Mary Wickham Bond, *How 007 Got His Name* (London: Collins, 1966) p. 21.
12. Ian Fleming, 'How to Write Thrillers', p. 17.
13. From John Pearson, *The Life of Ian Fleming* (London: Jonathan Cape, 1966) pp. 273–4.
14. Bennett and Woollacott, p. 163.

8

The Great Game? The Spy Fiction of Len Deighton

DUDLEY JONES

Two topics have exercised a powerful grip on Len Deighton's literary imagination: World War II and espionage. The former has given rise to three novels (*Bomber, SSGB* and *Goodbye Mickey Mouse*) and three works of non-fiction (*Fighter, Blitzkrieg* and *Battle of Britain*); the latter has resulted in fourteen spy novels including the recent *Game Set and Match* trilogy. In assessing Deighton's prolific output it may be appropriate to employ the distinction made by Graham Greene between novels and 'entertainments'. Many regard *Bomber*, a graphic account of a single bombing raid over Germany, as his finest achievement and *SSGB*, an imaginative projection of what might have happened if Britain had collapsed in 1940 and been occupied by the Nazis, has also enjoyed critical acclaim.[1] Deighton will probably be remembered best, though, as a writer of spy fiction – a series of extraordinarily successful novels established him as one of the most important and influential contributors to this popular literary genre. These 'entertainments' with their ingenious plots and laconic humour, are lighter in tone than the 'war' novels even though there is clearly an attempt to extend and deepen the range of his spy fiction in the *Game Set and Match* trilogy.

It is a critical commonplace to say that *The Ipcress File* (1962) and le Carré's *The Spy Who Came In from the Cold* published a year later, changed the face of spy fiction and in some respects it is obviously true. Although *The Ipcress File* lacked the sustained intensity of le Carré's novel, the two books had features in common. Both represented a reaction to the glamorous presentation of espionage in Ian Fleming's Bond novels. Deighton's anonymous hero and le Carré's Leamas provided a sharp contrast to the jingoism, élitest attitudes and ostentatious consumerism of James Bond. In place of the surrealistic exploits of Bond, one had the apparently authentic documentation of the squalid, down-to-earth existence of spies; the moral certainties of 007 were exchanged for ambiguities, cynicism and, especially in le Carré's case, disillusionment.

To a large extent these differences can be accounted for by changes in the social and political climate. The egalitarian and meritocratic outlook of Deighton's hero, for example, is articulated earlier in Hoggart's *Uses of Literacy*, his anti-establishment feelings echo Jimmy Porter's frustration in *Look Back in Anger* and his technical skills anticipate the emphasis by the Wilson government on technological revolution. Perhaps the most important influences, however, on Deighton (and le Carré) were the Burgess, Philby, Maclean affair and the erection of the Berlin Wall. With the Burgess, Philby, Maclean affair, the focus shifted from an external enemy – the power-crazed megalomaniac threatening the survival of the free world in Fleming's scenarios – to the enemy within. The emphasis was upon moles and double agents; the central theme became, and remained, betrayal.

The Berlin Wall established a literal and symbolic barrier: it divided East and West Berlin and stood as a permanent reminder of the ideological divisions of the Cold War. And Checkpoint Charlie offered novelists and film makers a marvellous dramatic focus for the exchange of spies and desperate bids for freedom.

Although Berlin is not used as a location in *The Ipcress File* it does feature prominently in novels that will be examined later in this article – *Funeral in Berlin* and the *Game Set and Match* trilogy.

The success of *The Ipcress File* surprised everyone including its author.[2] It displays the characteristic features that were to become the hallmark of Deighton's spy fiction. The story is told by a first person narrator, a narrative mode adopted by Deighton in nearly all his spy novels. It is presented in the form of a dossier, a secret file, to the Minister of Defence, and the following novels, *Horse under Water*, *Funeral in Berlin* and *Billion Dollar Brain* were offered as secret files Nos. 2, 3 and 4. Like its successors *The Ipcress File* is liberally sprinkled with footnotes suggesting the author's authoritative knowledge of espionage. In addition a lengthy appendix includes a mix of 'factual' information about such matters as the calibre of Smith and Wesson revolver ammunition and fictional background to some of the characters in the story.

This blurring of the boundaries between fact and fiction would appear to be quite deliberate and to constitute one of the ways in which this writer constantly teases and plays games with the reader. No doubt Deighton was amused to learn that American customs officials called in the FBI because of his use of faked facsimiles in *An Expensive Place to Die* of what appeared to be top secret documents.[3] Again, the reader inclined to dismiss General Midwinter and his private army in *Billion Dollar Brain* as an entertaining but entirely unbelievable creation, may be given pause for thought by the apparently authentic Appendix 3 which provides detailed information on Privately Owned Intelligence Units.

If at times Deighton seems to be trying to persuade his readers he is writing 'faction', in other ways he is at pains to emphasise the fictionality of his narrative. The use of ironic epigraphs for chapter headings for example: in *The Ipcress File* he employs astrological signs and forecasts ('Aquarius [Jan 20–Feb 14] someone else's forethought may enable you to surprise a rival'); in *Funeral in Berlin* chess moves and terminology ('Roman Decoy: a piece offered as a bait to save a hazardous situation'); and in *Funeral in Berlin* extracts from nursery rhymes ('A Master I have and I am his man / Gallopy dreary dun'). Even in a novel as carefully researched and richly documented as *Bomber*, Deighton, in his subtitle, alerts the reader to the fabricated nature of his tale: 'Events relating to the last flight of an RAF Bomber over Germany on the night of *June 31st* 1943' [my emphasis].[4] Finally, the ingenious and complicated plots with their twists and turns, bluffs and double bluffs invite the reader – as in a 'whodunit' or a chess problem – to predict the next move and respond accordingly.

Although it may be wrong, as Lars Sauerberg points out in *Secret Agents in Fiction*, to assume that the heroes of Deighton's stories are actually different manifestations of the same man, the correlation between the hero's personality and background in *The Ipcress File* and that of later narrators, plus the use of the same Intelligence unit location and personnel, encourages such an assumption.[5] Even Bernard Samson who, unlike previous incarnations had not been to university, appears to follow in a direct line from the hero of the first novel – a fact acknowledged by Deighton.[6] When we first meet the narrator of *The Ipcress File* he is transferring from Military Intelligence to a civilian Intelligence Unit – WOOC(P). He is 26 years old, 5'11" tall, 'muscular inclined to overweight'. He seems to be from a working-class background, is bright and has won a mathematics prize in his fifth year at a Burnley grammar school. In *Spy Story* we learn that he has acquired a degree in mathematics and economics from a provincial university. Resentful of the privileges conferred by birth, class and a public school education, he employs a cynical humour to dissociate himself from the Establishment:

'You are loving it here, of course?' Dalby asked.

'I have a clean mind and pure heart. I get eight hours' sleep every night. I am a loyal, diligent employee and will attempt every day to be worthy of the trust my paternal employer puts in me.'

'I'll make the jokes,' said Dalby. . . . Dalby tightened a shoe-lace. 'Think you can handle a tricky little special assignment?'

'If it doesn't demand a classical education I might be able to grope around it.'   (*The Ipcress File*, p. 10)

The hero, claims Sauerberg, is a representative of the post-war meritocracy who found it extremely difficult to obtain society's recognition. 'The new men of the meritocracy were well-educated and needed for the rapid developments everywhere but their "fault" was that they were not born with any kind of privileges'.[7]

In his foreword to the Silver Jubilee edition of *The Ipcress File* Deighton says: 'My enthusiasm for Raymond Chandler, Evelyn Waugh and Somerset Maughan are perhaps evident'. Certainly in this and later novels, the influence of Chandler is marked: it's present in the thumbnail sketches of settings, in the vivid character cameos and especially in the laconic humour of the narrator. Readers undoubtedly came to expect, and derive pleasure from, these Chandleresque qualities.

There are, however, the kinds of weakness one would expect from a first novel. The emphasis on brainwashing techniques about which there was considerable discussion when the book was being written, now seems somewhat dated. More importantly the concluding explanation of the Ipcress conspiracy provided by the hero for the benefit of his assistant Jean (and the reader) is a clumsy device reminiscent of the denouement of Agatha Christie's 'whodunits'.

By the time of Deighton's third novel *Funeral in Berlin* such clumsiness has largely been eliminated. The narrative techniques have been refined and the style is assured. The story is swift-moving and the dialogue crackles with wit and vitality. Interestingly (and untypically) Deighton experiments with the subjective first-person narrator form inserting 'interchapters' in which events are viewed from the perspective of different characters within the novel.

In the story Colonel Stok of Red Army Security, a recurring figure in Deighton's early work, agrees to sell to the West, for a price, an important Russian scientist. The Gehlen Bureau, a West German fascist organisation, involved in setting up the deal stipulates that papers must be provided in the name of a Czech, Louis Broum. Only towards the end of the book does it become apparent that different groups are competing to secure these papers because they will enable the bearer to tap the wealth immured in a Swiss Bank since the war. The hero also has to contend with a glamorous Israeli agent who wants to divert the scientist (a specialist in germ warfare) to Israel. Stok's plan to convey the scientist in a coffin with a false bottom is eventually revealed as a hoax – the coffin contains only Communist propaganda leaflets. Typically in this convoluted plot, nothing is what it appears to be and no one can be trusted.

Issues such as the ethics and legitimacy of espionage and intelligence-gathering organisations which are largely ignored in *The Ipcress File*, are briefly touched upon in *Funeral in Berlin*. When Jean, the hero's assistant, challenges his bending of Interpol regulations, he argues that it's not the role of their department to make political decisions – that is the function of Parliament. Jean feels this is ironic coming from him because 'When Parliamentarians wake up in the small hours of the morning bathed in sweat and screaming you are what they were dreaming of' (*Funeral in Berlin*, p. 212). The hero defends his position, claiming that 'the moment we notice someone who isn't frightened that this set-up and all the other set-ups like it are a threat to democratic parliamentary systems – we fire him' (Ibid., p. 213). This notion of self-scrutiny and of eternal vigilance in the face of threats to democratic freedom isn't entirely convincing, especially since he goes on to admit that there is a danger that the people who finance his department may feel they should be immune from surveillance. When Deighton's heroes are confronted by the complexities of ethical and political problems, they tend to fall back upon the code of professionalism. To some extent the professional can absolve him/herself from moral and political judgements: getting the job done efficiently brings respect from fellow professionals and becomes an end in itself. Talking to a Czech officer, Colonel Stok declares that the hero 'is a professional just like you and me. Professionals never make problems' (Ibid., p. 197).

One of the impressive features of the book is the way in which Deighton captures the atmosphere of both West and East Berlin. The skilful depiction of a variety of locations soon becomes another hallmark of Deighton's spy fiction: he was able to draw profitably on his experience as an airline steward flying on BOAC's long distance routes to Africa, Japan and Australia with frequent stop-overs at places en route – *The Ipcress File*, for example, moves between London, Beirut and an atomic missile test base in the Pacific. Deighton's agents swiftly traverse the international stage of espionage pausing in major cities like London, Berlin, Prague, Leningrad and Helsinki to negotiate, make deals, exchange information and sometimes people. Such trading often takes place in back streets or quiet suburbs and the author functions as an unobtrusive but expert guide.

Berlin, however, seems to have a particular fascination for Deighton. He returns to it again in the *Game Set and Match* trilogy where, though the action moves between Berlin, Mexico City and London, it is Berlin that provides the recurrent focus for some of the most dramatic events in each book. Berlin clearly appeals to Deighton because, as a divided city, it presents starkly the opposition between the communist and capitalist political systems and the Wall is a tangible and symbolic reminder of that opposition. But it goes beyond this – as least as far as the trilogy is concerned – because the internal divisions of the city reflect the divided self of the hero, Bernard Samson.

In one sense the spy is like an actor: there must always be an element of schizophrenia in his make-up as he is continually obliged to assume new identities. The problem is compounded for Bernard who, despite his British nationality and his home and work-base in London, feels little sense of belonging to his native country – his roots lie elsewhere.

Having been brought up in Berlin and attended school there, Bernard feels a genuine attachment to Germany. He speaks fluent German, knows Berlin intimately and obviously resents being overlooked for promotion to resident Head of the German Desk. An English colleague asks him if he is German and he says to Werner, his friend since childhood: 'I look at myself and I wonder where I can call home' (*Mexico Set*, p. 244). In the final part of the trilogy it doesn't occur to the old lady 'Tante' Lisl (for whom Bernard has a deep affection) and her friend Herr Koch to think of him as German and he reflects: 'I was devastated by the rejection so implied. This was where I had grown up. If I wasn't German in spirit what was I? Why didn't they both acknowledge the truth? London was a place where my English friends lived and where my children were born but this was where I belonged' (*London Match*, p. 371). Also, although Bernard as an agent never wavers in his loyalty to British Intelligence he identifies strongly with his Soviet counterpart, Erich Stinnes. When Werner points this out he denies it but Werner goes on to enumerate the similarities in their background, and the denial lacks conviction. In *London Match* that identification is openly acknowledged by Bernard. He goes on to say of Stinnes: 'I respected his professionalism and that coloured all my thoughts and my actions' (p. 132). That respect is mutual: when Bernard's superior complains that he should have 'winged' rather than killed a KGB hitman in a gun battle, Stinnes rises to Bernard's defence: 'What Samson did was just what I would have done. It's what any really good professional would have done' (Ibid., p. 240). As in other Deighton novels the qualities of the good pro are constantly being expounded in the trilogy – once again professionalism is being accorded a primary value. When mistakes occur, sometimes with tragic consequences, it's because of the interference of amateurs.

The *Game Set and Match* trilogy revolves around the defection of Bernard's wife Fiona, a Senior Intelligence Officer, to East Berlin, and the subsequent 'fake' defection of Erich Stinnes, a Soviet agent who Bernard has to 'enrol' in order to allay suspicions about his own loyalty. When Bernard realises – after considerable damage has been done – that Stinnes has been deliberately planted by his wife to destabilise British Intelligence, he is exchanged for Bernard's friend Werner who has been arrested for spying in East Berlin. The central theme of the trilogy is betrayal. In Bernard's case the feeling of betrayal is exacerbated by the fact that it is both personal and political.

The intention seems to be to develop this theme, a familiar one in Deighton's spy novels, in greater depth and explore in more detail both the relationships between the main characters and ethical and political issues raised by espionage. Unfortunately these intentions are only partially realised. At the personal level they are vitiated by Deighton's weakness in portraying mature relationships between men and women. In an interview he said that the espionage element in the Samson books was still there but that the trilogy is: 'as much about a marriage as about spying. When Samson's wife defects, it's his response to her personal betrayal of him which, I think, keeps readers interested'.[8]

In one sense this is true: the crisis of confidence brought about by his wife's defection, the threat both from Fiona and her father to Bernard's custody of the children and his continuing need to prove his loyalty, does sustain the reader's interest. However, because Fiona is not sufficiently developed as a character, her defection always seems like a functional device enabling the writer to focus on its consequences for Bernard. It is true that there are some brief but effective scenes of married life where Deighton deftly conveys Bernard's love for his wife and the insecurity caused by his suspicion that she is having affairs with other men. Again, his growing fear that she might be the mole at the heart of British Intelligence, his desire to warn her, giving her time to escape before exposure, is handled with characteristic skill and economy. However, even allowing for the restricted perspective of first-person narration and for Bernard's failure to penetrate his wife's cover, the motivation for Fiona's defection is never adequately developed. Part of the problem is that Deighton's females tend to be *types* rather than fully realised creations. Fiona is the beautiful, intelligent career woman who betrays her husband and country; Werner's wife, Zena, is the capricious and acquisitive schemer, using her seductive wiles to dominate Werner and entice Stinnes; and Gloria who appears in the second and third volumes of the trilogy is a familiar type from earlier novels, a glamorous young woman captivated by the middle-aged, overweight hero – a menopausal male fantasy. The one exception is 'Tante' Lisl Hennig who owns the shabby hotel in Berlin in which Bernard's father had been billeted after the war and where Bernard stays when he is on an assignment in Berlin. Significantly Lisl is a lonely character whose beauty has faded and she is drawn with great delicacy and affection. She is in fact so much a part of the hotel (she is unable because of arthritis to leave it) that Deighton's description of the physical surroundings becomes a subtle way of sketching in our knowledge of the character:

There had been few changes made in this 'salon' since Lisl was a child in a house with five servants. There were photos on every side: sepia family groups in ebony frames, faded celebrities of the thirties. Actresses with long cigarette holders, writers under big-brimmed hats, glossy film stars from the UFA studios, carefully retouched prima donnas of the State Opera, artists of the Dada movement, trapeze performers from the Wintergarten and nightclub singers from long-vanished clip joints. All of them signed with the sort of florid guarantees of enduring love that are the ephemera of show business.   (*Berlin Game*, p. 98)

A little further on in this scene description and dialogue blend to produce a rounded portrait:

She switched on another light. A large plant in an art-nouveau pot cast a sudden spiky shadow on the ugly brown wallpaper. She turned to see me better, and part of her pearl necklace disappeared into a roll of fatty muscle. 'There will always be a room for you, Liebchen. Give me a kiss'.

But I had already leaned over to give her a kiss. It was a necessary ritual. She had been calling me Liebchen and demanding kisses since before I could walk.

'So nothing changes, Lisl,' I said.

'Nothing changes! Everything changes, you mean. Look at me. Look at my ugly face and this infirm body. Life is cruel, Bernard, my sweetheart,' she said, using the name I'd been known by as a boy. 'You will discover it too: life is cruel'.   (Ibid., p. 99)

Deighton's general failure in the trilogy, though, to develop characters and relationships in greater depth may also be explained by his fidelity to the conventions of the popular genre in which he is working. The swift pace of the story, the convoluted plot, the dramatic set pieces – which are after all the things that we and Deighton know he can do well – tend to preclude the time and space needed to establish and sustain characterisation.

When one turns to the treatment of ethical and political issues, there are once again unresolved problems. Deighton's spy narrators display little trust in their superiors – the greatest threat to their survival generally comes from their own rather than the enemy's side. A deep-rooted cynicism about the reliability and the competence of British Intelligence prevails and the hero rails against the injustices and inequalities of the class system. There is an increasing scepticism about the motives of spies and the moral justification for espionage (of course there's nothing new about this – it's the territory explored by *The Spy Who Came In from the Cold*). In *Mexico Set* Bernard says to Werner: 'It's the same everywhere: bribery and corruption. Twenty or more years ago when we first got involved in this business people stole secrets because they were politically committed or patriotic. . . . How many people are like that nowadays? Not many' (p. 239).

Later he observes 'The job I do is not strictly legal. I cannot afford the luxury of a clear conscience ' (Ibid., p. 240). What is curious, in view of these doubts, is the manichean view of East and West that comes across in the trilogy and in earlier novels. In the final analysis, the East stands for evil and the West for good; Russia and the Eastern bloc represent an inhumane, totalitarian suppression of all freedoms while the West for all its materialism is the repository of individual liberty. Bernard, discussing with his boss Dicky Cruyer the possible enrolment of Stinnes, declares that he is 'one of a top level élite in a totalitarian state where there are no agonising discussions about capital punishment, or demos about pollution of the environment or the moral uncertainties of having atomic weapons' (Ibid., p. 124). and this view is echoed by Dicky when Bernard raises the problems facing defectors to the Soviet Union: 'All they have to offer is a perverted ideology and a medieval system based on privilege and obedience. We have a free society; a free press, freedom to protest, freedom to say anything we like' (Ibid.).

These sentiments are not challenged by Bernard and they don't seem to be undercut by irony. Now Deighton has warned his readers that he employs an unreliable narrator and they should not assume that the narrator's view can be equated with the author's.[9] It is nevertheless difficult not to see the above views as carrying an authorial endorsement. Ironically – and if Deighton is aware of the irony he doesn't signal it to the reader – only a few pages earlier Werner has drawn attention to the social inequalities in Mexico suggesting the country is on the brink of revolution. The peasants, he argues, are exploited by Western capitalism:

. . . four out of ten Mexicans never drink milk, two out of ten never eat meat, eggs or bread. But the Mexican government subsidises Coca Cola sales. The official explanation is that Coca Cola is nutritious. . . . And now that the IMF have forced Mexico to devalue the peso, big US companies – such as Xerox and Sheraton – can build factories and hotels here at rock bottom prices, but sell to hard currency customers. Inflation goes up. Unemployment figures go up. Taxes go up. But wages go down.' (*Mexico Set*, p. 114)

Unfortunately this kind of economic and political analysis doesn't feed through to discussions about the conflicting ideologies of the capitalist and communist systems. There is no consideration of Marcusian theories of repressive tolerance, no suggestion that the freedoms referred to by Dicky Cruyer are undermined by the realities of economic power.

What does receive a sharper cutting edge in *Game Set and Match*, however, is Deighton's attack upon the public school/Oxbridge/Old Boy Network. The ironic jibes of the Other Ranker about the officer class and the Establishment have been a source of pleasure from *The Ipcress File* onwards. They represent an oblique criticism of the class system. The foibles of the upper middle-class with their country weekend parties are satirised in the trilogy with the usual deadly accuracy. At the same time the attack is broadened. In *Berlin Game* Bernard reflects that for a Soviet defector, the prospect of facing a 'highly competitive, noisy, quickmoving kaleidoscopic society and braving its dangers – sickness, crime, poverty – could be traumatic' (p. 259). One senses that the meritocratic narrator (and the author?) values that society and accepts its dangers as long as he can complete on equal terms. If privilege – in the shape of class and education – is allowed to gain an unfair advantage in the competition, there is the danger not only that an Establishment amateur will threaten the efficiency and survival of the technical professional but that the ruling class, those in positions of power, will become complacent, sheltered from the realities of life outside their élite circle and resistant to egalitarian reforms that challenge their privilege. When Stinnes tells Bernard that he is lucky not to have a party system working against him all the time Bernard replies: 'We have got it, it's called Eton and Oxbridge' (Ibid., p. 297). Deighton also suggests that the public school can breed a fascist mentality. Bernard comments that a colleague called Henry Tiptree had the glossy polish that the best boarding schools can sometimes provide: 'Such boys quickly come to terms with bullies, cold showers, corporal punishment, homosexuality and relentless sport but they acquire the hardness I'd seen in Tiptree's face'.

Behind the haw-haws and schoolboy smiles, Bernard concludes, was an 'expensively educated storm-trooper' (*Mexico Set*, p. 227).

In a celebrated article entitled 'Narrative Structures in Fleming', Umberto Eco compared the narrative movement in the Bond novels to a game of chess with a sequence of nine moves the order of which was subject to change in individual stories.[10] He also suggested that similar kinds of pleasure were generated by reading Fleming and watching the Harlem Globetrotters play basketball: the outcome in both cases is not in doubt; our interest and enjoyment lies in watching the skills and intricate manoeuvres of the players. The analogy with games like chess or basketball is clearly appropriate in the context of Deighton's novels and the reader is explicitly invited to participate in the fictional game situation through the use of chapter headings which in *Funeral in Berlin*, for example, relate to chess and in *Spy Story* to wargaming. Such an invitation may appear to be signalled through the title of the *Game Set and Match* trilogy but the author's intentions here are clearly different. This is a more serious engagement with espionage themes and the gaming metaphor is employed in a less playful way to register the hero's moral weariness, his abandonment of any position of ethical superiority. In *London Match*, Bernard's girlfriend Gloria passionately condemns moles, calling them traitors, bastards who should be shot. The depth of her feeling surprises Bernard, who replies: 'It's all part of the game' (p. 251). When she rebuts this pointing out that the mole's betrayal leads to people being tortured and murdered, he says that perhaps the mole is only doing what he thinks is right and then reflects: 'I didn't exactly believe this but that was the only way I could do my job. I couldn't start thinking I was part of a struggle against evil or freedom against tyranny' (Ibid., p. 251).

This is a significant concession. In the past Deighton's heroes may have maintained a cynical detachment, an irony that distanced them from an unthinking allegiance to the 'Free World' but there had always been a sense of the hero engaged in precisely that struggle of freedom against tyranny. Now that his belief in the justness of his cause has been abandoned, the hero falls back again on the notion of professional competence: 'The only way I could work was to concentrate on the nuts and bolts of the job and do it as well as I could' (Ibid., p. 251).

Some of the wit and vitality of Deighton's earlier spy novels is missing from the trilogy. There is the sombre recognition that espionage, Kipling's 'Great Game', is a deadly one characterised by betrayals that have far-reaching and disastrous consequences. Bernard's dismissal of the traitor's duplicity as simply part of the game suggests the extent of his disillusionment and invites a critical revaluation both of espionage and those who practise it.

NOTES

1. *Bomber* is included by Anthony Burgess in *Ninety-Nine Novels: The Best in English Since 1939* (London: Allison & Busby, 1984).
2. Preface to the Silver Jubilee edition of *The Ipcress File* (London: Collins, 1987) p. viii. All other quotations from the work of Len Deighton are from the following editions: *Funeral in Berlin* (London: Jonathan Cape, 1964) p. 212; *Mexico Set* (London: Panther, 1985) p. 244; *London Match* (London: Hutchinson, 1985) p. 371; *Berlin Game* (London: Panther, 1984) p. 98.
3. A. Masters, *Literary Agents: Novelists Who Spied* (Oxford: Basil Blackwell, 1987) p. 259.
4. The prodigious research carried out for *Bomber* is indicated in the acknowledgements at the end of the book and in his Preface to the Silver Jubilee edition (London: Collins, 1987).
5. L. Sauerberg, *Secret Agents in Fiction* (London: Macmillan, 1984) p. 108.
6. Interview with Len Deighton, (1 October 1983) p. 11.
7. Sauerberg, p. 108.
8. *Mail on Sunday*, (22 March 1987).
9. Preface to Silver Jubilee Edition, *The Ipcress File*, p. vi.
10. Umberto Eco, 'Narrative Structures in Fleming' in *The Role of the Reader* (London: Hutchinson, 1981) pp. 144–75.

9

Are You Telling Me Lies David? The Work of John le Carré

MICHAEL J. HAYES

'Your name is David Cornwell?'

'Yes . . . and no'.

'Yes and no? What does that mean?'

'My name is David Cornwell, but you as critic are interested only in John le Carré, my other name'.

'You don't like critics'.

'Even the word makes my whippets growl'.[1]

'Aren't you being unfair? After all a critic might be an ideal reader, or even Eliot's mild mannered man exercising a certain braggadocio from behind the refuge of his typewriter'.

'Which are you?'

'I'm neither, I'm an interrogator. You might say my role is that of one of Bakhtin's hoods. Something intrigues me, I start digging. At the moment my tradecraft bears the marks of my spymaster, Bakhtin.

'How conspicuously fashionable!'

'Somewhat like yourself Mr le Carré conspicuously fashionable, also like yourself disguised. Not so much a hoodlum as a hooded figure bearing an allegiance, as I have said, to Bakhtin. At the same time through the folds of the hood the words sometimes fumble and are distorted. My excuse, my alibi if you like for an imperfect relationship with my spymaster'.

'All right, you're an interrogator, why investigate me rather than Conrad, Deighton or Greene?'

'Fair question. Novels despite appearances to the contrary are an invitation to a dialogue. They may look rather like texts in one voice, the monologues of their authors, demanding only

113

acquiescence or denial, but in fact "The novel can be defined as
a diversity of social speech types . . . and a diversity of individual
voices, artistically organised."[2]

The novel is a symphony of affirming, denying and interroga-
ting voices, each one inviting interchange. But I find the inter-
changes within your novels problematic, they demand
investigation. They leave behind them silences and cacophanies
which deny or even negate the individual authentic voice. If we
take the end of *A Perfect Spy* Magnus dies "like somebody who
is a little deaf, straining for a sound" (p. 606).[3] Jack Brotherhood,
source and origin of so much traffic, is standing still while "the
fools on the roof were shouting at the fools in the square"
(p. 607). Only Mary, of all the voices, affirms, albeit tetchily her
continuing willingness to enter into dialogue, "of course I will"
(p. 607). Magnus, having at last orchestrated the voices of his
life, their lies and whispers, in a written version, kills himself.
The word in all its complexity written by Magnus to save his
son Tom, to afford him a bridge to "walk over to get from Rick
to life" (p. 205) serves at the same time to negate Magnus himself.
King Lear suffers to learn what Cordelia's silence at the beginning
of the play really means, he dies but he has learnt. Magnus only
suffers an endless trial of deception by words, both written and
spoken, and then dies to an accompanying silence broken only
by the shot exploding in his right ear.

The dialogues, or networks as you might call them, are
destroyed. The lines of communication, the discourses, are one
by one rolled up to be succeeded by a negative silence; the line
goes dead. Time and again we are forced to ask if anything can
be rescued or is the situation really as bad as the night Bill
Haydon was unmasked?'

'Critics have been through this stuff a dozen times, the files
are getting worn with being so continually thumbed through.
What more do you think you're going to find, what more can
you write? Picking over stuff from over twenty five years in
order to make theories without substance, bit like Peter Wright.
Stuff it, sport. That's my advice. Pop it up the old back passage.
Best place for that one.'

'Upper crust vulgarity David.'

'Not David, John.'

'Of course, I apologise, page one hundred and nine, *The
Honourable Schoolboy*.'

But of course I know that, having undertaken to engage the author in a fictional context, though expressing real views, I end up pretending to outwit myself. As Magnus learns if you want to deceive successfully 'The art of it was to forget everything except the ground you stood on and the face you spoke from at that moment' (p. 132). Does David Cornwell believe that, or believe that John le Carré thinks that, or is it only Magnus who believes it, or is it the other narrator created by le Carré to frame Magnus's story who believes it?

If we think not of the words themselves but of the use of words as the necessary approach to language there are strong suggestions that the conman, the spy and the novelist share the same skills. Further I think David Cornwell's novels explore the awful possibility that to use language is inevitably to deceive.

In his two earliest novels, *Call for the Dead* and *A Murder of Quality*, le Carré sets out to prove himself as a popular storyteller. He pays close attention to the expectations created by the genre, telling his tale within conventions that readers will recognise and that will encourage maximum participation. There are of course problems in the concept of genre but here I am using the term in such a way that it 'functions much like a code of behaviour established between the author and his reader'.[4] By choosing to write in a way already popular le Carré almost guarantees himself an audience but at the expense of 'a whole series of prescriptions and restrictions'.[5] What is interesting though is that even as he chooses a popular, comfortably predictable way of telling his story he, at the same time, subverts it. Even in his use of the familiar apparatus of a popular form he demonstrates its fragility, its arbitrariness.

As Kingsley Amis for example was quick to point out *Call for the Dead* opens with a strong reminder of the 'whodunit': a mysterious suicide that may be murder. Even the use of Smiley as the investigator follows the classic line of twentieth-century lay detectives such as Miss Marple and Lord Peter Wimsey. This use of non-professional detectives generally frees the inquirer to pursue leads with greater freedom than a serving policeman would have. It is interesting that where P. D. James uses a serving policeman, Adam Dalgliesh, he is often released from the conventional constraints by some device, such as being on holiday or being related to the victim. In Smiley's case however the freedom from constabulary constraints is replaced by the even more peremptory demands of his political masters.

Another feature of the detective novel with a lay hero is that the hero has to have some link with the professionals. This not only provides access to forensic evidence gained by the police but also on occasion gives the hero a conventional foil to engage in speculation and discussion about the crime. In *Call for the Dead* this role is filled by Mendel, whose retirement during the course of the novel puts his skills at the disposal of Smiley.

The disruption of the convention is effected by the manipulation of the story into a spy thriller. A murder mystery with a violent denouement that in its atmospheric chase through fog-bound London and final struggle on the houseboat looks back to the spy adventures of the early part of the century.

A Murder of Quality appears much more squarely in the detective story mode. The public-school setting is as isolated as the conventional country house, expensive hotel or English village. The body in the conservatory with footsteps in the snow leading only to the scene of the murder, even the victim's portent of danger sent to *The Christian Voice* are all devices familiar to readers of the genre. But is the story really presented as innocently as it seems? Might it not be that the very obviousness and abundance of the anticipated paraphernalia suggest parody?

Part of the fun of the genre is to see the familiar tricks turned to new ends and given a new slant. The guilty party for example varies from being the least obvious to the most obvious. Fielding is the most likely candidate for the murderer, and when it does turn out to be him we would not think it amiss, but for the fact that it is the final trick in a rather ostentatiously marked pack. I hesitate to assert that the book is a parody, but the author's very self-conscious use of the genre suggests a lack of conviction, a sense perhaps that the real thing lies elsewhere.

This notion is strongly reinforced by le Carré's next book *The Spy Who Came In from the Cold*, about which Kingsley Amis perceptively comments, 'if ever a book was a farewell to a subject and genre it was *The Spy Who*'.[6] Certainly the book marks an important turning point. Where the main impetus in the earlier books appears to be the need to write books here the authentic voices begin to speak. What I mean is best demonstrated by looking at contrasting examples, the first taken from *A Murder of Quality*, the second from *The Spy Who*.

It was a peculiarity of Smiley's character that throughout the whole of his clandestine work he had never managed to reconcile the means to the end. A stringent critic of his own motives, he had discovered after long observation that he tended to be less a creature of intellect than his tastes and habits might suggest; once in the war he had been described by his superiors as possessing the cunning of Satan and the conscience of a virgin, which seemed to him not wholly unjust.   (p. 79)

There is an artificiality of a rather pedantic kind here posturing as the wit of an intelligent wag. Who is actually speaking? Who knows about his 'clandestine work' and his moral dilemma over ends and means? Why should such a relatively common dilemma be a 'peculiarity of Smiley's character' rather than simply a feature, or a trait? Who is the piler-up of clichés, such as 'stringent critic', 'after long observation,' and 'a creature of intellect'? One could go on to ask about the superior who is supposed to have produced such a strained description of Smiley, and finally wonder at the awful clichéd double negative 'not wholly unjust'. There is no flow of voices here, no unified orchestration of narrator, Smiley and his wartime superior into an artistic whole. What dominates is an idea of Smiley which the author is struggling to convey through an elaborated code wrenched into a semblance of urbanity. It may well be that it is this grotesque singularity of voice just as much as the abundance of genre devices that leads me to suspect a parody.

He [Control] was shorter than Leamas remembered him; otherwise just the same. The same affected detachment, the same donnish conceits; the same horror of draughts; courteous according to a formula miles removed from Leamas' experience. The same milk-and-water smile, the same elaborate diffidence, the same apologetic adherence to a code of behaviour which he pretended to find ridiculous. The same banality.   (p. 18)

Here the description works because it blends a range of observations that derive from the languages and viewpoints of different speakers at the same time doing so in the tone of a semi-official report. The opening physical observation is Leamas's. The next sentence derives from the colleagues of similar public school, university background to Control, friends and acquaintances who would know enough about him to be in a position to tease his 'donnish

conceits' and 'horror of draughts'. The third sentence is the inner
voice of Control fastidiously revealing his knowledge of himself;
appropriately for a spymaster it involves reflection and self-
reflection. The final summing-up is offered by the author in the
spirit of collusion with the reader. As readers we are not forced to
perceive 'banality'; it is voiced for us as our mutual conclusion.

The apparatus and subject matter no longer dominate this book
as they did the former two. In *The Spy Who* it is the set-piece
dialogues with their revelations, discoveries and implications that
give the book its energy. It may be looked at as the story of Leamas,
a courageous but not very subtle man, capable of profound
sympathy, who is always one step behind the ramifications of
what is being said. A man who understands the meaning but fails
to realise how far that meaning can be subverted by other dialogues
taking place elsewhere.

When Control interviews Leamas about the destruction of his
East German network he suggests that Leamas may have had
enough, 'one has to come in from the cold' (p. 19). Leamas
understands what Control means, or rather he literally 'sees' what
he means, but he is unable, perhaps unwilling, to continue the
dialogue. ' "I can't talk like this, Control," Leamas said at last.
"What do you want me to do?" ' (p. 19). Ironically what Control
wants him to do is open a discourse with the opposition. The plan
is to bluff the other side into believing that Mundt, their deputy
head of the Department for the Protection of the People, is a spy.
Leamas, it is implied, is specially chosen for the job because it was
Mundt who destroyed his network. He is really chosen because
he is someone who uses discourse rather than engaging in it. By
this I am suggesting that while he is open to the nuances of
relationship that can develop out of dialogue, he holds on to the
meaning he is given as if it were a sacred trust.

Crucial to the working of the plot are Leamas's dialogues with
Fiedler, the deputy head of security. Fiedler debriefs him when he
pretends to defect and it is through Fiedler that the seeds of doubt
can be sown. 'Espionage is a crime almost devoid of evidence,
which is why intuition, for better or worse, always has a large part
to play in its successful detection'.[7] There is not scope here to
explore in detail the dialogue between Leamas and Fiedler. Suffice
it to say that through its progress an intimation forms in Leamas
that Fiedler is his ally. This feeling is strengthened not only by
their mutual suffering at the hands of Mundt but by their access

through dialogue to each other. Both men actively seek to bring about a reaction in the other. Leamas has his 'job' to do, namely to activate suspicion in Fiedler while Fiedler wishes to find in Leamas what Leamas is not 'conscious of knowing' (p. 127).

> Responsive understanding is a fundamental force, one that participates in the formulation of discourse, and it is moreover an active understanding, one that discourse senses as resistance or support enriching the discourse.[8]

In many ways we are looking at the classic interrogator and prisoner, hostage and captor relationship. The undoubted impact derives from the evolution of the exchanges played out against the reader's knowledge of ulterior motives. The shock is not that of 'the terrible clarity of a man too long deceived' (p. 217); we have already understood what is going on. The shock is the demonstration of the ambivalence of the dialogic relationship. Leamas's sense of the use and validity of language is destroyed and all he has left is visions of suffering humanity and an obtuse devotion to Liz. Since dialogue has lost its meaning for him when Liz dies, he has nothing; he gives himself up to death amid the 'shouting, English, French and German' (p. 240).

Accepting that language is a focus of interest for le Carré certain enquiries emerge from his early books. He is clearly interested in genre, he uses recognisably popular genres to support his efforts to become a storyteller. But he does not do so uncritically and he reacts against the constraints imposed by playing with, even mocking, their conventions. Gradually out of the kind of fictions he writes the nature of dialogue emerges as a central problem. It dominates *The Spy Who* but it apparently offers no more stable ground for communication than did genre.

Leamas, in *The Spy Who*, is the outsider who is manipulated by the establishment. His human sympathies and understanding of how language between people works are betrayed and subverted by intentions of which he has no knowledge. Le Carré is interested in the use and preservation of power by a self-perpetuating élite and particularly how it is effected through the medium of language.

Being a novelist this theme of language necessarily relates, reflexively, to his own use of language as well.

In *The Looking-Glass War* the focus shifts from the outsiders to the insiders, to the preservation of power by the privileged few. As such the book has no heroes and only two protagonists and possibly three if we count Taylor, Avery and Leiser. These three are used to explore different kinds of dialogue employed by outsiders in their relations with the powermasters. Interestingly, even the masters of the game are seen to be engaged in a power struggle between themselves, the old guard deriving their authority from the Second World War and the new deriving their authority from the Cold War. Taylor is disposed of quickly, a low ranking functionary sent on a mission for which he has no aptitude. His ineffectual behaviour in the airport bar veering from bumptious and aggressive with the barman to subservient with his contact the pilot Lansen speak clearly his incompetence. He is flung out of the novel as peremptorily as he is thrown out of life by the car that kills him.

Avery, trying to 'reconcile an Arts degree with an uncertain provenance' (p. 25) sees being 'on the team' as a way of belonging. The old brigade accept him as the new boy, but do not hesitate to remind him that he does not have their shared wartime background that would make him fully one of the elect. It falls to him to be Leiser's companion in training but not on the human terms which Avery understands, 'He's an agent. He's a man to be handled, not known' (p. 121). It is that lack of genuine feeling which Avery never does understand. When Leiser, in spite of the Vopos closing in, continues radioing back from East Germany, nobody listens, nobody cares and only Avery mourns, 'sobbing like a child' (p. 231).

Fred Leiser is doubly the outsider. He might have worked for the department during the war, undertaking dangerous missions in the field, but he does not have the background and, as a Pole, English is not even his first language. Rather like Leamas, and later Harting, Leiser upholds an ideal of honour which the duplicitous world of espionage could never maintain. When Haldane says condescendingly of him to Avery 'And remember he's British: British to the core' (p. 130), he is speaking more truly than he realises. Lacking the nuances of language and ambivalences of feeling he remains faithful to a past ideal, 'held by some private discipline, a man once more intent upon appearances, conscious of tradition' (p. 237). Of course the gesture is futile, the quest was only ever a rumour in the first place, the real story lies in the great game that the principals are playing elsewhere to ensure their existence.

I suggested earlier that le Carré seems, in some senses, to undermine his own novels. In *The Looking-Glass War* the elaborate fiction of military operations is swept away in the ridiculous futility of the mission. All that is left is the shadowy manoeuvring between Control and Leclerc for power. The real story, the substance, is on the margins and as readers we are, possibly mockingly, fed the sensation and the sentimentality.

The Looking-Glass War is a deception, le Carré the conjuror shows us Fred the rabbit – only to make him disappear, revealing glimpses of the real trick elsewhere. In *A Small Town in Germany* the author is in crisis, searching for his missing novel. Stated baldly like this the comment seems merely modish, but it can be unravelled to sound plausible and, I believe, revealing. I have so far tried to demonstrate that a major current in le Carré's work is suspicion of language. Suspicion of the forms of language needed to establish communication (such as the generic form for writing novels) and suspicion of individual's usage, where characters are either heartless and lying, like Control and Haldane, or limited and deceived like Leamas and Leiser.

This view has in it the seeds of a serious problem, the familiar logical contradiction. If I write a book expressing the view that 'all language is deceptive' what is the value of the book? Either it is itself an act of deception, or the statement is wrong and the book erroneous. I am a liar or a fool.

A Small Town in Germany and *The Naive and Sentimental Lover* can be seen as addressing just this problem. Up to this point the main strength of le Carré's novels has been in the dialogue, not just dialogue between characters but writing about communication as essentially verbal rather than written. There have been some occurrences of written material in the novels, none odder perhaps than Smiley's retelling of the novel in the so-called report contained in Chapter 17 of *Call for the Dead*, but they have tended to be slight. *A Small Town in Germany* is different.

From the opening of the book written texts create tension, the midnight streets are empty but the written slogans shout their political messages. After the prologue the first character to speak is Meadowes, the Chancery Registrar, whose records are to figure so largely in the book. Basically the situation is that, 'Forty-three files [are] missing, not one of them below confidential. One green classified Maximum and Limit, gone since Friday' (p. 47). Their absence has been discovered in the wake of the disappearance of Leo Harting, a refugee like Fred Leiser, who works for the British Embassy in Bonn. Harting has been either ignored or looked down on for the twenty years he has worked for the British in one temporary post after another. He is an enigma. 'We know nothing about him. He's not even carded. As far as we're concerned he doesn't exist' (p. 47).

Alan Turner is sent from England to track down Harting and cover up the mess which everyone believes will result from Harting's assumed defection. But just as Harting is an outsider, a displaced person, so too is Turner in his own way. Harting's 'English was never perfect' (p. 66) but then Turner's does not quite fit either, though for other reasons. Bradfield, Head of Chancery, is the voice of the establishment:

> They were glaring at one another across centuries of suspicion: Turner clever, predatory and vulgar, with the hard eye of the upstart: Bradfield disadvantaged but not put down, drawn in upon himself, picking his language as if it had been made for him.   (p. 58)

We have two extremes, Bradfield on whom the language, its use and nuances, sits easily: Harting on whom the language has never quite fitted. In the middle is Turner, skilful in his use of language but wielding it like a weapon, rather than communicating with it as if it was one with his being. In a very real sense the book is about a writer, Turner, seeking an absent novelist.

Harting is the novelist. He is recorded several times as a good storyteller, 'He had a lovely way of narrative, Leo did' (p. 84). Not only that but in Bakhtin's terms he is an ideal novelist, for 'He could do all the voices, Leo could' (p. 99). His novel is whatever it is he has found in the files, and as the novel we are reading proceeds it becomes clear that his novel derives from the continuation of the past, including his own past, into the present.

Turner too is a constructor of narratives. His search for Harting is a reconstruction of embassy life, with its deceptions and falsities. The difference is that Harting has created his 'novel' outside the text whereas we see the process by which Turner works within the novel. The forerunner to Harting's disappearance is the Thursday absence. In Turner's endless questions and reconstructions, 'where did they meet? where did he unpack those files and letters and breathlessly recite his intelligence?' (p. 161), we see the attempted formation of a continuous and consistent text of Harting's absence.

A number of times Harting's ability with language is commented on, his ability to write reports (p. 110) his ability to convince his hearers (p. 216). But the insider's comment, Helen Bradfield's judgement, is that 'it was all fake. He was on guard. He listened to his own voice the way he listened to yours' (p. 237). The lower grades in the Embassy may admire Harting's language abilities, but the establishment view remains that he is a fake. That is why he himself feels that his words fail him and that at the end it will not be the telling but the action which will succeed. In pursuit of the action he dies.

Just as the slogans on banners dominate the beginning of the book so Turner's cry 'Leo' is drowned by the chants of the mob at the end. Reports of the truth are silenced, as Turner is silenced by Bradfield who, when he suggests admitting Harting's disappearance, says 'I will not have it said' (p. 206), or are drowned by 'The music [that] had risen to a single note, a raucous, crude, deafening roar, a call to battle and a call to anger' (p. 318).

A Small Town in Germany is rich in voices, cautious speakers like the caretaker, and Praschko, hovering between speech and writing. But here I am concerned with how David Cornwell's invention John le Carré writes about language, particularly language as novel. In this book we have someone, Harting, who has something important to say. What he has to say is that the establishment is in league with the barbarians and all the Turners in the world cannot save him. Bleak as this conclusion may seem something positive has happened. The novel is the story of Turner's retrieval of the authentic text. Muddied and untidy it may be; nevertheless its word is rescued though its author dies.

Le Carré's next book *The Naive and Sentimental Lover* has generally had a bad time from the critics. In commenting on the book's gaucheness one is reminded of the nineteenth-century critic who wrote of one of Disraeli's novels that it appeared to have been written for a wager, to see how much balderdash the public would accept. But in pursuing le Carré's quest to find out what he is doing when he writes novels the book is complex and full of interest. It compares the maker with the creator.

The tone is reminiscent of *A Murder of Quality*, pretentious and arch: 'He called his process taking the feel of the place. It was one he had rehearsed often and which involved the sampling of many intangible elements' (p. 17). If we can accept the banality of Cassidy's 'taking the feel of the place' as telling us about Cassidy we cannot accept it being matched by the author's cliché-ridden commentary which follows, with its odd inclusion of the unfocused word 'intangible'. But if one puts this aside there is a fascinating comparison between the maker of things and the maker of novels. A comparison deepened by Cassidy's fascination with Shamus, his flirting with being a novelist himself. Again though we have a pessimistic ending, not because he finds writing 'a lonely business' and 'tiresomely elusive' (p. 429), nor because he does not read Shamus's latest book *Three for the Road* but because language and being are confirmed as separate. As Sandra says 'The truth is you . . . . Not what you say' (p. 329). Shamus's credit is not as a maker of fictions but as 'the taker and challenger of life' (p. 431).

Le Carré's next three books, a trilogy featuring Smiley and published under the joint title of *The Quest for Karla* appear largely to shelve the problematic nature of language to concentrate on the social, political and individual themes that are such an important ingredient in his work. Certainly the genre of spy fiction is ironically handled through the persona of Jerry Westerby in *The Honourable Schoolboy* but the central concern with language seems to hark back to *The Spy Who*.

The books are an endless store of varied dialogues handled with great skill ranging through classes and even through the shades of Empire. They are a culmination in a way of le Carré's early work, even characters like Mendel, are brought back for the feast. There is though a weakness; the dialogues do not speak for themselves as they do for instance in the work of George V. Higgins. Rather le Carré guides us through them in case we miss the point. Sometimes he does this by setting the scene and the characters so elaborately that the dialogue is merely a narrative device, as with Ricki Tarr and Connie Sachs, to push on the story rather than the dynamics of the story itself. At other times he painstakingly constructs the inner directions ' "May I ask you something, Mikhel?" Smiley said, selecting a line that was oblique to the main thrust of his enquiry' (*Smiley's People*, p. 115), so breaking the tension of our response to the writing. It is rather as if the conjuror told us the rabbit was coming from the tail of his coat as he produced it, the sleight of hand is brilliant, but we are still being patronised.

To some extent I am breaking faith with Bakhtin's method. Le Carré's orchestration of dialogue from different strata of society and between different strata is masterly. But I have a suspicion that le Carré's dislike of critics is not the scorn of the creative for the parasitic but the dislike of rivals. The books are a disquisition on dialogues with commentary – dressed as novels. Looking at the latest two books *The Little Drummer Girl* and *A Perfect Spy* the tension of his own dialogic enquiry into the nature of language returns.

In these latest novels, le Carré has returned to the investigation, among others, of the nature of fiction. Not simply scrutinising the use of fictions but, more significantly for a novelist, asking what does it mean to participate in the fictioning process? Is a fictionist, like the fathers of Charlie and Magnus, like the fathers of Philby and Cornwell, basically a conman?[9]

Alongside this question, which I have tried to show as manifest in different ways through le Carré's books, is the accompanying question: Is the use of language between people basically a con? Is to use language necessarily to lie either by deliberate intention, or inadvertently, through the manipulations of those who have the power to ordain the context? Is Cornwell like Philby, not merely in having a conman for a father, but in needing to provide a critique of society, Philby doing so through his espousal of Marxism in his 'silent war', Cornwell doing so through his novelist, the deceptively square le Carré?

Throughout the books the world of theatre and acting provides an image of the third rate and the false. The Weybridge Repertory Theatre in *Call for the Dead* is the stereotype of all that is supposed to be worst in theatre. Even the production of *Edward II* towards the end of the same book only serves to provide a rather dreary background contrasting with that 'improbable romantic' and genuinely 'unforgettable figure', Dieter. These larger set-pieces are accompanied by many pejorative descriptions which use theatre to indicate the meretricious and insincere. The heroine of *The Little Drummer Girl* is an actress, Charlie, and a large part of the motive force of the book is the contrast and comparison of theatre with what le Carré calls the 'theatre of the real' (for example p. 292, p. 522).

The contrast is between the tatty touring companies that Charlie belongs to and the major Israeli deception that she joins with director/producer Marty Schulmann, in order to further the fight against international terrorism. Of course such a contrast is too easy, the theatre world invoked by le Carré too stereotyped and too predictable. What is really interesting is the comparison, between theatre and life. 'Theatre should be useful. It should make people share and feel' (p. 122), but this is said at the same time that this goal is actually contending with the means employed. Theatre is (in a sense) a con and the performers 'trained to pretend', so that, 'how can one believe anything' (p. 335). It is a situation fraught with paradox: a deception to reveal truth, just as the killing is to save lives, 'We save innocent life. Assuming I deliver the explosive, that is' (p. 268).

The verbal paradoxes become, like the world of espionage itself, unbearable. We are in what 'Angleton called "the wilderness of mirrors," where defectors are false, lies are truth, truth lies, and the reflections leave you dazzled and confused'.[10] The diary that the Israeli intelligence team fake for Charlie constitutes a 'story within the story within the story' (p. 274). The only resolution is to break the mirrors of lies and have recourse to deeds, for Khalil 'The guerrilla is the great actor of the world' (p. 484). Becker says of Charlie 'She's voting with her actions. Not with her words' (p. 465). At the end of the book Charlie goes back to the theatre of words but she is haunted by the images she has brought back from the theatre of the real. When she actually catches sight of Joseph, who is not Joseph at all but Gadi Becker, she dries in mid-performance. Her role collapses, the individual voice collapses 'I'm dead she kept saying, I'm dead, I'm dead' (p. 522). But as we see from the punctuation it is not just Charlie's own voice we hear, rather a medley of voices counterpointed by an interior monologue supervened by the voice of the narrator.

Of all le Carré's books *A Perfect Spy* is the bravura performance. The death of Magnus discussed briefly at the beginning of this essay, shocks and saddens us as it does because it is also the despair and death of the narrator. If this statement is to be any more than a trick of rhetoric, a lie or a rather loose metaphor it needs explaining.

Magnus and the narrator are the same, they share the same multiplicity of voices, they share the same touchstone of value and they experience the same tyranny. Magnus is the narrator's *alter ego* in that he lives out the experiences of the novelist, whose autobiography is the novel. Repeating Bakhtin, who has been invoked as the guiding spirit in this taking of 'backbearings' through le Carré's files, 'The novel can be defined as a diversity of social speech types (sometimes even diversity of languages) and a diversity of individual voices, artistically organised'.[11]

The novelist then is adept at mimicry, at reproducing different voices. Just so Magnus from the opening of the book is seen as endlessly amenable, the master of whatever voice is needed, 'Magnus of course is in whatever mood he needs to be in' (p. 22). 'Magnus has a lot of ways of talking' (p. 66). This facility has a price, it divides you into pieces none of which ever quite belongs to you, just as Magnus is divided 'after the great Pym share-out' (p. 36). Does the novelist, endlessly iterating other voices, never quite belong to himself?

The literature held up for admiration in le Carré's books is seventeenth-century German literature. Probably the most famous novel of that period, *Simplicissimus*, is the totem of the bond between Axel and Magnus, its significance reinforced by its being the key to their communication. One of the great novels of Europe, its value is that it embodies the spirit and reflects the essential culture of its troubled times through the life of its hero. Without passing a comparative judgement on the two books *A Perfect Spy* similarly gives us a life which takes us through a period of great change. At the end the central characters might be said each to have 'sat down to my books, which were now both my work and my delight',[12] and from this process to have completed the discovery of themselves. Both decide to leave the world, Simplicissimus for a hermitage, Magnus for death.

But these two signs of unity between the novelist and his protagonist, namely their shared capacity to recreate diverse voices and their shared totemism of the same literature, are complemented by a third – a shared fear of the same tyranny of the language they have learnt. Magnus's habits of deception have been learnt from Rick, Rick who so ably trims his voice and cadences to the person he is talking to. His struggle to gain a life of his own is the story of the book. When Magnus writes, 'Life began with Lippsie' (p. 93), it began not only because of love but because she 'taught him writing' (p. 125). It is the beginning of a long slow emancipation from Rick which is only completed with the writing of the book, 'Word for word the truth. No evasions,

no fictions, no devices. Just my over-promised self set free'
(p. 36).

The significance of the need to break free of the ideological
constraints of the discourse of others is best expressed in this
passage from Bakhtin:

> The tendency to assimilate other's discourse takes on an even
> deeper and more basic significance in an individual's ideological
> becoming, in the most fundamental sense. Another's discourse
> performs here no longer as information, directions, rules, models
> and so forth – but strives rather to determine the very bases of
> our ideological interrelations with the world, the very basis of
> our behaviour; it performs here as authoritative discourse, and
> an internally persuasive discourse.[13]

This exploration of Magnus's struggle to free his consciousness of
Rick's influence, to determine his own idealogy, is paralleled by
the author's struggle, proposed through this essay, to break free
of what he sees as the evasiveness, the duplicity, the con of
language. At the end the hero welcomes silence, the author stops
writing, only the indeterminateness of the book remains. Of course
as long as readers are prepared to enter into a dialogue with the
book its voices live again, their murmur drowning the growl of
the dogs.

Le Carré favours the downbeat ending, I don't. Speaking of
writers Elias Canetti says:

> He should be able to become anybody and everybody, even the
> smallest, the most naive, the most powerless person. His desire
> for experiencing others from the inside should never be deter-
> mined by the goals of which our normal, virtually official life
> consists; that desire has to be totally free of any aim at success
> or prestige, it has to be a passion in itself, the passion of
> metamorphosis.[14]

NOTES

1. Dennis Monaghan, *The Novels of John le Carré*, (Oxford: Blackwell,
   1985) p. ix.

2. Mikhail Bakhtin, *The Dialogic Imagination*, ed. M. Holquist (Austin: University of Texas Press, 1986) p. 262.
3. Quotations from the works of John le Carré are from the following editions: *A Perfect Spy* (Sevenoaks: Coronet, 1987); *The Honourable Schoolboy* (London: Pan, 1979); *Call for the Dead* (Harmondsworth: Penguin, 1987); *A Murder of Quality* (Harmondsworth: Penguin, 1986); *The Spy Who Came In from the Cold* (London: Pan, 1965); *The Looking-Glass War* (London: Pan, 1967); *A Small Town in Germany* (London: Pan, 1970); *The Naive and Sentimental Lover* (London: Pan, 1973); *Smiley's People* (London: Pan, 1981); *The Little Drummer Girl* (London: Pan, 1983).
4. Hugh Dubrow, *Genre* (London: Methuen, 1982) p. 2.
5. Ibid, p. 9.
6. Kingsley Amis, *What became of Jane Austen?* (Harmondsworth: Penguin, 1981) p. 75.
7. Peter Wright, *Spycatcher* (New York: Viking, 1987) p. 300.
8. Bakhtin, *The Dialogic Imagination*, pp. 280–1.
9. David Leitch, interview with John le Carré published in *The Sunday Times Colour Supplement*, September 1987.
10. Wright, *Spycatcher*, p. 305.
11. Bakhtin, *The Dialogic Imagination*, p. 262.
12. H. J. C. von Grimmelshausen, *The Adventurous Simplicissimus*, tr. A. T. S. Goodrick (Lincoln: University of Nebraska Press, 1986) p. 354.
13. Bakhtin, *The Dialogic Imagination*, p. 342.
14. Elias Canetti, *The Conscience of Words and Earwitness* (London: Picador, 1987) p. 163.

10

Reading John le Carré

RICHARD BRADBURY

John le Carré's writing about George Smiley spanned nineteen years, from his first appearance in *Call for the Dead* to, presumably, the end of his career at the conclusion of the Karla sequence. As such, he is the central figure in a group of novels which employ the developments in superpower politics over the last thirty years as a background against which to articulate a more or less coherent world view. Despite the success of the relatively early *The Spy Who Came In from the Cold*, it was not until the quest for Karla trilogy had been completed and the two BBC serialisations of *Tinker, Tailor, Soldier, Spy* and *Smiley's People* had been shown that George Smiley, thinly disguised as Alec Guinness, became, albeit briefly, a media star and the novels began to attract serious critical and scholarly attention. This lack of concern was primarily caused by le Carré's choice of an 'unliterary' form, the spy novel, which stood beyond the confines of the 'great tradition' as studied in much of the English academy. Indeed, despite its undeniable weakness as a novel, it seems to me that *The Naive and Sentimental Lover* was used as an occasion by a number of critics to chastise le Carré's pretentions (as they saw them) towards writing Literature. Since the successes of the Karla trilogy and the development of a serious methodology for the study of popular literature, however, his work has been the subject of three important studies.

Nevertheless, Peter Lewis's explanation of his reasons for devoting space in his work to the early novels, namely that they had been ignored in favour of exhaustive investigation of the works from *The Spy Who Came In from the Cold*, remains true today. My purpose here, therefore, is to examine George Smiley's early manifestations and the ways in which le Carré used the early novels to lay stylistic and thematic foundations upon which he then elaborated the later and more widely known works. From his first appearance as the 'breathtakingly ordinary' figure at the beginning of *Call for the Dead*, Smiley has been employed by le

Carré as the representative of English middle-class common sense. The function of this essay, then, is to unpick the threads of George Smiley's early career and show how he has developed into the representative of those most ideological strategies: the denial of ideology and the use of doubt as a mechanism for the maintenance of the status quo.

Smiley's denial of ideology consists of his constant appeals to normality. He increasingly sees what exists as the only possibility, and therefore defends that despite any moral or ethical qualms he might have. Rigby's office is the early reflection of this – a room which both mirrors and is mirrored by the normality of the man who occupies it – and the later absence of any ideologically based defence of the precepts of the Western politicians is its completion. The place of doubt in this model is in its filling of the void left by the absence of any ideological certainty or absolutism. In this way Smiley becomes the personification of moral and political pragmatism and, as such, the 'living centre' of the novels; the character with whom the reader is 'required' to identify.

> When Lady Ann Sercomb married George Smiley towards the end of the war she described him to her astonished Mayfair friends as breathtakingly ordinary. When she left him two years later in favour of a Cuban motor racing driver, she announced enigmatically that if she hadn't left him then, she never could have done; and Viscount Sawley made a special journey to his club to observe that the cat was out of the bag. (*Call for the Dead*, p. 7)

This first paragraph of le Carré's first novel introduces us to a number of crucial facts about Smiley; his ordinariness, his marriage to Lady Ann Sercomb and the distance which exists between his social position and the Sawley family as the representatives of the semi-aristocratic wing of the old ruling class. I emphasise this here because one of the most striking features of the early novels is their acute sense of the finer distinctions which produce the cultural labyrinth within which social class operated (and operates) as a mechanism of inclusion and exclusion. Le Carré's own involvement with, interest in and finally distance from, the institutions of the English ruling class has given him a particularly acute sense of the nuances they employ to distinguish between themselves and others.

The first of these three elements is Smiley's constant source of defence throughout the novels. He is not painted in the flamboyant colours of Ian Fleming's two-dimensional moral and political absolutist adventurer Bond, but is very much part of the world of England in the early 1960s. Unimpressive is an adjective employed to describe his appearance on numerous occasions. He is 'the most forgettable man' (*A Murder of Quality*, p. 24). he is the epitome of the middle class, of the petty bourgeois.

As such, Smiley occupies a position which is deeply contradictory. Recruited into the Service in the thirties, he is a part of the tradition of amateurism which is being replaced by a bureaucratic machine in the post-war years. He is closely related to the heroes of the work of John Buchan and Erskine Childers by their shared amateurism, but is at the same time at a distance from them in that for Smiley espionage is a profession. He is, therefore, the bridge between the amateurism of the years before World War II and the developing business of spying in the years after. Hence, the drift from *espionnage* as excitement to spying as a boring, repetitive job which was one of the first markers of le Carré's fiction. As such, he was recognised as a realist and his work has continued to have an air of realism, even down to the (invented) argot with which his characters describe their work.

This dividedness is also a reflection of the ideological position he occupies, as he negotiates his way in this first novel between the pre-war view of the world and the developing understanding of the post-war period. The history of Smiley's relations with Dieter are indicative of this, as he changes from a friend to an enemy partly because of his socialism, partly because of geographical accident, and partly because of the expediencies of power politics.

> This was a new world for Smiley: the brilliantly lit corridors, the smart young men. He felt pedestrian and old-fashioned, homesick for the dilapidated terrace house in Knightsbridge where it had all begun.   (*Call for the Dead*, p. 13)

Old-fashioned, perhaps, because he is not completely in tune with the new world-view and he can therefore retain an attachment to that pre-war world through his relationship with Dieter Frey, in which shared experience can supplant ideological differences. This, in turn, leads to Smiley's guilt after having killed Dieter because the latter 'had remembered their friendship when Smiley had not'

(*Call for the Dead*, p. 143). For a moment, an emotional response supplants ideological positions.

But this disturbance at the end of *Call for the Dead* is short-lived and vanishes as completely as the possibility of Smiley's reunion with Ann which flickers across the last pages of the book. By the beginning of *A Murder of Quality*, Smiley is back within the boundaries of a domestic dispute amongst the English ruling class and restoring normality to the perch from which it had been displaced by the murder of Stella Rode. Hereafter, Smiley may have extreme doubts about the morality, ethicality or even simply the purpose of what he is doing, but these doubts are subsumed within a conventional view of the political world as divided between East and West. For Smiley, the understanding that there is no qualitative difference between either the systems or their managers – a point to which the later works return a great deal – is less important than the public fiction that there is.

In the same way, his relationship with Lady Ann Sercomb, which both begins and ends *Call for the Dead* has ceased to be a living emotional commitment by the beginning of *A Murder of Quality*. Ann disappears from the novels until the Karla trilogy, and returns then only to haunt Smiley through her infidelities. But the memory of the wedding, of his albeit brief connection to the ruling class, returns to haunt him in the form of social humiliation. That he stays in the Sawley Arms hotel in Carne, that Shane Hecht publicly upbraids him for his attempt at upward social mobility, these and other markers of the gulf between Smiley and the denizens of Carne echo around the fringes of this second work and give the book a quality of social criticism beyond the often remarked-upon parallels which le Carré draws between the world of espionage and the world beyond. Smiley accepts that his place is to defend the social order represented by Carne even as he accepts that he is not a part of that world.

This divided view is at the root of his scepticism, and echoes his producer's opinions on that most English institution, the public school.

Eton, at its worst, is unbelievably frightful. It is intolerant, chauvinistic, bigoted, ignorant. At its best, it is enlightened, adaptable, fluent and curiously democratic. (*Listener*, 5 Sept 1974)

Smiley accepts the ends for which the English ruling class exists, namely the maintenance of the world order, but cannot come to terms with the reflection of those ends in their domestic means. It is precisely the mechanisms that these people maintain at home which Smiley most despises. The conclusion to this line, as it develops and grows through the later works, is Smiley's increasing disbelief in any constant which can act as an anchor for his consciousness other than his own intellect. As readers, we come increasingly to rely on that intelligence to guide us through the labyrinthine plots of the novels as they tear away at the ideological preconceptions of both characters and readers.

At crucial moments in the Smiley novels, however, even the home, that heart in the heartless world, becomes a site of danger for Smiley. Fennan is murdered by his wife as she attempts to protect her identity as the East Germay spy; Stella Rode is murdered within her own home; Smiley's vulnerability in the Karla trilogy flows directly from Ann's infidelities and this, in turn, generates the ambiguity at the end of *Smiley's People* as Karla drops Ann's cigarette lighter at Smiley's feet. Even that supposedly most secure redoubt from the ravages of politics, the emotional world, becomes cast into doubt. As the committedly doubting inhabitor of this world Smiley becomes the exemplary contemporary character for le Carré.

We should be clear, though, that this quasi-existential situation has its roots in a series of historical phenomena. As a product of the post-war years, le Carré was subjected to the 'lunatic ideological reversals' which constituted the move from hot to cold war. The bombers of Berlin in 1945 became the organisers of the Berlin airlift in 1948. The 'communism' of the East was excoriated by comparison to the freedoms of the West, even as both the old, and a series of new, undemocratic institutions reared their public heads in Britain and the USA. In the wake of Suez, this combined with an almost frantic clutching at a past similar to that portrayed in *A Murder of Quality* and began to percolate through the media of the time. At the same time, the climate of 'unideological' rebellion is familiar from the writings of the angry young men, and le Carré is a part of this generation. As the wartime certitudes were replaced by either another set of cynically produced political and social simplicities or by a confused and confusing set of positions, the index of revolt placed a high premium on a rejection of ideological standpoints. The point is, of course, that without an oppositional ideological position, these rebellions became absorbed into the conservative project of revitalising that which exists simply by accepting that the present status quo is a given. The work of John Osborne is a proof of this point.

What Smiley represents in the first two novels is the re-installation of the normalities of what is, essentially, a deeply conservative view of England in which anything disruptive is a frightening menace. The major advance from here to *The Spy Who Came In from the Cold* is the abandonment by the central character of any belief in the inherent rightness of the British way of life. As that book demonstrates, which side of the ideological or geographical line one stands is accidental and one's actions are shaped by a developing awareness of that contingency. But of course Smiley makes only the briefest of appearances in this work and his two final cries – 'Jump, Alec! Jump, man!' and 'The girl, where's the girl?' – are indicative of the positions rejected by Leamas when he climbs back into East Berlin because they represent the West as a haven and the completion of the mission as paramount. The rejection of ideology and the nihilistic conclusion of the book are intimately intertwined, but both these are products of the book's historic moment in the crisis of Conservative politics between 1956 and 1964.

George Smiley, however, avoids these conclusions by continually separating means from ends. The ends are identified as the defence of the stability of the English ruling class and in this cause the use of any means is justified.

> It was a cheap trick to play on a man who had suddenly lost his wife. Smiley knew that. . . . He acknowledged that in calling on Rode under any pretext at such a time he was committing a thoroughly unprincipled act. It was a peculiarity of Smiley's character that throughout the whole of his clandestine work he had never managed to reconcile the means to the end. . . . once in the war he had been described by his superiors as possessing the cunning of Satan and the conscience of a virgin, which seemed to him not wholly unjust. (*A Murder of Quality*, p. 79)

In *The Spy Who Came In from the Cold*, *The Looking-Glass War*, and *A Small Town in Germany*, Smiley is absented from the process of gradual realisation that the accepted political divisions in Europe are a fiction concealing the fundamental congruencies of East and West. But when he returns centre-stage in the Karla trilogy Smiley too has come to an acknowledgement of this and the only difference remaining between him and the other characters is that he retains an allegiance to the familiar and known territories of the West.

Both of the early works begin with a version of the opening strategy le Carré was to perfect in the later novels. The plot begins with a disruption of normality and concludes with the restoration of that normality through the intervention of Smiley. To make the challenge to the existing state of affairs more visceral, and therefore less obviously ideological, le Carré repeatedly demonstrates that Smiley is not the disinterested analyst but is a part of the action as it unfolds and is effected by it. He kills Dieter at the end of *Call for the Dead* and is badly frightened by the 'feel' of the Rode house at night in *A Murder of Quality*. He feels disgust for all those around him at the conclusion of *A Murder of Quality* and breaks his fingers when he punches Dieter in *Call for the Dead*. Nevertheless, Smiley represents an intellectual defence of the world view of the English ruling class and their allies within the worlds of both domestic snobbery and world politics.

The stylistic element by which le Carré's opening chapters are controlled is a feature that has become a marker of his work and, for some critics, a constant source of annoyance. Here we get his parcelling-together of large quantities of necessary background information so as 'to set the scene' or to display his knowledge of a particular setting. Indeed, this feature has been picked out to prove that the difference between 'Literature' and popular fiction is based wholly on the capacities of the individual writers. To which I would simply reply that almost exactly the same strategy is at work in the novels of Dickens. The question at issue here is not that of the relative merits of abstract literary style, but of the position of that style in relation to the socially determined boundaries of what is or is not a 'literary' form. That le Carré writes within the form of the spy novel automatically debars him in some circles from being capable of, or even from having the aspiration towards, writing 'serious fiction'.

While, on the one hand, this often leads to clumsy formulations, its purpose is clear. It is to give that normality of which I have already written a 'solidity' so that it is unnecessary to defend it in overtly political terms. It exists, it is there before us in the text and the forces of opposition committed against it are consigned to being not of that world; alien to it, frequently precisely because of the insubstantiality of the ideology on which they rest. In this way, le Carré creates a universe in which England becomes the known, the familiar, and its enemies come to occupy a shadowy position at the edges of that shared environment.

That this is the mechanism at work is best revealed in these early novels because they take as their referents an England which has been radically altered since the moment of writing. Thus, the referents which le Carré takes for granted as being part of the creation of that shared world are strange to the contemporary reader. As someone who grew up in Dorset, this is most obvious in the description of Smiley's journey from Waterloo to Carne along the now-destroyed Yeovil to Bournemouth line of the Somerset and Dorset railway. That reference inevitably returns this reader to the vanished social world of rural England twenty-five years ago. Presumably, for a London reader the continued existence of certain now-demolished buildings in Cambridge Circus in *Tinker, Tailor, Soldier, Spy* operates in the same way. The point of this is that le Carré employs these descriptions to create a world with which his contemporary reader feels familiar and any disruption of which intrudes into the reader's sense of normalcy.

Beyond this, the ways in which le Carré connects the shared social world of his readers to the world of his characters while at the same time creating an environment peculiar to these figures serve to convert plots of deceit and betrayal into metaphors for our social interaction. Le Carré was explicit about this in an interview when he said:

> the figure of the spy does seem to me to be almost infinitely capable of exploitation for purposes of articulating all sorts of submerged things in our society   (*Listener*, 22 Jan 1976)

The distinction between Smiley and le Carré is crucial but often ignored. Partly, no doubt, because it is not consistent and emerges only at moments of wider social description and can, therefore, be (wrongly) seen as extraneous to the 'plot' of the fiction. The point is, of course, that it is precisely the fashion in which this field is constructed which distinguishes le Carré's work from the 'run of the mill' thriller in which plot is all. The other extreme from his work is Fleming's construction of a world which is unreal despite the fidelity of its surface details, because the Bond novels consistently avoid making any connection to a social reality. They drive towards a setting which is familiar only because the labels on it are recognisable. Everything else in it is, literally, fabulous and fantastic.

On the other hand, le Carré's work is more 'realistic' because it demonstrates an awareness of the contradictions inherent in the world in which we live. Beyond the accuracy of detail which gives the books a contemporary 'correctness', there is a clash, dramatised repeatedly in le Carré's work, between ideological assumptions and the day-to-day business of living one's life which reinforces the substantiality of the sensual, as opposed to he ethereality of theoretical or ideological explanations of the world. Thus, Dieter Frey is the 'enemy' in *Call for the Dead*, in that he is the East German spymaster in London but he is also an old acquaintance of Smiley's, always referred to as 'Dieter' and mourned by Smiley at the end of the novel – even though it is Smiley himself who has killed Dieter:

> Dieter was dead, and he had killed him. . . . And Dieter had let him do it, had not fired the gun, had remembered their friendship when Smiley had not. They had fought in a cloud, in the rising stream of the river, in a clearing in a timeless forest: they had met, two friends rejoined, and fought like beasts. Dieter had remembered and Smiley had not. They had come from different hemispheres of the night, from different worlds of thought and conduct, Dieter, mercurial, absolute, had fought to build a civilisation. Smiley, rationalistic, protective, had fought to prevent him. "Oh God," said Smiley aloud, "who was then the gentleman?"   (p. 145)

I quote this at length not simply to point up the irony of George Smiley quoting from John Ball's sermon of rebellion, but also because of its similarity to that line which stands so close to the thematic heart of the Karla trilogy, when Smiley asks Karla if it isn't time 'to recognise that there is as little worth on your side as there is on mine?'

The same is true in *A Murder of Quality*, when Smiley intrudes into the closed world of Carne Abbey – an institution dedicated to 'keeping the new world out and the old world secure' (p. 84). Persistent references to the nineteenth century in the initial descriptions of Carne, combined with the image of the boys rushing to perform the rituals of public school clearly situate Carne as a point in the past, as part of a society the urban environment has surpassed but on which the structures of an earlier time have a significant hold. The division of Carne between not only town and gown but also Church and Chapel produces a pattern of social differentiations across which the intruder from the present cuts in order to restore normality but also to introduce a new order. If Rigby and his office are described thus: 'the very ordinariness of the man and his room identified him with the society he protected' (p. 36), this gives us a clue to his inability to solve the crime. He stands too close to the social order which is, ultimately, the cause of the crime. Smiley, as a geographical and social outsider, can see to the heart of the crime but even then his commitment to the maintenance of public social proprieties leads him to attempt to offer Fielding the 'gentleman's way out'.

In all of this, the function of le Carré's narrative voice is central because it plants a procession of adjectival and adverbial landmines designed to blow off the clay feet of the Carne School habitués. While Peter Lewis correctly identifies a satirical tone in much of le Carré's descriptions of the institutions of the English ruling class he fails to see that le Carré identifies patterns of behaviour, the social mechanisms they develop in order to exclude those not of their class, rather than anything about their ideological motives, as central to his intense dislike of these people. Again, it is the means rather than the ends which are criticised.

The real distinction between le Carré and Smiley, though, is revealed by their respective positions within the narrative. Smiley endures the social assaults and humiliations in order to arrive at his conclusions; he is involved in the forward motion of the plot. Le Carré, on the other hand, defends Smiley through his use of the satirical description of the environment in which his hero is operating. Our position as readers in this nexus is as intermediaries between these two positions; invited to identify with Smiley as our intellectual and physical guide through the labyrinths but at the same time invited to cast knowing glances at our hero's weaknesses. This is a question of degree, rather than of principled difference, but it is still useful to a reading of the novels.

11

The Well-Wrought Structures of John le Carré's Early Fiction

DAVID SEED

During an interview in 1986 John le Carré was confronted with the suggestion that the public considered his plots too complicated. His response was categorical: 'I do not agree. The people who offer that complaint are not prepared to make any intellectual effort . . . I am convinced that the reader likes to work a little and at the end is happy to have resolved a somewhat complex story'.[1] An extreme of complexity was reached in *Tinker, Tailor, Soldier, Spy* (1974) whose unusual intricacy was subsequently explained by le Carré as follows:

> In the novel the facts of the affair were presented as a deliberate jungle; as a devilish, perverse chaos which only Smiley could resolve. This is a perfectly normal feature of the detective story and, in the convention, requires Poirot, or Holmes, or whom you will, to call everyone together and explain who precisely was in the woodshed at three a.m., and for what fell purpose, and why it is that only the great man himself was able to come up with the solution. The audience does not really *follow* the arguments, but it derives a vicarious sense of accomplishment, which is musical rather than rational, from somebody else's spurious arithmetic . . .[2]

Le Carré's linking of his own fiction with detective stories suggests that he is putting a very high premium on information – on its release, coherence and connection through a character like George Smiley whose prime function is explanation. Such a character is obviously designed as a mediator between the reader and obscured narrative fact, and his activities will bring this hidden information to the surface. We will thus be presented with the story of the unfolding of a story, a double narrative working simultaneously on two different levels. In what follows I shall be examining the different ways in which le Carré handles his plots in the novels up to *A Small Town in Germany* (1968), considering the role of mediator-characters and variations on expected patterns to events.

A key figure who has clearly had an impact on le Carré's sense of plot is Somerset Maugham. Le Carré has described the latter as the 'greatest craftsman of our century' and wrote to Maugham's biographer Ted Morgan to admit: 'the Ashenden stories were certainly an influence in my work. I suppose that Maugham was the first person to write about espionage in a mood of disenchantment and almost prosaic reality'.[3] Apart from issues of tone Maugham's insistence on craft and structure was vitally important. He saw plot as a 'line to direct the reader's interest' and from the French and Chekhov formed an artistic purpose based on a clear single continuity: 'I wanted to write stories that proceeded, tightly knit, in an unbroken line from the explanation to the conclusion'.[4] This principle is repeated in *A Writer's Notebook* (which was read approvingly by le Carré) and in his preface to *Ashenden* (1928), a series of interlocking stories centring on the activities of a British agent based in Switzerland. Here Maugham draws a Jamesian distinction between the 'random' and 'structured' schools of fiction, arguing that the former is all very well for short effects but that any degree of length 'needs a supporting skeleton'. He continues: 'The skeleton of a story is of course its plot. Now a plot has certain characteristics that you cannot get away from. It has a beginning, a middle and an end. It is complete in itself'.[5] When interviewed on BBC Radio shortly after the success of *The Spy Who Came In from the Cold* le Carré declared an intention which virtually echoed Maugham, a felt need to create a 'single narrative form, to make order out of chaos, to give the thing a beginning a middle and an end',[6] although his narrative structures rarely have such a rigidly Aristotelian pattern. In Maugham's stories Ashenden is a writer as well as a secret agent and this enables Maugham to introduce a self-reflexive dimension to his narratives, especially where Ashenden is trying to locate himself within larger sequences of action: 'he never had the advantage of seeing a completed action. He was concerned with the beginning or the end of it, perhaps, or with some incident in the middle. . . . It was as unsatisfactory as those modern novels that give you a number of unrelated episodes and expect you by piecing them together to construct in your mind a connected narrative'.[7] Maugham limits us to Ashenden's perspective and creates local reversals and anti-climaxes some of which rebound ironically on him and others of which thwart the reader's desire for glamorous action. Of le Carré's critics only Eric Homberger has pointed out the importance of Maugham's character for the former's fiction: 'Ashenden, like Smiley, made the process of understanding, the immersion in the mentality of his opponent, the central drama of effective counter-espionage'.[8] The first part of this statement is the most helpful since Maugham undoubtedly helped le Carré to compose narratives based extensively on investigation, analysis and the patient reconstruction of plot; and to guide him away from spy fiction based on glamorous action. A statement made in le Carré's second novel stands as a general gloss on his own works: 'The byways of espionage are not populated by the brash and colourful adventurers of fiction' (*A Murder of Quality*, p. 83).[9]

Le Carré's first novel, *Call for the Dead* (1961, temporarily retitled *The Deadly Affair*) combines espionage with the formula of a whodunit and thereby confirms Eric Homberger's general point that 'his characters and his plots are with very few exceptions always rooted in the past, a past which declines to stay buried: it must be dug up, sifted, reinterpreted for clues to the meaning of the present'.[10] In surveying the general patterns of detective fiction Tzvetan Todorov draws a crucial distinction between the story of the crime and the story of its investigation. The former is a hidden plot, initially inaccessible to the reader, whereas the latter is the 'mediator between the reader and the story of the crime'.[11] Todorov is too hasty in his dismissal of the investigation as a purely functional convenience. It will be argued that on the contrary the inquiry enacts the novel's construction of a plot, scrutinising itself in the very process of that construction. The issues around which the plot revolves are whether Samuel Fennan, a Foreign Office employee, was a spy, and secondly whether he really did commit suicide. The figure who attempts to solve these questions is George Smiley who will play a major role in le Carré's 1970s trilogy *The Quest for Karla*.

The most startling structural aspect of *The Call for the Dead* is the fact that the opening chapter delays the introduction of the narrative proper by giving an ironic summary of George Smiley's social and professional career up to that point. If Peter Lewis is right that le Carré is wilfully diverging from an expected pattern then this delay gives Smiley (the investigator) priority over the *subject* of investigation in spite of the apparent ironies levelled against him.[12] When his divorce is described le Carré seems to caricature his fate:

> And so Smiley, without school, parents, regiment or trade, without wealth or poverty, travelled without labels in the guard's van of the social express, and soon became lost luggage, destined, when the divorce had come and gone, to remain unclaimed on the dusty shelf of yesterday's news. (*Call for the Dead*, p. 7)

With masterful economy le Carré divorces Smiley from the British establishment (represented by his wife and her circle) and from the present to suggest a solitary figure at odds with his contemporary professional context. The metaphor in this passage is particularly well-chosen because Smiley's own enthusiasm for travelling gives a hint to the reader that he has avoided social fixity (and in that respect contrasts strongly with the English stereotypes who appear in this novel). The ironies of the chapter move Smiley to the margin of the intelligence service – it is no surprise that he resigns quite early in the novel – and prepare us for the essentially individual nature of his investigation. By temporarily privileging character over plot-sequence le Carré firmly distinguishes his own novel from a kind of thriller-writing he described in a 1974 interview as 'books which are written in such a mechanical way that you impose upon the characters forms of behaviour'. He went on to give the following example: 'you have to get the parson into the woodhouse at 2 a.m. in order to kill the duchess. Now that is a book where the plot is imposed upon the characters'.[13] By contrast Smiley's method of investigating the Fennan case follows a course dictated by his preliminary character-sketch.

Before his death Fennan had been investigated by Smiley for holding Communist sympathies and le Carré here blurs any sharp distinction between the hidden and latent plots. The two levels of investigation displace the reader even further back in time to the 1930s which proves to be a crucial decade in the hinterland to the novel's action. Just as the reader is uncertain over chronology so the issue of the plot turns out to be more complicated than a simple death. Since Smiley was in the unique position of investigating Fennan he alone can appreciate the disparity between their interview (which cleared him) and Fennan's suicide. A routine visit to console his widow actually begins to multiply the discrepancies (why did he ask for an early morning telephone call if he was going to commit suicide?) and spurs Smiley on in an investigation which his superior officer Maston strongly discourages ('We're not policemen, Smiley'). Here a major ironic theme in le Carré's works emerges for the first time: the search for truth is usually conducted against an official insistence on secrecy which is designed to avoid administrative embarrassment. Smiley pursues this search through a series of interviews which establish his credentials as an analyst. In the first chapter of *Call for the Dead* le Carré mimics an external visual perspective on a silent Smiley whereas in the bulk of the narrative the perspective is *from* him, and the investigation demonstrates his acumen through speech, through knowing which questions to ask. As this investigation proceeds, however, it becomes obvious that Smiley needs an assistant and le Carré supplies one in the person of Mendel, an inspector in Special Branch who is coming up for retirement. Mendel, like Smiley, embodies a professionalism while being on the margin of his profession and he functions entirely as an extension to Smiley's search. It is discovered that the Fennans have a connection with the operations of East German spies in Britain one of whom batters Smiley unconscious. This misfortune immobilises him for a considerable part of the novel, confirming Smiley's primary role as a sifter and interpreter of information, a role which he partly fulfils through dialogue and partly through composing a series of written résumés of the information discovered. These constitute narrative cruxes every bit as dramatic as more violent events because they focus the enquiry on specific points of fact.

The summaries represent the novel's whole purpose in miniature since they assemble information in the most logical and dispassionate way and that very act of ordering leads to new discoveries. Thus Smiley links his own attempted murder with the death of Fennan by the fact that someone saw them together and recognised Smiley as an intelligence agent. On a very much smaller scale Smiley is performing a function here which anticipates his presence in say *Tinker, Tailor, Soldier, Spy*. As le Carré subsequently explained, 'I needed Smiley to take them [readers] by the hand and ask questions on their behalf, solve the mystery for them'.[14] Smiley leads the action remorselessly towards its ultimate goal of uncovering the hidden plot and making it explicit. The true resolution of the novel comes when he sits down to write out a final accurate summary of the main facts.

The progression through the plot towards this summary sounds like a gradual shift from *sujet* to *fabula*, but the novel brings into question the true nature of the plot and the true focus of importance. For one thing le Carré seems uncertain how much scope for physical action to give Smiley. Although Mendel takes over the drudgery of the investigation and is physically powerful it is Smiley who eventually kills his opposite number in East German intelligence, Dieter Frey. The logic to this action arises from a submerged psychological theme in the novel, namely whether Smiley's profession has led to a dissociation of feeling from reason. This is the charge which Elsa Fennan levels against him but ironically it is exactly his feelings of scruple which induce him to believe her 'admission' that her husband was a spy when in fact she was the agent. In Chapter 14 Smiley contemplates a rococo porcelain group from Dresden with the objectivity he lacked in the earlier scene and by so doing achieves the climactic realisation which would put all the events in their proper relation to each other. This is simultaneously an insight into order and into himself: 'He saw how he had been the fool of his own sentiment, had played false with the power of his mind' (*Call for the Dead*, p. 122). The Dresden figurines trigger off memories of when Smiley was recruiting agents in the 1930s. One of these, Dieter Frey, can now be seen for the first time in the novel and emerges from the past as a satanic but romantic anti-self to Smiley which must be destroyed. Fennan's fate has by this stage been long forgotten and he has been kept firmly in the background so that an ultimate confrontation can emerge between Frey and Smiley. Given the nature of the novel this opposition between attacker and defender, man of action and man of reflection can never substantiate itself. Le Carré does not give himself room to render this contrast except through rhetoric out of key with the main narrative ('they had come from different hemispheres of the night').

A Murder of Quality (1962), as its very title suggests, stays closer to the pattern of the whodunit and in so doing avoids some of the awkwardness of le Carré's first novel. This time Smiley's role is firmly limited to that of investigation and the action is distanced from the world of espionage to such an extent that Smiley's background becomes an irrelevance beyond explaining tenuous connections between himself and some of the other characters.

Like *Call for the Dead* this novel opens with a pointedly ironic description of the West Country public school which will be the main setting. The greatness of Carne School, we are told, 'is little short of miraculous. Founded by obscure monks, endowed by a sickly boy king, and dragged from oblivion by a Victorian bully, Carne had straightened its collar, scrubbed its rustic hands and face and presented itself shining to the courts of the twentieth century' (*A Murder of Quality*, p. 9). The cumulative force of le Carré's sarcasm repeatedly undermines the school's pretensions to status and tradition, suggesting the very opposite qualities of provincialism and obscurity. Although the narrative revolves around a murder the descriptive details offered the reader are constantly in excess of what the mystery might demand and thus suggest that the novel is partly a period and local study. The ironies le Carré directed against a certain level of society in *Call for the Dead* are now focused more powerfully on a specific institution and Smiley's observations on character and place perform the function of confirming those ironies. A mockery of Carne turns out to be the means of solving the murder-mystery; revelation shades into exposure.

In many ways *A Murder of Quality* conforms to the pattern of whodunit as outlined by Todorov. It virtually starts with the completion of an 'absent' series of events culminating in the crime: the murder of the wife of a teacher. It pursues a second narrative devoted to uncovering the former series and uses such traditional devices as the principle that 'the tenor of each piece of information is determined by the person who transmits it' in order to pace out the gradual release of information.[15] Setting (the school and its immediate surrounding) imposes a firm boundary on the action and it is made clear from the beginning that the cast of characters (and therefore suspects) is limited. By contrast *Call for the Dead* uses chronological regression to displace the reader into different levels of the past and to introduce its key antagonist long after its narrative has got under way. In the second novel le Carré develops Smiley's enquiry through a series of interviews with the school staff which apparently culminate in the successful arrest of Crazy Jane, a local character. It is blatantly obvious that she is the wrong suspect, partly because her arrest occurs so early and partly because she cannot act as a conduit for information on the hidden plot. An increase in new evidence and the device of a second murder (this time of a schoolboy) confirm the irrelevance of Jane and lead the narrative into a revelation (a subsidiary one, it seems) of a master's sexual weakness for young boys. At every point in this narrative le Carré attempts to balance the reader's suspense (fed by cliff-hanging chapter endings) against constructive inference. Passages of dialogue thus alternate with passages of reflection where Smiley even analyses the processes of his own thinking: 'It had been one of Smiley's cardinal principles in research . . . not to proceed beyond the evidence. A fact, once logically arrived at, should not be extended beyond its natural significance' (*A Murder of Quality*, p. 98). Smiley's caution tugs against le Carré's arrangement of the narrative which deliberately feeds the reader false clues, premature confessions and conclusion, and misleadingly seems to underline certain characters as key suspects.

Smiley's efforts to bring the truth to light involve him in the progressive exposure of the Carne teachers as driven by the unflattering motives of snobbishness or escapism. Rode can only emerge as the likely murderer of his own wife Stella because of the strong class-antagonism which existed between them. But even this is a false trail. As Peter Lewis has pointed out, le Carré further complicates our reactions by 'making the murdered Stella so unsympathetic that the murderer seems justified', but adds that this reversal is not a moral one since Fielding, the actual murderer, is also a corrupt individual.[16] Revelation of the murderer's identity involves revelation of his motive which was to keep his homo-sexuality hidden. In other words the investigation was by its very nature hostile to Carne's institutional tendency to keep such matters hidden.

The same anti-establishment animus becomes even more hostile in le Carré's next two novels although the structural method he uses has changed considerably. *The Spy Who Came In from the Cold* (1963) and *The Looking-Glass War* (1965) replace investigation with plots which exploit the ignorance of their characters. In both novels a sequence of action fulfils itself in such a way that the protagonists only realise its true nature towards the end of the narrative when it is too late for them to do anything about it. Revelation of pattern and structure becomes pointedly ironic because of this ignorance, an ignorance compounded by the fact that the protagonists must act. They are not there to investigate an earlier sequence but to participate in a current plan with information supplied on a 'need to know' basis. Since the perspective of *The Spy Who* is limited mainly to that of Alec Leamas, a British agent completing his career in the field, then the reader will be debarred from gaining extensive information unlike le Carré's first novels where Smiley uncovers even more information than that possessed by the intelligence establishment. Predictably this puts far more weight on the gaps between the blocks of narrative. Le Carré of course has been preoccupied throughout his career with the limits of what is known within the context of espionage. In his 1968 introduction to *The Sunday Times* 'Insight' team's biography of Kim Philby, le Carré repeatedly compared the book to a novel characterised by absences: 'This book is massively incomplete . . . we should never forget the gaps . . . it is arguable that even the principle character is still missing.'[17] By the latter le Carré means Philby's recruiter and it was the absence of such details which spurred his imagination on to create the convoluted plot of *Tinker, Tailor, Soldier, Spy* and the psychological sophistication of *The Perfect Spy*, both novels making use of the Philby case.

The Spy Who Came In from the Cold begins with an ending. The death of Alec Leamas's agent Riemeck at a Berlin check-point is the last in a series just as Leamas's job to dispose of his East German opposite number Mundt is to be his last before he comes in from the cold, that is, from operations in the field.[18] The novel assembles an astonishingly varied sequence of entrances and exits which all belie the title's suggestion of a hostile exterior contrasting with a hospitable interior. The sequence of action where Leamas functions as protagonist (instead of just observer as at the check-point when Riemeck is shot) begins in a flat which is 'small and squalid, done in brown paint with photographs of Clovelly'. Once he has got to know Liz Gold, a naive Communist and worker in the same London library, she invites him to her equally anonymous bed-sitter. The apparent depths of Leamas's decline are reached when he spends a short period in a London prison. From the day of his release onwards his contacts with East German agents develop through a series of entries to the flats of Ashe and Kiever and to Peter's Dutch bungalow. The laconic chapter-headings ('Contact', 'The Third Day', etc.) make it clear that a sequence is taking place, a sequence glossed explicitly as a 'progression in quality' to reflect the hierarchy of the intelligence service. Chapter 10 marks the turning-point in the novel since Leamas is now taken out of Holland on a passport which expires during the narrative. Although he talks of 'going home' in the novel no interior adequately embodies the comfort he desires. All the flats described are anonymous, furnished perfunctorily and therefore the stop-ping-off points in an essentially transient existence. It is only after Leamas has left and thus receded into a distant image, that Liz can use her room to try to live over again her memories of their intimacy. When Leamas is taken into East Germany the farmhouse where he is held reminds him of the Circus (the British intelligence service) although his bedroom is 'like something in prison camp' (*The Spy Who Came In from the Cold*, p. 126); and when he is knocked unconscious by Mundt memories of past captivity blur into the present as he imagines himself back in the London prison. Le Carré skilfully weaves variations on the theme of autonomy here by suggesting differing degrees of confinement. Indeed the novel repeatedly appears to alternate captivity with release, at the same time complicating the alternation by questioning the nature of his release. The open wooded countryside where Leamas has his conversations with Fiedler at one and the same time suggests the distance he has come from a familiar supporting context and also functions as a misleading prelude to Leamas's interrogation at the hands of Mundt. During his journey to the East Leamas is reminded of Arthur Koestler's captivity narrative *Darkness at Noon* but at least in this novel the relation of captive to captor remains stable. In *The Spy Who* identities are constantly shifting. Mundt the interrogator then becomes the accused in a secret trial and finally the liberator in opening up an escape route for Leamas and Liz into West Berlin.

These shifts in role and the spatial ambiguities of the novel's settings all bear on the dramatic irony in the plot, the irony of a character's unconsciousness of how his or her subsequent fate will develop. In this sense the opening chapter is predictive. It looks forward to Leamas's own death and will bring his comments about agents getting involved with women to bear on his own Achilles' heel – his relationship with Liz. In an interview of 1964 le Carré described the organisation of the book in the following way: 'I wanted to lead him [the reader] into a cosy adventure story and then implant a feeling of alarm as he read on, so that things consistently turned out differently all the time. Make an equation and reverse it, make another equation and reverse that. Finally, let him think he'd got nearly to the solution of the main equation, and then reverse the whole thing'.[19] Peter Lewis has pointed out that the 'groupings of characters and the patterns of opposition stand out clearly from the texture of the novel' but this is only true if we try to imagine the structure of the novel synchronically.[20] A

vitally important part of *The Spy Who* involves the gradual perception of structure as the novel progresses and le Carré's limited
perspective ensures that this is going to be an arduous and
disconcerting process.

The complexities start towards the end of Chapter 2 when
Control (Leamas's superior) tells him that he has a plan to discredit
Mundt and invites Leamas to his house to discuss the details. We
infer that the plan has been finalised in the gap between this and
the following chapter when le Carré begins to make use of what
John G. Cawelti and Bruce A. Rosenberg have happily called
'rumour-devices'.[21] At the beginning of Chapter 3 the perspective
has been shifted to a collective view of Leamas from the Circus,
but with a rhetoric ('seemed', 'as far as could be judged', etc.)
which leaves a margin open for the revision of impressions. At
this point we are temporarily manoeuvered into the position of
Leamas's observers whether they are colleagues or enemy agents
and, since we know that a plan is being pursued, we know
how untrustworthy appearances are. Our vulnerability from the
limitations of information is underlined by the kind of narrative
comments which le Carré uses throughout the book. When Leamas
is about to leave Holland he hears that a newspaper article has
run that he is being sought by the British police. His reaction is an
attempt at self-reassurance: 'Control had done it. Control had
started the hue and cry. There was no other explanation' (*The Spy
Who Came In from the Cold*, p. 101). Juxtaposed to this chapter is an
account of Circus officials visiting Liz which concludes 'It was very
strange'. Both these examples represent a character's specific
and limited response to particular events. Within the ostensible
contrasts set up by the novel Liz clearly represents the innocent
whereas Leamas is the hard-boiled worldly-wise professional.
However the juxtaposition of the two chapters actually questions
this contrast. Leamas's lack of certainty implies that he has only a
limited knowledge of Control's plan, a suspicion confirmed by the
visit of British agents to Liz's flat. This in turn implies that Control
(whose very title implies a principle of action) might be using her
unbeknown to Leamas. The reactions quoted above then become
important for what they do not say, for the possibilities they still
leave open.

Betrayal is central to le Carré's oeuvre and is introduced strategi-
cally in his novel through Leamas's suspicion that Riemeck has
been given away by his lover. This preliminary information estab-

lishes the need for Leamas's cynical pose although, as Tony Barley has shown, the novel questions this pose through a whole series of interrogation scenes.[22] Leamas proves to be every bit as innocent as Liz in assuming that his own side will not betray him and that their relationship is somehow exempt from the machinations of espionage. This relationship plays such an important part in the novel that le Carré became quite anxious when it was neglected in critical comment on *The Spy Who*, insisting: 'It is a very romantic story: two people fall in love and one has to betray the other and both of them, in a sense, perish in a mental institution'.[23] The Cold War's capacity to divide is symbolised in the novel by the Berlin Wall which le Carré saw as an 'image of a physical division through a living city'.[24] Perhaps as a corrective le Carré seems to overstate the centrality of the romance in *The Spy Who*, which functions partly in order to break down once and for all Leamas's confidence that he can use the role of a disillusioned defector as a mask for his feelings. Liz's introduction into the East German hearing swings our attention round from Mundt to Leamas as if he were on trial, and le Carré seems to return to romantic adventure in having Leamas and the girl escape. But such a conclusion would smack of Ian Fleming and once again expectations are reversed. Liz is shot (deliberately?) and Leamas deliberately commits suicide because he cannot find a preference between the one side of the Berlin Wall and the other. Tony Barley suggests that he has found a 'tiny no-man's land' but Leamas's problem is that there is no space available in between the collapsed antitheses of East and West.[25]

Leamas starts his last operation from a position of apparent knowledge. As he is being questioned he can stand back from the immediate situation to predict what is going to happen ('they would know it was a gamble'). Conversely the interrogator Peters can view Leamas as a typical defector and phrase similar predictions as likely hypotheses. The process of interrogation simultaneously supplies the reader with a lot of information predating the immediate narrative and (through the interrogators' emphases) keeps the reader's attention concentrated on a number of specific areas which have not been described before, such as Leamas's activities in the Circus banking section. On his journey east Leamas thinks back to his conversation with Control about their plan when the latter declared: 'Fiedler is the acolyte who one day will stab the high priest in the back' and it is Fiedler who later tells Leamas: 'you have told us all you are *conscious* of knowing' (*The Spy Who Came In from the Cold*, pp. 119 and 127). The ironies multiply at this point since Leamas does not make a full confession until the trial. Fiedler's statement is relevant to the reader because it hints at unconscious concealments and unconscious admissions. The different stages of Leamas's questioning draw explicit attention to the assimilation, selection, and organisation of material, in other words to the process whereby plot is apprehended by the reader. In le Carré's first two novels investigation is concentrated in the character of Smiley whereas now this activity is spread through a series of characters culminating in a secret tribunal. The trial of Mundt ironically confirms Fiedler's words to Leamas because it occasions a 'false' summary of events from the former (Mundt has been secretly taking money from the British) and a second counter-summary from Mundt (this was all a plot hatched by the British which implicates Fiedler). At this point the full meaning of Control's statement about Fiedler becomes clear in a moment of realisation: 'suddenly, with the terrible clarity of a man too long deceived, Leamas understood the whole ghastly trick' (*The Spy Who Came In from the Cold*, p. 217). The third possibility (that the scheme was made deliberately blatant in order to *protect* Mundt, who is a British agent) is not made explicit here. The chapter-ending highlights Leamas's insight but defers revealing it to the reader for several pages. Here we must draw a distinction between two kinds of pattern which have emerged. The first is the internal structure of Control's plan; the second is the formal pattern of ironies set up by the novel as a whole. Although Leamas now understands the former he has yet to conclude the sequence of ironies with his death. The effect is of an expanding series of frames; Fiedler's summary of events is contained within the larger set of correspondences and ironies.

The Looking-Glass War (1965) is certainly one of le Carré's most biting novels because it repeatedly contrasts intelligence plans with their actual outcome in order to show the blindness and high proportion of sheer fantasy in those plans. The two parts of the British intelligence establishment – the Circus and the 'firm' – are presented as rivals, the former dominating the field and the latter having been reduced to a research organisation. The Second World War functions as a major reference-point to this intelligence unit since the war puts a halt to its progress and in its subsequent stagnation it is sustained only by a worn-out traditionalism. The signs of this tradition are petty office rituals and a speech-idiom characterised by slang and circumlocutions which are constantly described as antiquated. This idiom is ominous because it has cut itself from the outside world and now serves the main function of reinforcing the solidarity of the unit. Against this set of self-enclosed expressions le Carré places the voices of the women in the novel who, whether secretaries or wives, ask direct questions which expose the weaknesses and absurdities in the unit's verbal conventions. The women characters collectively extend the implicit ironies in passing narrative comments, bringing them to bear explicitly on such issues as the identity of the unit's enemies. To take one example from le Carré's detailed descriptions of London: 'it was a large building, very ugly in its way, the beginning of a new world, and at its feet lay the black rubble of the old' (*The Looking-Glass War*, p. 42). This attention to urban redevelopment alerts the reader to exactly the historical changes which the unit has been unable to digest. The signs of this temporal paralysis are verbal as when the unit's supervisor Leclerc tells an operative's widow that her husband has died 'gallantly'. Her response is angry and relevant to the perspective of the novel as a whole: 'What do you mean gallantly? . . . We're not fighting a war. That's finished, all that fancy talk' (*The Looking-Glass War*, p. 73).

In spite of such explicit comments, which le Carré reinforces with ironic epigraphs from Kipling, Buchan and Rupert Brooke, the unit cannot believe that it is finished and devises an operation to send an agent into East Germany to verify reports of a new rocket base. This plan is described at length in the third section of the novel as an exercise of nostalgia, a way of reviving fading memories. Even before the plan is formulated details in the agents' speech and the physical appearance of their offices repeatedly displace the reader into the past and reduce their actions to what Tony Barley has called 'fantasies of purposeful behaviour'.[26] Le Carré himself has explained the unit's staff as people 'marooned by dreams of war which they've had to leave behind . . . they were looking for an enemy and they thought they had found [one] in the rockets in East Germany'.[27] The scheme to send an agent east can thus be read as wish-fulfilment, a collective desire to repeat the excitement of discovering the V-2 sites on Peenemünde, and every detail of the operation from the old-fashioned radio equipment to the return to a secret location near Oxford presents the plan as an anachromism.[28] Here the significance of the novel's title emerges. Operation Mayfly is a reflection or attempted repetition of earlier operations in quite different historical circumstances. Like the personnel of the unit Mayfly is the imitation or continuation of a lost original.

The Looking-Glass War is divided into three sections each described as 'runs', i.e. operations in the field. The first and shortest, like the opening of *The Spy Who*, describes a flawed meeting. Taylor the operative is due to give money to a pilot in exchange for a film he has taken of the suspected rocket sites but when the latter arrives he throws secrecy to the winds and talks openly about the operation. Taylor's panicky realisation that planning has collapsed ('this wasn't the way it was supposed to happen') is ironically confirmed when he is run down by a car just outside the Finnish airport where the meeting took place. The second 'run' is made by John Avery to collect Taylor's body and effects. Avery is an important character because he is too young to have acquired completely the mentality of the unit. On his flight to Finland he reflects with pride on the privilege of knowing his colleagues but this satisfaction is rudely shattered when things start to go wrong with his attempted recovery of the film. Embarrassing discrepancies over Taylor's passport, etc. begin to multiply and induce disenchantment with his own service. In this section le Carré alternates blocks of narrative in London with blocks from Finland in order to undermine the sense of home which might motivate the members of the unit. Thus Chapter 7 closes with Woodford's sense of familiarity with London, 'an old athlete on an old track.' This security is explicitly contrasted with Avery's utter isolation in Finland which drains his enterprise of any possible glamour. Just at the point where Avery's thoughts turn to England le Carré suspends his narrative and jumps to a studiously bleak image of London suburbia. The structure which now begins to emerge in the novel involves oppositions. On the one hand the unit's plan is a projected plot but in each of the first two sections the projections fail to materialise. Because all three sections have similar titles le Carré tacitly invites the reader to put a rather different predictive significance on to events. If the first two runs fail then surely the third will also. Against the unit's naively linear plot le Carré constructs a counterplot, a set of devices which fragment that projected sequence of action and which question the anachronistic attitudes underlying it. Apart from alternation of action le Carré uses repetition with, for instance, the report on the rockets from an East German engineer. This is produced by Leclerc as the main justification for Mayfly but Avery later reads a report of Soviet tank-trials with exactly the same technical data which has been discredited as spurious. Or again repetition can suggest surveillance and impending capture. Does Avery see the same old Citroën in Finland as the one which killed Taylor? When the former is alone in his hotel room he hears a footstep and rustle of clothes in the corridor, exactly the same sounds which Leiser, the Mayfly operative, hears on the verge of his arrest by the Russian authorities.

Whereas the intelligence unit tries to imagine that the 'Jerries' are still the enemy le Carré smothers this opposition by introducing a variety of quite different contrasts: between male and female, young and old, insider and outsider. Towards the end of the third section the East German police pick up Leiser's radio transmissions. At the beginning of Chapter 21 the Americans have also taken a fix and the mirroring between these two scenes amplifies a common interest strengthened by hints within them that the Circus deliberately went along with Mayfly, informing the Russians so that the unit would be discredited once and for all. This possibility remains a matter of suggestion as does Leamas's final insight in *The Spy Who* and a margin of uncertainty persists to the end of both novels because the ultimate force guiding events cannot be absolutely proven. Patterns and repetitions can thus function as the structural equivalents for le Carré's characters' sense of entrapment. In a 1977 interview le Carré reflected: 'I suspect we are all overkeen to interpret life as a conspiracy', adding 'but, then, in an age of Watergate, it's true'.[29] Even more important, a sharp political irony emerges through the structure of this novel and the preceding one. Reversals in the plot of *The Spy Who* undermine Leamas's capacity to maintain a clean sense of 'sides' and the emergent parallels in the novel's action imply a similarity of methods in East and West. Similarly, in *The Looking-Glass War* the series of 'runs' suggests repetition or, more ironically, mimickry and the verbal similarity between Control and Smiley (functioning here as an owlish commentator) on the one hand and the East German and Russian authorities on the other implies that the novel's opposition between professionalism and amateurishness cuts across the East–West divide.

With *A Small Town in Germany*, le Carré's last novel of the 1960s, he returns to the investigation plot, but with the complication that it is the investigation of an investigation. Leo Harting, a minor

official in the British embassy in Bonn, disappears with a secret
file and is initially taken to have been a Communist spy. David
Turner, a combination of Smiley and Mendel from *Call for the Dead*,
is brought in to solve the mystery and discovers that Harting was
himself investigating the Nazi past of a West German politician
named Karfeld. These two characters, as Peter Lewis points out,
are much discussed within the novel but make virtually their only
appearance in the prologue where the absence of names reduces
them to the roles of hunter and hunted.[30] Instead of the lateral
complexities discussed in the preceding two novels le Carré now
creates at least four distinct levels of plot. On the surface is Turner's
investigation of Harting in the present of the novel which lasts for
about one week. In the course of this investigation Turner uncovers
administrative ineptness and the personal weaknesses of the
embassy personnel. In this respect Turner's boorishness provides
le Carré with an agency for puncturing the facade of clannishness
maintained by the British expatriate community in Bonn and
thereby confirms the ironies which le Carré levels against their
ritualism.[31] At a third level Turner gradually reconstitutes Harting's
own investigation and at the deepest level of all Karfeld's participation in a Nazi euthanasia scheme.

It should have become apparent already that these plots are
intricately connected with the present moment in Bonn. No other
novel of le Carré's takes so many bearings from contemporary
history. Britain's wooing of West Germany in negotiating their
entry into the EEC, the resurgence of Nazism and the statute of
limitations, and the student protests of 1968 all play their part here
as a determining context to the action. Even the landscape is a
historical one, full of echoes from Germany's past and signs of the
present like the giant Coca-Cola advertisement which flashes over
Karfeld's rally. Le Carré exploits the reader's implied knowledge
of the Second World War to hint at parallels between this rally and
Hitler's address or between the burning of books by contemporary
students and by the Nazis, but refuses to draw any firm conclusion
from these parallels. On the contrary he assembles opposing
explanations of the same historical phenomena to force a gap
between events and their explanation.

As Turner proceeds with his investigation through a series of
interviews he has to assemble an identity for Harting out of the
different partial accounts, drawing the reader's attention to salient
points along the way. If he is the protagonist his antagonist is

Bradfield, the head of Chancery, who is professionally committed to a creed of surfaces. Whereas Turner's function is to bring information into the light of day, Bradfield maintains a steady hostility towards the process whereby the novel's plot takes shape. At issue is not truth but what can be publicly admitted. 'I will not have it *said*!' Bradfield exclaims to Turner. Despite this opposition Turner even induces Bradfield's wife to admit that she was Harting's lover, but his is essentially a subsidiary revelation in a novel where personal actions and desires give way to the political necessities of the moment. As usual le Carré builds up a false hypothesis about Harting's actions which is dismissed around the middle of the novel: 'Nothing worked, nothing interlocked, nothing explained the *energy*, nothing explained itself. He had constructed a chain of which no one link was capable of supporting the others' (*A Small Town in Germany*, p. 167). The central weakness is the assumption that Harting is a spy. Only after he has discarded this possibility can Turner begin to retrace the former's investigation of Karfeld and uncover his plan to assassinate him. The last revelation to take place in this novel is of the contents of the secret file Harting took, namely that the British Government has been having secret discussions with Karfeld. This discovery really implies the expendability of Harting who dies obscurely in the crowd at Karfeld's rally. Given a collusion to stifle memories of Germany's past his investigation of Karfeld is doomed and quixotic.

For all his emphasis on story-telling in his interviews le Carré is remarkably consistent in creating plots which turn out to be far more complicated than suggested in the openings of his novels. This same gap between expected plot and actual developments forms the basis of 'Dare I Weep, Dare I Mourn?', a short story published in 1967. The subject concerns a prosperous Lübeck grocer (Dieter Koorp) whose father dies in the East. When Koorp hears that he is required to collect the body he angrily protests at the inconvenience since he appears to value his own routine above everything: 'He was a meticulous man: meticulous as he took his knife and beheaded his egg at twenty minutes past eight that morning in early January: meticulous as he put down his spoon and with surgical precision slit open the letter'.[32] Le Carré's particularity ironically mimics Koorp's fussy style and draws explicit attention to it, 'meticulous' echoing through the story like a refrain. The first reversal occurs when Koorp goes to his father's house and finds him alive, the report of his death being a ploy to smuggle him into the West. The second reversal occurs gradually during Koorp's journey towards the border when he fails to open his father's coffin for air. By summarising his thoughts le Carré sets up a grotesque disparity between Koorp's care over his driving and his indifference to his father. When the border guards open up the coffin his father is indeed dead, killed by Koorp's timidity. The concluding statement of the story, 'a man feels for his father', is belied by the implications of the narrative which convert the narrative into an ironic study of temperament. Given its brevity and its nature this story cannot carry the explicit references to how plots are constructed which occur in all the novels discussed here.

Le Carré repeatedly strikes a balance between search-narratives directed towards the uncovering of information and the adoption of limited perspectives which will retard this process. This balance ensures a tempo slow enough for hypotheses to be formed, rested and reshaped as the action progresses. This 'retardatory structure', as Meir Sternberg has explained, allows the reader's expectations to take shape and creates a 'more colorful play of hypothesis and effect'.[33] Kim Philby has recently commented on le Carré's novels: 'I thought the early ones were excellent but then they started to get a bit too complicated for me.[34] But then even Philby could be mistaken about the apparent simplicity of le Carré's early fiction.

NOTES

1. Pierre Assouline, 'Spying on a Spymaker', *World Press Review* 33 (August 1986) 60.
2. 'At Last, It's Smiley', *Sunday Telegraph Magazine* (21 October 1979) 108.
3. 'What Every Writer Wants', *Cornhill Magazine* 1050 (Winter 1966/1967) 406; Ted Morgan, *Somerset Maugham* (London: Jonathan Cape, 1980) p. 313.
4. W. Somerset Maugham, *The Partial View* (London: Heinemann, 1954) p. 123.
5. W. Somerset Maugham, *Ashenden, or The British Agent* (London: Pan Books, 1955) p. v.
6. Interview by Leigh Crutchley, BBC Radio, 13 October 1965.
7. *Ashenden*, p. 13.
8. Eric Homberger, *John le Carré* (London: Methuen, 1986) p. 36.
9. Quotations from the works of John le Carré are taken from the following editions: *A Murder of Quality* (Harmondsworth: Penguin, 1964); *Call for the Dead* (Harmondsworth: Penguin, 1965); *The Spy Who Came In from the Cold* (London: Pan, 1964); *The Looking-Glass War*

(London: Reprint Society, 1966); *A Small Town in Germany* (London: Pan, 1969).

10. Homberger, p. 43. The title of the novel was changed during the making of a film adaptation.

11. Tzvetan Todorov, *The Poetics of Prose,* translated by Richard Howard (Oxford: Basil Blackwell, 1977) p. 46.

12. Peter Lewis, *John le Carré* (New York: Ungar, 1985) p. 16.

13. Michael Dean, 'John le Carré – the writer who came in from the cold', *The Listener* (5 September 1974) 307.

14. Nicholas Wapshott, 'Tinker, Tailor, Soldier, Novelist', *The Times* (6 September 1982) 7.

15. Todorov, p. 46.

16. Lewis, p. 57.

17. Bruce Page, David Leitch and Phillip Knightley, *Philby: The Spy Who Betrayed A Generation* (London: André Deutsch, 1968) p. 10.

18. The various meanings of 'the cold' are discussed by John G. Cawelti and Bruce A. Rosenberg in their *The Spy Story* (University of Chicago Press, 1987) p. 169.

19. Jordan Bonfante, 'The Spy-Master Unmasked', *Life* 56 (28 February 1964) p. 41.

20. Lewis, p. 69.

21. Cawelti and Rosenberg, p. 168.

22. Tony Barley, *Taking Sides: The Fiction of John le Carré* (Milton Keynes: Open University Press, 1986) Chapter 2.

23. Dean, p. 306.

24. Crutchley interview.

25. Barley, p. 46.

26. Barley, pp. 57–8.

27. Crutchley interview. The agency's isolation is indicated by, among other things, repeated monastic analogies.

28. Here the historical precedent outweighs the uncertainty of the photographic evidence. The sceptics over the aerial photographs of Peenemünde (a method then in its infancy) were proved wrong.

29. Philip Oakes, 'Goings On: Hard Cash and le Carré', *The Sunday Times* (11 September 1977) 35.

30. Lewis, p. 100.

31. It is no accident that the Chancery guard should be John Gaunt, named after Shakespeare's spokesman for the English landscape. Other Shakespearian parallels in the novel ironically evoke a sense of mission and of embattlement.

32. 'Dare I Weep, Dare I Mourn?', *Saturday Evening Post* (28 January 1967) 54. One of the lugubrious ironies of this story is that the suggestion of Koorp being an executioner, far from being just a stylish trope, is possibly confirmed in the action.

33. Meir Sternberg, *Expositional Modes and Temporal Ordering in Fiction* (Baltimore: Johns Hopkins University Press, 1978) p. 161.

34. Phillip Knightley, 'Philby: No Regrets', *The Sunday Times* (10 April 1988) C2.

12

Professionalism and Popular Fiction: The Novels of Arthur Hailey and Frederick Forsyth

DUDLEY JONES

The nineteen-sixties and seventies saw the publication, in Britain and America, of a number of academic studies drawing attention to the growth in size and power of professional groups in society. Sociologists like Daniel Bell regarded that growth as symptomatic of the transition from an entrepreneurial capitalism to a corporate or monopoly capitalism. This change signalled a new phase of economic development – the 'post-industrial' society – in which, says Bell, the 'central person is the professional for he alone is equipped by his education and training to provide the kind of skills which are increasingly demanded'.[1] The notion of a transcendent professional class, although challenged by some sociologists, was not confined to academic circles. It was a view widely held on both sides of the Atlantic, and Harold Wilson's reference in the 1964 Election campaign to 'the white heat of technological revolution' and the subsequent creation of a Ministry of Technology, reflected a public awareness of the rapid pace of technological development, the spectacular achievements of space programmes and the importance of professional expertise in a variety of fields.

The glamour and the 'personal service' ethic associated with successful professionals encouraged the media to draw upon their ranks in its search for popular heroes: in medicine Doctors Kildare and Casey; in law Perry Mason; and in the police force the new career men of *Softly, Softly* and the tougher professionalism of Regan in *The Sweeney*. Even managers, engineers and accountants assumed prominent roles in television series like *The Power Game*, *Mogul* and *The Brothers*.

Elements of professionalism could also be located in a range of popular fiction in this period including *The Godfather*,[2] *Jaws*,[3] and the spy fiction of Fleming and Deighton. The attitudes and values associated with the professional received their most direct expression, however, in the novels of Arthur Hailey and Frederick Forsyth and this essay will consider how those concerns were articulated and how the work of these bestselling authors related to the contemporary sociological debate surrounding the concept of professionalism. To provide a context for this discussion, I want to examine some of the key issues in this debate.

Broadly speaking, sociological opinion was divided into two camps: the pro-professional[4] and the anti-professional.[5] The former, often associated with a functionalist approach, tended to reflect the professions' own views about their role and status in society. The latter argued that claims for the growth of the professional classes had been exaggerated since the statistical evidence on which these claims were based took insufficient account of the way 'relabelling'[6] had upgraded the jobs of those aspiring to professional status. This criticism drew attention to a problem which had caused considerable disagreement among sociologists, namely the vexed question of what constituted a profession. Attempts were made to overcome this problem by adopting what was called the 'inventory approach' to identify the core elements that distinguished the professions from other occupations. Esland lists some of these:

> one of the most important features of professional practice which is singled out . . . is the service ethic. Members of professions are typically seen as motivated by altruism and a high respect for confidentiality in their dealings with clients. Also important is the right of professions to determine their own code of practice, standards of education and training. . . . A third significant feature of professional activity is the fact that it is often based on specialist knowledge and technique – usually acquired over a long period of education. Because of this, professions claim to act as guardians of this knowledge and the means of access to it.[7]

Knowledge is a form of power and to ensure that power was used in a responsible way, the practitioner's behaviour was controlled by an internalised code of ethics and by voluntary associations. Barber maintained that prestige and honour – the symbols of work achievement – were associated with community interest (as opposed to self-interest) and were more important to professionals than monetary reward.[8]

Clearly the 'inventory approach' had in mind some kind of ideal model based on the classical professions – law and medicine; proponents of that approach therefore tended to be pro-professional in their attitudes. The anti-professional group, on the other hand, argued that these 'ideal' characteristics identified in the inventory were designed to foster an ideology of professionalism, and that the inventory approach failed to distinguish between the symbols of a profession and the reality.

A number of the 'ideal' characteristics were subjected to critical analysis. The service ethic, for example, portrayed professionals in a very favourable light with their selfless devotion to the clients' interests setting them apart from other kinds of workers. Unfortunately it was difficult to reconcile this alleged altruism with 'the ever increasing exposés of the backstage activities of the professions regarding fees and fee-splitting, unnecessary referral and intervention, ritualistic procedures or billing for work that was never undertaken'.[9]

The legal profession, in particular, was attacked for its failure to measure up to the service ethic. Thorn, in his analysis of the US legal system, showed how the law favoured the rich at the expense of the poor and his strictures were obviously applicable to the British legal system:

> Not all clients are equal in the eyes of the legal profession. The fee-for-service favours those who can pay and the poor often go without help of lawyers. . . . When they do seek private legal services, the poor usually end up with lawyers who are at the lower end of the profession in quality and training. . . . In law, as in medicine, the success of a professional is gauged by his income and the status of his clientele.[10]

It was argued, moreover, that the public's willingness to believe in the altruism and selfless dedication of the professional reflected the pervasive ideology of trust embodied in the maxim 'credat emptor' (let the taker believe in us) as opposed to the business motto of *'caveat emptor'*. This trust, says McKinley was partly maintained by concealing the self-interest and corrupt practices of professionals – a process described as 'insulation from observability'.[11] Such insulation was defended by some on the grounds that it enabled the profesional to make effective decisions based on specialist expertise and experience, without interference from ignorant lay people. It was one of the ways therefore in which autonomy – an essential element of professionalism – was protected. A more jaundiced view was that insulation enabled human errors that would threaten professional credibility to be quietly covered up ('physicians bury their mistakes'). It was also pointed out that most professionals were not independent practitioners but salaried employees within large organisations. This undermined the autonomy of the professional and raised the possibility of a conflict of loyalties: a corporate lawyer, for example, might be forced to choose between adopting practices that were ethically repugnant or losing his job.

Despite these criticisms, the ideology of professionalism successfully promoted an image of professionals as caring and efficient people to whom wide-ranging powers and responsibilities were justifiably delegated. I now want to examine the work of Arthur Hailey and Frederick Forsyth to determine whether their portrayal of professionals reinforced or challenged that ideology.

In an obvious and limited sense of the word Arthur Hailey and Frederick Forsyth are 'professionals' since, for both of them, writing is a full-time occupation. There are other ways, however, in which their approach to writing novels can be said to be professional. The importance which professional groups place upon research, specialist knowledge and technical expertise has already been referred to and it is reflected in the extensive planning and preparation that goes into a Hailey or Forsyth novel.

Arthur Hailey, for instance, decides on the major theme of a novel, carries out exhaustive research for a year and then a further six-months' planning before he begins writing. Forsyth's obvious familiarity with his subject matter is derived largely from his experiences as a journalist. As a Reuter's reporter his coverage of the OAS campaign against de Gaulle in Paris provided him with the necessary background material for *The Day of the Jackal*.[12] His preparations for *The Dogs of War* can only be described as bizarre.[13] During the Nigerian Civil War, which he covered as a BBC reporter, he became very concerned by the tragic plight of the children of Biafra and his sympathies clearly lay with the Ibos and their leader, General Ojukwu. When he returned to Britain he recruited a band of mercenaries and then planned and financed an unsuccessful coup against Equatorial Guinea. According to a *Sunday Times* 'Insight' report the intention behind this amazing project was to provide a homeland for Biafran refugees and a base for the defeated Ojukwu, who would take over as the new President.[14]

Hailey's early background was also in journalism. After leaving the Royal Air Force in 1947 he worked as an assistant editor on a Canadian trade magazine before becoming a full-time writer. The experience gained in journalism had an important influence on both Hailey and Forsyth and this is reflected in the amount of factual information their work contains and the feeling of a close correspondence between fictional situations and factual events. In Forsyth's case, this sometimes prompts the question: is one reading a documentary account or a work of fiction?[15] In Hailey's novels the detailed, realistic description of an institution or industry (*Hotel*, *Wheels*) serves as the dramatic focus for the intersecting biographies of a group of characters.

The documentary approach of both writers takes three main forms. The first can be described as 'faction' – the deliberate blurring of the boundaries between fact and fiction. This is often achieved by juxtaposing real incidents and people with fictional ones so that the reader becomes confused about the status of characters and events within the novel. This device is used to good effect in the opening of *The Day of the Jackal* where Forsyth draws on an actual assassination attempt on de Gaulle to establish a documentary, 'feel' to the activities of the Jackal.[16] In *The Odessa File* there is a meeting between the hero, Peter Miller,· and Lord Russell of Liverpool, and *The Dogs of War* includes references to the Poseidon shares fiasco and a dossier of well-known mercenaries.[17]

Another 'factional' device occasionally used by Forsyth is the footnote. In *The Day of the Jackal*, for example, he refers in a footnote to the demolition of a building noted by the Jackal on his visit to Paris. This is clearly factual information and the incorporation within a novel of a convention associated with academic texts further elides the distinction between fact and fiction. As Erving Goffman says about a similar usage in a Len Deighton novel: 'the

footnoter *is* the writer . . . [the] footnote is hardly necessary except
to trick the reader into giving greater realness to the story and
knowledgeability to the teller than might be generated by a
conventional format'.[18]

Hailey also mixes 'real' and fictional characters. In *Airport*, Mel
Bakersfield, the airport general manager, has a signed photograph
of John F. Kennedy in his office. The photograph revives memories
of an invitation to the White House: 'The meeting with the
President had gone well . . . J.F.K., Mel found, shared many of
his own ideas . . . as time went on he drifted into one of those
easy going relationships which J.F.K. encouraged among those
with expertise to offer him'.[19] Again, in *Wheels*[20] Ralph Nader
and his attacks upon the car industry figure prominently, and
considerable attention is paid to the attitude and policies of
the 'Big Three' motor corporations – General Motors, Ford and
Chrysler.

The second type of documentary technique employed by Hailey
and Forsyth is the detailed account of technical operations or
business practices. This involves the kind of reportage one would
expect from a former trade magazine editor and an experienced,
investigative journalist. In *The Day of the Jackal* Forsyth provides a
three-page-long, detailed description of the special rifle commis-
sioned by the Jackal.[21] The writing here (as in so much of Forsyth's
work) is clear, precise, matter of fact, there are no stylistic
embellishments – the language is that of a technical manual.

Forsyth's description of the assassin's rifle achieves a marriage of
form and content. The prose style perfectly mirrors the meticulous
precision and professional detachment of the hired killer.

There's a danger, however, of lengthy description of complex
operations becoming exhaustive and tedious. *The New Statesman*
confidently asserts that 'what keeps you reading *The Dogs of War*
is its detailed dwelling on the plotting of the coup', but the
tendency to dwell at length on the intricacies of setting up a
shares company or the problem of obtaining end user licences for
purchasing weapons, threatens to become an obsession.[22]

Documentary-style passages are also a familiar feature of the
Hailey novel. Generally his detailed descriptions of big-business
procedures and industrial/technical operations can be justified on
the ground that they are integral to the plot. Thus the need to
discover the identity of a bank thief in *The Moneychangers* leads to
a description of a bank audit; and in *Airport* an account of the

complex demands made upon the air traffic controller enable the reader to appreciate he pressures that have brought Keith Bakersfield to the point of suicide.[23]

At times, however, Hailey chooses the most inopportune moment to introduce passages of information. In a skilfully prepared, tense scene towards the end of *Airport*, the saboteur succeeds in detonating the bomb in the airliner. With the passengers facing death through oxygen starvation, Hailey, instead of conveying the necessary information in a few sentences, suspends the narrative to insert a lecture on the inadequacy of the regulations concerning oxygen masks.[24] A page further on, with disaster still imminent, the reader is given an account of the way simulators prepare pilots for this kind of emergency.

Generally, Hailey and Forsyth are accomplished storytellers who know when to introduce reportage and how much to include. Their lapses may, however, be significant: it's almost as if they feel called upon to *display* their knowledge *as evidence of their professional competence* – to establish their authority as guides in areas remote from most readers' experience.

The question of the writer's authority is related to the third kind of documentary technique. This is what I want to call 'insider knowledge' and it goes beyond the simple documentation of the processes involved in a car assembly line or making a bomb. Close observation, attention to detail, assimilation of facts are not sufficient to give you 'insider knowledge'. When you engage a lawyer it's not simply because he knows more law than you do – it's also because he possesses certain kinds of privileged information denied to the outsider. Those who have gained access to the 'inner circles' of institutions, are entitled to demand trust: *credat emptor*. In *Airport* Hailey shows how 'insider knowledge' can be used to advantage.

> Liquor for first class passengers was free; tourist passengers paid a dollar a drink (or the equivalent in foreign currency) unless they took advantage of a piece of inside information. The information was that stewardesses were issued almost no change, their instructions were to give the passenger his or her drinks free. Some regular travellers had drink free for years in the tourist class, merely by proffering a fifty or twenty dollar bill and insisting they had nothing smaller.[25]

This is just the kind of information to appeal to the middle-class consumerists. Hailey also gives an insight into the 'perks' available to stewardesses – the wine and food, for instance, not consumed by passengers is appropriated by them.

Forsyth, in his novels, demonstrates this insider knowledge by his mastery of esoteric facts relating to criminal activities in general and the international underworld and secret service organisations in particular. In *The Day of the Jackal* he tells the reader:

> although beloved of novelists as a crime-busting force, the Sûreté Nationale itself is simply the very small and meagrely staffed office that has control over the five crime branches that actually do the work. The task of the Sûreté is administrative, like that of the equally mis-described Interpol, and the Sûreté does not have a detective on its staff.[26]

The 'beloved of novelists' is a nice touch; it suggests not only Forsyth's superiority to other commentators (unlike them, he's an 'insider') but also perhaps that he is as much an historian as a novelist.

If I appear to have laboured the documentary techniques employed by Hailey and Forsyth it's because I feel they embody deeply ingrained habits of thought and a pervasive ideology. The 'facts' obtained from a reading of the novels cited reflects, for instance, a concept of knowledge purveyed by TV quiz programmes like 'Mastermind' (BBC): 'In Mastermind terms knowledge is a thing which can be possessed. Possession is demonstrated by skill and agility in the use of 'facts'. The overview of knowledge implied is that of a constellation of rigidly defined subjects with a content of facts'.[27] The connection with professionalism – the body of knowledge to be absorbed, the specialist divisions within it, the successive examination hurdles facing the would-be practitioner, hardly needs stressing.

The notion, moreover, that there is an objective reality 'out there' which can be transported unmediated to the printed page seems to be implicit in this emphasis on documentation; it reflects a positivistic, commonsense view of the world. The 'fact' is unambiguous – it may be difficult to uncover but the trained observer can bring it to light. There's a revealing passage in *Wheels* where Hailey describes the making of a *cinema verité* film about Detroit.

When he was sure of the reaction Gropetti would spring instantly back so that the camera – already operating at the director's covert signal – would catch full facial expressions and spontaneous words. Afterwards with limitless patience Gropetti would repeat the process until he had what he sought – a glimpse of personality, good or bad, amiable or savage, but vital and real, and without the clumsy intrusion of an interviewer.[28]

While acknowledging the mediating influence of the director, Hailey can describe the result, apparently without irony, as 'vital and real'. Later, when Gropetti is interviewing a black assembly-plant worker, we are told that, 'though the young black worker's words were simple and sometimes stumbling, they conveyed reality and a true picture of himself'.[29] This stresses the essential neutrality and objectivity of the camera and its recording function. The assumption behind this naturalist aesthetic is that the film becomes more neutral and unbiased as the recording technique becomes more transparent.

It's possible, I think, to establish a link between these attitudes and the working methods and political philosophy of the professional. The professional tends to see himself as politically neutral, as standing 'outside the system', and facts are regarded as unproblematic.

The inclusion of the Jackal and Carlo Shannon amongst a gallery of professional types may seem questionable. After all, one is a hired killer, the other a mercenary – these occupations hardly come within the category of traditional professions. Hailey's characters on the other hand are drawn almost without exception from the established professions: doctors, surgeons and pathologists in *The Final Diagnosis*; corporation vice-presidents and design directors in *Wheels*; bank executives in *The Moneychangers* and politicians and lawyers in *In High Places*, and a wide range of executive and technical professions in *Airport*. Women also are shown occupying professional positions: Edwina D'Orsey in *The Moneychangers* is manager of FMA's main downtown bank and Dr Lucy Grainger in *The Final Diagnosis* is an accomplished surgeon.

Forsyth's assassins and soldiers of fortune appear to have little in common with Hailey's respected community figures. What they share, however, are professional skills – skills endorsed by their authors and by society. John Cawelti, in *Adventure Mystery and Romance*, refers to the frequent appearance of what he calls the Enforcer figure: 'The Enforcer is most commonly an assassin though in some cases he is a professional thief. His central characteristic is a ruthless and brilliant professionalism. . . . He is a man who applies the cool and detached rationalism of the professional specialist to matters of extreme violence and illegality.'[30]

These qualities are constantly stressed in the portrayal of the Jackal. Colonel Rodin, operations chief of the OAS, discussing the possibility of hiring an assassin to kill de Gaulle, concludes, 'In order to get the level of skill and of nerve necessary for this kind of operation we must engage a true professional'.[31] The skills which distinguish the Jackal's performance are no different from those of other more conventional professionals: thoroughness, attention to detail, a capacity for absorbing information, quick decision-making and technical expertise. The Jackal cannot afford mistakes; his survival depends upon the precision of his planning. We see this in his calculation of the angle of fire and the meticulous adjustment of the telescopic sights on his rifle. The arranging of a series of false identities shows a shrewd assessment of the dangers ahead – he's prepared for every contingency. His research into de Gaulle's life reveals a professional's ability to assimilate facts: 'He read voraciously and planned meticulously, and possessed the faculty to store in his mind an enormous amount of factual information on the offchance that he might later have a use for it'.[32] His technical efficiency is demonstrated both in his detailed specification for the rifle ('it's a pleasure to do business both with a professional and a gentleman', comments the Belgian armourer) and in the swift, expert killing of the forger who tries to blackmail him: 'His right hand slipped around the Belgian's neck and out the other side, and with it he gripped his own left bicep. The left hand was placed against the back of the forger's head. He gave one short, vicious twist to the neck, backwards, upwards and sideways.'[33]

Like James Bond, the Jackal's technical expertise extends to the sexual arena. Colette, the French Baroness who has allowed herself to be seduced by the Jackal, reflects on the night's lovemaking: 'He had been good, this English primitive, hard but skilled, knowing how to use fingers and tongue and prick to bring her on five times and himself three'.[34]

'Cat' Shannon in *The Dogs of War* has the same technical skill (and sexual attraction) as the Jackal. On the surface, at least, they are in the same business – the only difference being that the Jackal operates alone, and Shannon is the leader of a small group of highly trained men.

If the Jackal stands as a representative figure in the Forsyth novels embodying the skills associated with the professional, he has his counterpart in the Hailey world in the character of Joe Patroni in *Airport*.

Patroni is the maintenance chief at Lincoln International. As the airport's chief troubleshooter, he is renowned for his technical abilities and unconventional behaviour: 'Legends had grown up around Joe Patroni: some professional, others personal.'[35] His is the classic rags-to-riches story which proves that professionals don't always come from a middle-class background. He has risen to the top through natural ability. Starting out in life as a garage mechanic, he wins both the garage and an ancient biplane in a dice game. Later, after studying at night school, he becomes first an airline head mechanic, then a foreman with 'a reputation as a top-notch trouble shooter' and finally secures his present job with Lincoln International.

The skills that have made Patroni a top professional are exemplified in an early scene. Summoned to an airport to rescue a stranded jet which is blocking a runway, Patroni is caught up in a traffic jam. A massive articulated lorry – victim of the snowstorm that threatens to paralyse the airport – has jack-knifed and rolled over. Immediately Patroni takes command, supervising the police and ordering tow trucks. His assessment of the situation is quick and positive and the police officers defer to his obvious experience and practical know-how:

> Ten minutes later, working with the police, Joe Patroni had virtually taken charge. Two additional tow trucks, as he had suggested, were being summoned by radio. While awaiting their arrival, the driver of the first tow truck was attaching chains under Patroni's direction to the axles of the capsized tractor-trailer. The situation had already assumed a proficient, get on with it pattern – a trademark of any proceeding in which the energetic TWA maintenance chief became involved.[36]

Once again we see the qualities necessary for leadership in a complex, urban, technological society.

So far this study of fictional professionals has concentrated mainly on their technical and operational skills. Inasmuch as these skills are seen as essential to the smooth functioning of society, they are accorded a positive value. There are other issues, however, that are ultimately more important in defining a writer's attitude towards professionalism. To what extent, for instance, do the characters associated with professionalism conform to the requirements of an ethical code and how far is their conduct guided by a concern for the community interest? What freedom of action do they possess and how fulfilling do their lives appear to be?

I want to begin with Hailey's treatment of these issues because the service ethic and the professional's civic responsibilities are dominant themes which recur in all his novels. It could be argued that Hailey's presentation of professionals is balanced and objective and the frequent appearance of unethical practitioners in his work might appear to justify this claim.

Elliot Freemantle for instance, in *Airport*, shows how an unprincipled lawyer can deceive a gullible public. When residents close to the airport hold a meeting to protest about the noise of jets taking off and landing, Freemantle secures an invitation. It's clear that he is motivated purely by financial self-interest; to begin with, he doesn't even possess the specialist knowledge which the client has a right to expect from the practitioner: 'he had made a superficial study of the law, and recent court decisions, affecting noise and privacy – a subject entirely new to him – and when the committee arrived, he addressed them with the assurance of a lifetime expert'.[37]

Freemantle takes advantage of the notion of *credat emptor*. In talking to the angry residents he wilfully distorts the legal background, citing a number of cases where intrusion of property rights – including aircraft intrusion – resulted in court injunctions and financial compensation. Important factors which would invalidate his recital of precedents are ignored or suppressed. Freemantle hopes to make a financial killing by persuading his audience to engage his services on an individual rather than a collective basis. Significantly his efforts are frustrated by the intervention of the dedicated professional, Mel Bakersfield, who unmasks Freemantle's charlatanism in front of a large crowd and TV cameras.

Alan Maitland, the idealistic young lawyer of *In High Places*, stands in sharp contrast to Freemantle but here too there is an acknowledgement that the service ethic and a belief in justice do not always go hand in hand with legal practice:

> Alan Maitland had no callow illusions about the law. New as he was to its service, he was aware that justice was neither automatic nor impartial, and that sometimes injustice triumphed over right. He knew that social status had a good deal to do with crime and punishment and that the well-heeled who could afford to make use of all the law's processes were less likely to suffer direly for sinning than those less wealthy, who could not. The law's slowness he was sure, at times denied the innocent of rights, and some who deserved redress failed to seek it because of the high cost of a day in court.[38]

This passage suggests that Hailey's views are very much in line with those who criticise the 'ideal' model of the professional. Its force, however, is diluted by the succeeding paragraphs. These legal abuses, we are told 'pained [Maitland] deeply, as they pained many of his elder colleagues whose idealism had not rubbed off through the years at the bar'.

Already then there is reassurance: there are still many noble practitioners who will hold the banner of justice aloft. And what of the law? Well it has 'one great virtue'. It is there: 'It existed. Its greatest merit was its availability. Existence of the law was an acknowledgement that equality of human rights was a worthwhile goal. As to its defects, in time reform would come; it always has though it lagged behind the need.'[39]

This simple, meliorist doctrine is purveyed in all the Hailey novels. There may be faults in the system but dedicated professionals are capable of putting their own houses in order. In *The Final Diagnosis* O'Donnell, the president of the hospital medical board, reviews the abuses that have led to a baby's death and an outbreak of typhoid: 'More practically he reasoned: after today there must be many changes – not only those already exposed, but others they would uncover by diligent searching. They must probe for weaknesses – among themselves and in the hospital fabric. There must be greater self-criticism, more self-examination.'[40]

Reforms enacted from within, it is stressed, are preferable to those imposed from outside, since the latter might well be accompanied by state interference. In *Wheels* Hailey describes the archaic car-dealership system and concludes, 'if manufacturers and dealers acting together failed to initiate reforms in the system soon, it was certain that government would step in, as it had already in other industry areas'.[41] Alex Vandervoot, arguing for a socially-responsible policy on the part of his bank, makes the same point: 'Equally important: it is better to do this freely now than have it forced on us by regulation later'.[42] It is clear that state regulation is opposed because it would endanger the autonomy of the professional.

Vanderwoot is one of the 'good' professionals. What distinguishes Alex is his essential humanity, his concern for other people. His operational talents – 'experience and a flair for new technology – are not sufficient; the complete professional must embody the values of the service ethic as well as being technically proficient. Thus Hailey reinforces the ideology of professionalism. Alex is chosen by the ageing bank president, Ben Rosselli, as his successor because Rosselli wants to hand over to someone who will be 'more than a top technician. The kind of man I want to run the bank won't ever forget that small depositors – individuals – have always been our strong foundation. The trouble with Bankers nowadays is that they get too remote'.[43] 'Remoteness' is what makes Alex's rival, Roscoe Heywood, a 'bad' professional. Heywood is cold and detached; more concerned with balance sheets than human beings. When Alex and Roscoe, rival candidates for the vacant presidency, address the board meeting which will decide who shall be elected, Roscoe stresses that profitability is his number one priority. He criticises Alex Vandervoot's belief in 'corporate social responsibility', arguing that too many decisions in banking and in business generally are being excessively influenced by social issues.

Alex's speech in contrast sounds like a policy statement on behalf of the 'people caring' professions. He maintains that civilisation is changing and that what they are seeing is a social revolution of conscience and behaviour, whose driving force is: 'the determination of a majority of people to improve the quality of life, to stop spoilation of the environment and preserve what's left of resources of all kinds'.[44]

It's obvious where our sympathies are expected to lie, and the message comes across loud and clear: the successful manager – at whatever level – must combine intelligence and efficiency with humanitarian concern. The need for this duality of efficiency and humanity is constantly reiterated. We see it again in *The Final Diagnosis* where David Coleman, the brilliant young pathologist, lacks the warmth which his father possessed – it's not until his feelings are deeply aroused by the tragic and avoidable death of a baby (caused by his colleague's negligence) that he's able to examine the basis of his own detachment and arrive at a more tolerant understanding of others.

It's clear that even the good professionals experience crises when their vocational ideals and loyalties are tested. Such scenes occur in almost all Hailey's novels and represent a kind of biblical tempting. Kent O'Donnell in *The Final Diagnosis* is faced with a choice between love and vocational obligation. Having accepted the job of chief administrator at the run down, inefficient, Three Counties Hospital, he has achieved notable reforms. When he falls in love with wealthy socialite Denise Swayne, she agrees to marry him if he'll go to live and work in New York. Kent eventually rejects Denise not simply because her money and possessiveness threaten his independence but also because he recognises that much remains to be done at Three Counties.

Kent's situation again raises the question of the professionals' autonomy in these novels. It's true that their freedom of action is compromised at times by organisations and by the relationships of power within them. The dilemma is usually posed in terms of the financial constraints which interfere with their ability to carry out duties properly and efficiently. Kent O'Donnell, for example, when confronted by evidence of Dr Pearson's professional negligence, delays making a decision on his dismissal because he knows it could jeopardise the huge endowment promised by Pearson's friend which could dramatically improve the hospital's facilities. The delay proves to be a contributory factor in the death of the baby referred to earlier. O'Donnell reproaches himself: 'I could have fired Joe Pearson: there was plenty of reason to. But no! I dallied and procrastinated, playing politics, convincing myself I was behaving reasonably, while all the time I was selling medicine short'.[45]

Although Hailey brings these issues to the reader's attention, they are invariably resolved in a simplistic way. In this case Dr Pearson acknowledges his failure to meet the required standards of his profession and resigns. It's an emotional scene and there is another when his friend confirms the endowment and sets up a trust fund to help the father of the dead baby continue his medical studies. But there's no questioning in *The Final Diagnosis* of a system which makes hospitals dependent upon the financial contribution of individuals who thereby exercise power and influence within the running of the organisation. The problems are resolved by individuals – either in the shape of generous benefactors or determined and altruistic professionals.

The professional's autonomy can also be endangered by state interference. This is only posited as a threat though and, as we have seen, Hailey believes it can be averted by responsible and socially enlightened leadership.

Finally there is the question of how fulfilling are the lives of these people? – certainly the demands made upon the professional are severe. Invariably (as if to confirm the view of pro-professional sociologists) the professional's occupation is more a way of life than a job and cannot be confined to a nine-to-five working day. Inevitably, therefore, domestic relationships are strained: Alex Vandervoot feels his wife's mental illness and withdrawal has been brought about by his preoccupation with his job and Mel Bakersfield has drifted apart from his wife partly because his duties at the airport take up so much of his time.

The solution to these problems is often a relationship with a fellow professional who can understand and sympathise with the demands made by the Job. Thus Alex lives with Margot Bracken, a 'radical' lawyer and Kent O'Donnell deserts Denise Swayne for Dr Lucy Grainger, his attractive and faithful colleague. The career woman (we are reassured!) can achieve success without losing her charm and attraction. Dr Lucy Grainger is typical of the professional women in these novels: 'He [O'Donnell] liked her for many things, not least the way she could hold her own in what was sometimes thought of as a man's world. At the same time though she never lost her essential femininity.'[46]

The chances of fulfilment for the non-professional woman on the other hand appear distinctly remote. She seems doomed either to hover supportively in the shadow of great men or chafe at the sexual and social limitations imposed by her husband's job.

In general it is clear that if sacrifices are demanded of professionals, virtue is its own reward. This is perfectly illustrated by the doctor on board the crippled jet in *Airport*. He provides a model of the 'caring' professional and the satisfaction derived from serving the community:

> The only time he ceased practising medicine was while he slept. He enjoyed being needed. He acted as if his profession

were a prize he had won, which if not guarded, would slip away. He had never been known to refuse to see a patient at any hour or to fail to make a house call if sent for. He never drove past an accident scene as did many of his medical brethren, fearing malpractice suits. He kept conscientiously up to date. Yet the more he worked, the more he seemed to thrive.[47]

The good Samaritan echo is surely intentional, reminding us of the epiphanies that occur in many Hailey novels when one of the central characters acknowledges his own destiny within the profession and its glorious mission. Perhaps the most striking example of this occurs in *The Final Diagnosis*. In a scene where O'Donnell considers the hospital's future there is a series of hypothetical questions – expressed in language that has a dominantly religious ring: '(Is it in truth a place of healing? Or have we raised in folly, a white sepulchre – an empty antiseptic shrine?)' culminating in the affirmative statement: 'Let today, he thought, stand as a bright and shining beacon – a cross of sorrow, a signal for a new beginning.'[48]

The rhetoric is significant; it emphasises the key role of the professional in shaping the society of the future and establishes the notion of 'a calling' as the dominant way in which the professions are represented by Hailey.

The range of occupational types in Forsyth's novels is far more restricted than Hailey's and, since his characters don't represent the 'people caring' professions, the service ethic receives less attention. *The Day of the Jackal* certainly doesn't contain the kind of moral endorsement of professionals one finds in Hailey's work. The only kind of obligation the Jackal feels, is a contractual one towards his employer. He may derive satisfaction from his skill and efficiency in handling as assignment but there's no suggestion – as there is with Shannon in *The Dogs of War* – that the assignment is chosen on moral grounds. His killing is purely arbitrary; it is entirely dictated by the client's choice. Once the contract has been placed, the Jackal enjoys almost complete autonomy – he works alone and in secret and the client, unable to monitor his activities, is forced to rely on his professional competence. The question of loyalty doesn't arise because the Jackal knows that if he betrayed his employers he would become a marked man for OAS agents throughout the world.

The Jackal is portrayed in totally amoral terms. There's never any hint of condemnation by the author; on the contrary, he seems to admire the killer's technical proficiency and the reader tends to identify with the Jackal because, for large sections of the narrative, events are seen through his eyes. This identification and the flat, unemotional way in which the killings are described makes moral judgements seem irrelevant.

The Jackal, however, is not the only professional in the novel. He has his counterpart in the Police Deputy Commissioner, Claude Lebel.[49] Lebel lacks the flamboyance of the Jackal. He realises that ninety-nine per cent of police work is 'routine, unspectacular enquiry', and that the successful prosecutor of cases often depends on laborious checking and double checking. Systematically he proceeds with the task of tracking down the Jackal. Though he presents a contrast in style to the assassin, he is equally effective.

Since Lebel is a detective, it might be expected that he would embody the service ethic. He's conscientious, dedicated to the job and proves incorruptible in the face of bribes and threats. Here surely is a man like Alan Maitland who will uphold the ideal of law and justice. Instead the reader becomes aware that, once again, moral judgements are out of place. Lebel is no better and no worse than the Jackal. He has the same pride in his performance and loyalty towards his employer. It's not as if he regards de Gaulle as a saviour of his country whose life must be protected at whatever cost to human liberties. He is more conscious of the fact that failure to catch the assassin will jeopardise his career. When the politicians are willing to call off the search, thinking the Jackal had given up all hope of killing the President, Lebel is less sure and almost acknowledges a kinship with the Jackal:

> he . . . had an odd faith, that he could certainly never divulge, that the man he was hunting was another professional who would carry out his job no matter what.
>
> Over the eight days since this affair had landed on his lap he had come to a grudging respect for the silent, unpredictable man who seemed to have everything planned down to the last detail, including the contingency planning.[50]

The reader is more conscious therefore of rivalry between two highly-skilled professionals than of moral imperatives. This feeling is reinforced by horrific acts of cruelty on both sides: the Jackal's cold-blooded killing of anyone who obstructs his path is matched by the sadistic torture methods of the French secret service. It's as if the violations of the moral code on both sides cancel each other out. Like a Jacobean tragedy, one is left in a moral vacuum where the only concerns become technical and operational: who is to succeed in his mission – the Jackal or Lebel?

Forsyth is writing 'documentary' thrillers, not tense social melo-dramas like Hailey's, and it would be unwise to infer too much from his first novel.[51] Nevertheless what comes over strongly is that functional efficiency and technological supremacy are both primary values and ends in themselves. Altruism, and the notion of service to the community, is simply not represented.

It could be argued that these concerns are addressed in Forsyth's second novel, *The Odessa File*. In this novel Peter Miller, a German journalist, is attempting to track down Roschmann, a Nazi war criminal, who, it is later revealed, is in charge of a factory which is designing a tele-guidance system for Egyptian rockets. Odessa – the Organisation of Former Members of the SS – is arranging for the rocket heads to contain cultures of bubonic plague and irradiated strontium 90 so that when they fall on Israel they ensure the 'final and utter destruction of the Jewish race'.[52]

Miller's pursuit of Roschmann is justified not only on the ground of humanitarian justice but also because it helps to prevent an horrific act of mass destruction. Miller, however, is unaware of this plan and, though appalled to learn of the extent of Nazi atrocities during the war, his motivation is more personal and psychological than social: Roschmann, it is revealed at the end of the novel, had murdered Miller's father. As Miller says, he's sorry about the Jews but not that sorry – it's really his father's death that he wants to avenge.

Miller then is a good responsible journalist. His determination, resourcefulness and investigative research identify him as a profes-sional but the novel's conclusion makes it clear that there are different types of professionalism. Miller ignores the instructions of the secret Jewish organisation who have recruited him, and pursues his quarry independently. Rescued at the point of death by a tough, experienced Israeli paratrooper, he is given some advice, 'go back to Hamburg, marry Sigi, have kids and stick to reporting. Don't tangle with professionals again'.[53]

Forsyth's concern for the suffering inflicted on the Jews, however, is undermined by his efforts to apportion blame. He suggests that it was an unrepresentative group of degenerate criminals who were responsible, not the German nation as a whole. As Solomon Tamber – the Jewish concentration camp prisoner – says in his diary: 'I bear no hatred or bitterness towards the German people, for they are good people. Peoples are not evil; only individuals are evil'.[54] This point is echoed by Miller in his conversation with Roschmann: 'You smeared my country with your dirt. . . . You bastards used Germany and the German people until they could not be used any more'.[55]

One may not regard this individual theory of guilt as entirely satisfactory. The question of responsibility raises complex issues which can hardly be dealt with in a few sentences (as Forsyth does). In any case it's difficult to reconcile this analysis with other passages in the novel where Forsyth suggests there are national characteristics that make Germany specially vulnerable to fascist domination. For example, Forsyth, commenting on the title Werewolf adopted by the chief executive of Odessa, says: 'It had the advantage of being anonymous, symbolic and sufficiently melodramatic to satisfy *the eternal German lust for playacting*' [my emphasis][56] and we are told later that Odessa has succeeded in protecting members through its ruthlessness and the 'usual German cowardice when faced with a moral problem'.[57]

In *The Dogs of War* Forsyth returned to the subject of mercenaries though this time the central character, 'Cat' Shannon, appears to have a conscience and a philosophy that extends beyond self-interest and hedonism. Early on he stakes his claim as a professional. When Simon Endean, Sir James Manson's representative, who is engaging Shannon's services, questions the price quoted for a report on a military invasion of an African state, Shannon replies: 'You know perfectly well if your firm consult a lawyer, architect, accountant or any other technical expert you pay him a fee. I'm a technical expert in war. What you pay for is the knowledge and experience – where to get the best men, the best arms, how to ship them out etc.'[58]

So far Shannon sounds just like the Jackal but later when he begins to outline his philosophy to Manson's daughter he's shown to be more than an unfeeling technocrat. He places great emphasis on his autonomy – unlike the ordinary professional soldier, no one tells him when or where to fight or on which side: 'That's why we're outlaws; we fight on contracts and we pick our own contracts.'[59] Choosing his own contract enables him to fight for a cause he believes in. Shannon's analysis of society is based on money and power. A process of natural selection ensures that the people who get to the top are those who are prepared to fight – the 'predators' whose insatiable desire for 'increased profits and increased power' leads them to engage in imperialist wars on some trumped-up pretext of a just and glorious cause. Shannon despises this hypocrisy; the mercenary may fight for money, he says, but this is not the most important factor: 'Most of the best ones fight for the same reason I do; they enjoy the life, the hard living, the combat.'[60] The dangers of this life are infinitely preferable to the safe routine monotony of a commuter's nine-to-five existence.

It's not just the life and the combat that are important to Shannon though; there's an idealistic strain to his make-up. Commenting on the adage 'God is on the side of the big battalions' (the gospel of the rich and powerful), he says that perhaps God has something to do with 'truth, justice and compassion rather than sheer brute force and that truth and justice might possibly be on the side of the little battalions'.[61]

Since Shannon ultimately fights on behalf of one of these little battalions, the view of the mercenary being projected is that of a quixotic Robin Hood figure, but this is hardly consistent with the image one has of mercenaries from the news media and the ignominious failure of the real-life mercenaries recruited by Forsyth to seize power in Equatorial Guinea suggests there is often a wide gap between the expertise and efficiency of fictional mercenaries and their real counterparts. There's no reason, however, why Shannon shouldn't be portrayed as exceptional both in terms of his abilities and his social conscience. To establish the idealistic side of his character here is to prepare the reader psychologically for the twist at the end of the novel when Shannon betrays Manson and hands over power to the exiled African leader (whom one is obviously meant to identify with Ojukwu) and a democratic government.

Endean asks Shannon why he has betrayed Manson. The author's own experience as a reporter in Nigeria is reflected in the mercenary's reply. He describes how for two years he watched between half a million and a million children starve to death knowing that profiteers like Manson were really responsible; men who operated behind the visible front of indifferent politicians and

Foreign Office men and supported vicious and corrupt dictatorships in order to secure larger profits. 'I may be a fighter, I may be a killer but I'm not a bloody sadist', says Shannon.[62]

He points out that he and Endean are both mercenaries along with Sir James Manson and most of the people who have power in the world. But this is misleading. It suggests that all three are on an equal footing – this is patently not the case. Men like Shannon and Endean work for Manson; he is the one with the power. Although, in this case, the 'good' professional Shannon, emerges triumphant, it's a victory against the odds. As Shannon had earlier observed, it's the people with power and money who invariably win.

The question of how much satisfaction Forsyth's professionals derive from their work is a difficult one. As a writer Forsyth is more concerned with external events than exploring the inner lives of his characters and his characterisation tends to be two dimensional. In *The Day of the Jackal* he's able to turn this weakness into a strength because it's fitting that the Jackal should remain an anonymous character. He is, after all, a person without a name who nobody ever gets really close to. As far as motivation and fulfilment are concerned, Cawelti's comment that the 'Enforcer lives by a code that is deeply rooted in his profession and in the maintenance of his honour as a man of supreme skill and dedication to his role' certainly applies to the Jackal, Lebel and Shannon – and, to a lesser degree, Miller.[63] Miller can also congratulate himself on having unmasked a despicable war criminal and prevented the destruction of the Jewish race which, on reflection, is no mean achievement. Shannon, however, is the character who seems to experience the greatest degree of fulfilment: he enjoys his work and the life that goes with it, he has a moral code that enables him to kill without a bad conscience and he has the satisfaction of having led an exiled, suffering tribe into the promised land.

In most of these novels the hero is portrayed in a favourable light. At times it may be simply his operational skills that are regarded as vital to a complex, technological society. If you have a stranded jet blocking the airport run-way you get Joe Patroni to shift it. It's the obvious and logical thing to do. The danger with this kind of obvious, logical thinking is that it leads to a situation where 'purposive-rational action' (to use Jurgen Habermas's term[64]) becomes an end in itself, divorced from the social and political totality. It can then be seen solely in the context of limited practical objectives and judged by instrumental criteria. Thus 'purposive-rational action' offers itself as neutral and value-free whereas in fact its ideological content is hidden, not dissolved.

The distortions which arise from a partial contextualisation are apparent in *The Final Diagnosis*. Hailey acknowledges the dangers inherent in private financial endowments but the reliance of the medical system upon these endowments is never seriously questioned. Similarly in *Wheels*, the fact that people desire the freedom and mobility of the motor car is taken as sufficient justification for the continual growth of private car ownership.

The Dogs of War appears to avoid these dangers by situating Shannon and Manson's activities within the wider context of capitalist imperialism. Ultimately, though, Forsyth's political analyses both here and in other novels is undermined by the continual emphasis on process – on how things are done. What Forsyth seems to admire above all (and what is held up for the reader's approval) is Shannon's mastery of technology, weapons, business practices, the banking system, etc. This disturbs the balance of the novel – expertise becomes a primary value, an end in itself rather than a means to an end.

The need to establish professional attitudes and foster professional skills in contemporary society is never seriously questioned then by Hailey or Forsyth. Instead they construct a mythic image of the professional. He or she is associated with service to the community (or the client), dedication and integrity, expertise and knowledge, sexual attraction and virility and a glamorous lifestyle. 'Join the Professionals' proclaimed the Army recruiting advertisements in the 70s. The photo-collage of the advertisement portrayed a series of images in which shots of soldiers' technical expertise were juxtaposed with beautiful beaches in exotic locations. These images reinforced the association between professional skills and an exciting, glamorous way of life. But the images of the copywriter – and the novelist – are not created in a vacuum. They draw upon the existing symbols of a professional ideology to create fictional archetypes of immense social significance, and these archetypes in turn become part of the means by which that ideology is sustained and nourished.

NOTES

1. Daniel Bell, *The Coming of Post Industrial Society* (New York: Basic Books, 1973).
2. Mario Puzo, *The Godfather* (London: Pan, 1970).
3. Peter Black, *Jaws* (London: Pan, 1975).
4. This would include sociologists such as: B. Barber, 'Some Problems in the Sociology of Professions', *Daedalus* 92, vol. 4 (1963); W. J. Goode, 'Community within a Community: The Professions' ASR 22 (1957); T. Parsons, 'Professions' in *The Encyclopaedia of Social Sciences* (1968).
5. For example: T. Johnson, *Professions and Power* (London, 1972); J. McKinlay, 'On the Professional Regulation of Change' in P. Halmas (ed.) *Professionalisation and Social Change* (London, 1973).
6. K. Kumar, *Prophecy and Progress* (Harmondsworth: Penguin, 1978).
7. G. Esland, *Politics of Work and Occupation I*, Open University Units Block 4, 12–14, p. 20 (Milton Keynes: O.U. Press, 1976). Esland is not endorsing this view, he is simply reviewing different sociological approaches to professionalism.
8. Barber, (1963).
9. McKinlay, (1973) p. 68.
10. B. Thorne, 'Professional Education in Law' quoted in G. Esland, *Politics of Work and Occupation I*, p. 46.
11. McKinlay, (1978) p. 77.
12. Frederick Forsyth, *The Day of the Jackal* (London: Corgi, 1971).
13. Frederick Forsyth, *The Dogs of War* (London: Corgi, 1974)
14. *The Sunday Times*, 16 April 1978.
15. See, for example, M. Thompson-Noel's article 'Thrills and Rewards in Forsyth's Saga', *Financial Times*, 14 September 1974.
16. Forsyth, *The Day of the Jackal*, pp. 11–18.
17. Frederick Forsyth, *The Odessa File* (London: Corgi, 1974).
18. E. Goffman, *Frame Analysis* (Harmondsworth: Penguin, 1975) p. 44. It seems to me likely that in the example cited by Goffman, Deighton is entering into the 'game' of spy fiction and would expect many readers to recognise and enjoy this 'trick'.
19. Arthur Hailey, *Airport* (London: Pan, 1969).
20. Arthur Hailey, *Wheels* (London: Pan, 1973).
21. Forsyth, *The Day of the Jackal*, pp. 114–17.
22. Quoted on dust jacket of *The Dogs of War*.
23. Arthur Hailey, *The Moneychangers* (London: Pan, 1976).
24. Hailey, *Airport*, pp. 393, 395–6.
25. Ibid., pp. 127–8.
26. Forsyth, *The Day of the Jackal*, p. 181.
27. J. Tulloch, 'The Television Quiz and the Concept of Knowledge', *Screen Education* (Summer 1976).
28. Hailey, *Wheels*, p. 240.
29. Ibid., p. 245.
30. J. G. Cawelti, *Adventure, Mystery and Romance* (Chicago, 1976) p. 67.
31. Forsyth, *The Day of the Jackal*, p. 40.

32. Ibid., p. 61.
33. Ibid., p. 127.
34. Ibid., p. 293.
35. Hailey, *Airport*, p. 42.
36. Ibid., p. 47.
37. Ibid., p. 101.
38. Arthur Hailey, *In High Places* (London: Pan, 1976) p. 191.
39. Ibid., pp. 132–3.
40. Arthur Hailey, *The Final Diagnosis* (London: Pan, 1967).
41. Hailey, *Wheels*, p. 173.
42. Hailey, *The Moneychangers*, p. 133.
43. Ibid., p. 22.
44. Ibid., p. 131.
45. Hailey, *The Final Diagnosis*, p. 273.
46. Ibid., p. 10.
47. Hailey, *Airport*, p. 425.
48. Hailey, *The Final Diagnosis*, pp. 303–4.
49. In Jerry Palmer, *Thrillers* (London: Edward Arnold, 1978) there is an interesting analysis of *The Day of the Jackal* in which Lebel is characterised as a bureaucratic professional.
50. Forsyth, *The Day of the Jackal*, p. 317.
51. A categorisation employed by John Sutherland in his *Bestsellers* (London: Routledge & Kegan Paul, 1981).
52. Forsyth, *The Odessa File*, p. 72.
53. Ibid., p. 309.
54. Ibid., p. 35.
55. Ibid, p. 296.
56. Ibid., p. 122.
57. Ibid., p. 166.
58. Forsyth, *The Dogs of War*, p. 149.
59. Ibid., p. 222.
60. Ibid., p. 220.
61. Ibid., p. 223.
62. Ibid., p. 433.
63. J. G. Cawelti, *Adventure, Mystery and Romance*, p. 67.
64. Jürgen Habermas, *Towards a Rational Society* (London: Heinemann, 1971) p. 81.

13

Spy Fiction and the Vietnam War

JOHN SIMONS

Hollywood's many attempts to reproduce the political and cultural complexities of the Vietnam War can hardly be said to have been successful and, indeed, recent offerings are serious cause for concern to those who believe that history may serve as, at the very least, a tool by which the present may be made safer and the future a source of optimism. The films of the last decade, from *The Deer Hunter* and *Apocalypse Now* to *Full Metal Jacket*, have hardly raised themselves above the political level of John Wayne's notorious *The Green Berets* which at least had the excuse of being produced while the conflict was in full swing. As Jean Baudrillard has said: 'If one side won an ideological and political victory, the other made *Apocalypse Now* and that has gone right round the world.[1]

However much claims may be made both for the aesthetic importance or social relevance of some films in mediating the Vietnam experience both to veterans and to the post-war generation, the frank jingoism of the *Rambo* films and the prurient brutality masquerading as sensitive concern of *Platoon* have anchored the cinema in an adherence to a range of stereotypes which may easily be traced to mass cultural images of the Orient and to the man's world of barrack and battlefield. In spite of suggestions which have been put forward that the Vietnam experience was essentially different from other wars, especially in New Journalistic exercises such as Michael Herr's *Dispatches* or memoirs and novels by veterans, the war remains, as a phenomenon in popular culture, scarcely distinct from other representations of America at war whether the enemy be the indigenous population or Darth Vader's evil Empire.[2]

When the war is read through the spy novel this situation holds true and, indeed, the prevalence and persistence of some very old cultural stereotypes in this genre is quite remarkable. In this study

I will be concerned to survey a range of fictions which have as their centre political intrigue, secrecy and adventure.

Very few of the novels would satisfy Eric Ambler's pristine definition:

> a spy story is a story in which the central character is a secret intelligence agent of one sort or another.[3]

but Michael Denning has pointed out that studies of popular fiction can often collapse into listing and categorisations which do not ultimately help in the analysis of the texts.[4] However the fact that Vietnam becomes a space in which the political intrigue and secrecy involve the amateur spy who is not even a gentleman adventurer in the traditional British mould is important in signalling the problems that even the most basic pulps have in making directive statements about value to their readers. If the Vietnamese are almost always 'bad' it is far from the case that the Americans are always 'good'. Indeed the problem of the 'bad' American and the duplicity of the State's organisations (especially the CIA), in the ruthless manipulation of its own citizens, is constantly addressed even in the face of a sinister and cruel enemy. It does not need anything but the most basic knowledge of the political history of the Vietnam war in its popular manifestations on television and in mass demonstrations to understand that this crisis of values was precisely what confused the issue for the American public and that it was this confusion that stimulated the growth not only for a broad anti-war movement but also of a vibrant (if minority) counter-culture.

In the late nineteenth and early twentieth centuries the increasing numbers of Chinese citizens who came to work and live on the American mainland generated a rush of fiction that dealt with the fear of the 'Yellow Peril', the dread that the West would be swamped by an Asiatic horde if not through direct military conflict then through economic competition and miscegenation. Though the demographic fact is that the original myth grew up around a specifically Chinese immigrant labour force the irrational and racist fear of the East soon swelled to incorporate other Asian groups which were poorly differentiated, if at all:

> "All Asians look alike", the saying goes and indeed there has been little or no attention given to the vast differences which

exist between, say, the Chinese and Japanese with respect to food, dress, language, and culture. This blurring within popular culture has given us supposedly Chinese characters who wear kimonos; it is also the reason why the fast-food restaurant McDonald's can offer "Shanghai McNuggets" with teriyaki sauce.[5]

Plainly, however much the theme of the 'Yellow Peril' was proved, historically, to consist of unfounded fears, the experience of the Pacific War, Korea and then Vietnam did little to dispel its deep-seated appeal and enabled a resurgence of its stereotypes in a range of cultural artifacts.

It may truly be said that a defining feature of popular fiction, especially at the pulp level, is its reliance on stereotypes (arguably theorised by Eco in his distinction between 'open' and 'closed' texts[6]) and in 1939 George Orwell produced a brief typology of racial stereotypes as they appeared in British boys' weeklies. It includes the following: 'CHINESE: sinister, treacherous. Wears pigtail.'[7]

Cutting off the pigtail we will find little to distinguish between Orwell's thumb-nail sketch and the fuller treatment of the topic by William Wu on the same subject as it appeared in American popular fiction of the 1870s:

The prevailing stereotype of the Chinese immigrants at this time was that of a "coolie", or unskilled laborer. Coolies were considered physically small, dirty, and diseased. In manner, they were allegedly humble and passive, but also sneaky and treacherous. They supposedly all looked alike and were depraved morally, given to theft, violence, gambling, opium and prostitution. The most durable of their alleged traits was inscrutability, a quality that remains part of the Chinese American stereotype to the present.[8]

While the Chinese American remained a major element in popular fiction until the Second World War the stereotype changed little. This is because it grew up in response to the populist fear of the 'Yellow Peril' and while this remained a force, however increasingly unlikely, a stereotype helped to mediate and confirm it. The 'Yellow Peril' and its stereotype help to construct an alien who is to be resisted and, especially, to strengthen the perceived cultural norms of the majority.

In pulp spy-fiction which deals with Vietnam the stereotype of the Asian is maintained with remarkably little modification. In *The Dead and the Damned*, a novel so dreadful that its author W. Howard Baker takes cover behind the pseudonym Bill Rekab on the cover, we find the following:

> They were smooth. Smooth, bland smiles; smooth bland features; smooth, olive skins. Smooth! And at any time at all they were going to drop down from their stools and pad over to her table. They were going to clip out English words they could hardly pronounce from mouths in which were jungles of gold teeth.[9]

> Clearly Huang was one of those who preferred the more bizarre western styles, with western women inside them. Perhaps it gave him a sense of satisfaction to humiliate one of the race that had for so long dominated the eastern races.[10]

The inscrutability of the Oriental, carrying within his very mouth a mysterious and dangerous terrain, is placed together with the racial conflict which seems to be one of the few ways in which popular fiction can imagine Vietnam. In *The Dead and the Damned* a deep Vietnamese plot is unravelled by the professional agent Quintain who also rescues the American Angela Geddes from a terrible but titillating fate in 'the lewd embraces of Mr Huang – and even worse at the hands of his helots.[11] Little in this text rises above the stereotype but there is an attempt to site the encounter of the United States and Vietnam in a quasi-Spenglerian vision of eternal *Kulturkampf*:

> Some of those in Britain today will say that the United States isn't yet a nation old enough to blow its own nose, let alone the noses of other people. But who are they to talk? When Britons were still in the early Iron Age, China had a highly developed civilisation. They certainly haven't now, but they may have again some day. So much for the virtues of age.
>
> And sometimes in the East, life means nothing, even to those it belongs to, as we know from the suicide charges of the Korean war.[12]

The 'Yellow Peril' of the 1870s rears its head in the Vietnam of the

1960s. Huang's evil – and China, Vietnam and Korea are all lumped together as 'the East' – is seen not as a function of individual wickedness but as structural to a culture and a history against the threat of which the West must maintain a constant vigil.

In Edward S. Aarons's *Assignment Cong Hai Kill*, a novel about a professional spy (Sam Durrell's mission to bring back an American defector to the communists), the defector attains various Oriental features. In spite of the fact that his Colonel sees his bravery and ruthlessness as symbolising 'everything . . . that makes the Marines the fine body of men they are' his peer group identify his 'yellow eyes', his 'un-American' appearance which makes him 'more like our strikers than a white man'.[13] The defector's assent to the values of the East are somehow inscribed on his features. The racial transgression of the defector is prefigured in the face of the Thai terrorist who is busily trying to murder Sam Durrell at the beginning of the book: 'Durrell saw a skeletal face, a melange of racial strains in almond eyes, brown skin, a round shaven head.'[14]

While Rekab sees a threat of military and cultural conquest Aarons seems more concerned with the problems of miscegenation. The question 'Why are we in Vietnam?' seems easily answered in the terms of these pulp novels but it is an answer constructed not from any engagement with military pragmatism or political science but from the cultural stereotypes which the nineteenth century knew as the 'Yellow Peril' and the contemporary Pentagon knew as the 'Domino Theory'.

For Neil Elliot's hero Chris Lucas, a newspaperman embroiled in political intrigue at the highest level involving the CIA and KGB as well as the Vietnamese, the cunning of the Oriental is concealed by sexual attractiveness:

At the first floor landing, a lovely slant-eyed secretary greeted me.

"Ah, Mr. Lucas, we are so happy to see you!" She grinned and I was afraid she was going to clap her hands.

"Calm down, sister. Where's the prime?" She looked puzzled then caught my meaning and held out her hand to indicate that I should follow her.

"This way, please." I sized her up as I followed her. Tremendous hips for a Vietnamese and I had already noted unusually large breasts. Maybe I could use a secretary. It was something to think about.

She opened the door for me. As I squeezed past her, I took all of her bust with me. They were real, but I wouldn't have been surprised to find Made in Japan tattooed on their undersides. "Nice," I said. She blushed. "Prease [*sic*], Mr. Lucas. One could misunderstand." "Not likely," I laughed, and I pressed against her.[15]

Elliot's *Noisy American* trots out a sub-hard-boiled prose across an inconsequential plot. The passage here demonstrates the playing off of 'good' and 'bad' in the racial stereotype. Lucas is, I suppose, meant to be an admirable character so we do not find in this text the difficulties encountered by other novelists in dealing with the 'bad' American but in the presentation of the Asian we do find polarities which enable certain balances to be struck as individuals are plucked out of the inscrutable horde and endowed with some positive value. The *locus classicus* for this effect is the contrast of Fu Manchu and Charlie Chan: the one the evil genius of fiendish inscrutability the other the corpulent pidgin speaker who is both lovable and tough.[16] This possibility in the stereotype enables the norm to be further elevated by showing how the Asian may be 'saved' from his own culture by adopting some Western attitudes. Chan's goodness is thus mitigated by his incompetent English. As a Chinese Hawaiian Chan, in any case, occupies a half-way house. Similarly the figure of the Eurasian Nadya in *The Dead and the Damned* or the 'lovely half-caste' Yeu-Marie in Simon Harvester's pulp *Battle Road* serve not only to reinforce the stereotype of the sexy oriental put over by *The Noisy American* but also to function as helpers to the Western heroes. The part-Asians can be 'good' it seems, and their cunning is appropriate when used for the right purposes but one fears that this ability is shown to come more through the admixture of occidental genes than innate integrity.

If the pulp spy fictions of Vietnam are remarkable for their consistent deployment of an old racial stereotype more serious attempts to write novels of adventure and espionage are concerned with an exploration of the spy himself and the cultural problems of the West. Michael Denning has shown that in the British spy thriller the hero can either be a gentleman amateur or a dedicated professional. Either way, the ideology of the text whether it be devoted to the crypto-fascists of John Buchan or the cold warriors of John le Carré is directed towards a coherent exposition of an otherwise complex and morally ambiguous political formation. We may fear the ruthlessness of a James Bond but we have few doubts as to the probity of his political trajectory.[17] In the novels to which I am about to turn the American involvement in Vietnam is seen as far from morally and politically simple. Indeed, if there is a deployment of a stereotype it is that of the 'bad' American: the brainless military martinet, the corrupt politician, the callous CIA spook. Against these monsters – Neil Elliot's Chris Lucas is one presented as a hero – are pitched inadequate protagonists, morally ambiguous themselves, manipulated but representing through their very inadequacy a field on which the faceless men of the true intelligence service can be exposed.

I am going to discuss the protagonist in three novels and in every case he is a journalist of some kind. It is a commonplace that some sectors of the American military and political establishment felt that the public will to continue the war effort in south-east Asia was sapped and then undermined by the scale and nature of media coverage of the conflict.[18] Whatever the truth of this perception the fact remains that in the world of spy fiction where loyalty, value and morality can be slippery qualities it is the journalist, perceived subverter of the American bulwark against the 'Yellow Peril', who is loaded with the heroic task. The novelists strike back – hardly surprising as two of them, Robert Elegant and Charles Collingwood were journalists themselves – by portraying the seedy world of the emigré community and its dubious contacts with both East and West in a manner which is hardly flattering to the United States.

The journalist is, in any case, already a kind of spy. The profession involves itself in observation, scrutiny and the uncovering in the public interest of uncomfortable secrets. If for 'public interest' we substitute 'state interest' we have a reasonable job description for a spy. In *The Noisy American* Chris Lucas's status as a journalist enables him to gain access to Ho Chi Minh himself but his job acts as the flimsiest of covers for his real business as an adventurer. In novels like Robert Elegant's *A Kind of Treason*, Charles Collingwood's *The Defector* and Michael Wolfe's *Man on a String* the journalists become spies as part of the gesture with which they pick up their note-book or camera and we, as readers, have in the text the represented journalistic account of their exploits.

The journalists in this kind of story start out down on their luck or in the professional doldrums. They are thus easy prey to those who will blackmail them into joining the world of espionage. In *A Kind of Treason* Mallory, a best-selling author now running out of cash and about to retrieve his fortunes with a prestigious commission on Vietnam is threatened by the CIA:

> 'Your fat fee is ten thousand plus expenses. I'm prepared to add another ten thousand for a few bits of information that happen to interest me . . . that I don't want to ask anyone in Saigon to get. After you've agreed, I'll give you a little more detail . . . You don't *have* to do anything for me. If you don't, though, you won't be going to Vietnam for *Quest*. Your friend McAllen doesn't know it, but we planted the idea for this story – and your name too. We can easily unplant it.'[19]

In *The Defector* Bill Benson, a journalist of the highest integrity as well as considerable knowledge of Vietnam, is persuaded by a CIA contact to check out the validity of a rumour that a high-ranking North Vietnamese minister wishes to defect. He agrees to perform this small task out of genuine patriotism but when he arrives in Cambodia *en route* for Hanoi he discovers that he is expected to rescue the defector and that the CIA will ruin him by publishing a doctored tape if he refuses:

> 'Ned, I'll do anything to help my country, but I'm just a poor working foreign correspondent. Now, from that point of view, what's in it for me?'
> At this point I began to sweat. That bastard Bailey had had a tape recorder in his briefcase and had really done a job on the tape. I knew what came next. I had said I might sell my soul for a quarter of a million dollars. Sure enough, I heard it coming back to me.
> 'Let's say $250,000.'
> 'That's a bargain,' Ned Bailey said triumphantly.[20]

In both books the CIA is depicted as a duplicitous and heartless organisation which will not hesitate to destroy even United States citizens to achieve ends which seem far from obviously desirable in either the public interest or that of the state. Mallory's and Benson's missions are completed with results that are inconsequential or even counter-productive.

For example, Nguyen Van Thanh, the North Vietnamese minister in *The Defector*, after a perilous journey to safety in the South is immediately assassinated with the connivance of the CIA who now believe him to be a double agent. Collingwood, with his intimate knowledge of Vietnamese history, never makes the mistake of allowing Benson to employ the 'Yellow Peril' stereotype and is scrupulous in stressing the real differences between the south-east Asian countries but he encounters it in his CIA puppet masters:

> There was you, and that girl, and Muller, and the courier we used, and me, and the whole damned what is laughingly called South Vietnamese Intelligence Service. Let me tell you, something *always* goes wrong when that many people are in the know – especially if any of them are Vietnamese.[21]

The meaning of this is, of course, that the CIA are not attempting the domination of a real south-east Asian country. What they are attempting to engage with is a discourse of Vietnam ultimately culled from the hysterical popular culture of the late nineteenth century. This is confirmed in the CIA agent Lou Pfeiffer's cover as a dealer in fake Khmer antiquities. The export of Asian culture, although fake, forms part of a general cultural take-over; what is invaded is merely a discursive space, clearly false to Benson's educated eye but opaque to the intelligence agents. Benson even stays aloof from the attractions of the Vietnamiennes.

Benson's exemplary behaviour is almost matched by Mallory's in *A Kind of Treason*. He does the round of opium dens and brothels with a pack of jaded ex-patriate journalists in Saigon but falls in love with Tuyelle the Vietnamese mistress of an American officer of uncertain loyalties who has been killed in dubious circumstances. Mallory leaves the novel and Vietnam for a future with Tuyelle in America and Europe in a gesture of gentle expropriation but his conduct is seen as positively good in the text's own morality. The relationship is not based on a stereotyping of the Asian woman and, again, it is the politicians and ex-patriate capitalists who appear to inhabit the world of the 'Yellow Peril':

> 'On the Hill,' said the Senator, 'some of us tend to get impatient, to think these people here ought to get on with it instead of whining for more help and more money.[22] 'The Oriental is a simple man. Above all, he prizes unshakeable loyalty to friends

and implacable hostility to foes. We must be true, if we are to prevail.'[23]

Characteristically, these middle-brow novels pass off what are, essentially, the themes of the pulps onto the morally ambiguous representatives of the state. They show their unwilling spies to operate in a space fixed by military and political reality and not by a fantasy of power underpinned by fear of the alien. Thus the journalist brings back what is, to the CIA, news from nowhere, as the Vietnam of history does not exist for it. It was, of course, precisely this disjunction of perspective, the contest for the mastery of the signifier in Vietnam, which ultimately caused American commitment to wane.

Michael Wolfe's *Man on a String* sets a slightly different scenario. Here, the protagonist, Keefe, is a journalist whose permit is about to expire because he has lost his job. He is blackmailed by a South Vietnamese officer, Colonel Xe, whom he has previously crossed by publishing film of his torture of prisoners. He is sent to pick up a large sum of lost American money but is saved from Xe's treachery by military intelligence in the shape of the beautiful Colonel Margaret Eriksen who has previously seduced him (though he believes that he played a more active role in their encounter). Keefe lives with a Vietnamienne, Co, who is murdered by Xe but his use of stereotyping is restrained and complex. Here is his interview with Xe:

> 'Good evening, Colonel Xe.' He wasn't in uniform but I was sure it was the same guy.
> 'So you remember me?' He smiled. 'So many times Americans say all Vietnamese look alike.' He enjoyed his little joke . . .
> He heaved his bulk out of his chair and I saw how big a man he really was. Not just big for a Vietnamese but big for anywhere. Over six feet tall and close to 250 pounds, but it didn't seem to slow him down any. About forty-five or so without a gray hair in his close-cropped military crew cut. His almost coppery complexion and high cheekbones made it obvious that he had something other than lowland Annamese–Tonkinese in his pedigree.[24]

Wolfe draws attention to the racial obsession of the stereotype through the Colonel's joke but, at the same time, Keefe's meditation on Xe's pedigree reaffirms the concern for racial purity. One curious sequence is that in which Captain Ahn, Keefe's guide and guard, takes him to a secret village presided over by an old French colonial Bedaud/Be Do. He is half-tricked into having sexual intercourse with a young village girl and thus helps Be Do's project of keeping the closed community alive, 'to rebuild what the Americans had destroyed in their clumsy attempt to save it'.[25] Here miscegenation comes as part of an enlightened French colonialism which jars against the cynicism of the American ex-soldier Keefe.[26] At the end of the novel with Co, Ahn and Xe all dead Keefe yearns to return to the Utopia (literally, nowhere) of Be Do's village which contrasts with the ghastly world of south-east Asians perceived through the discourse of the western state:

> With their families scattered and their homes torn from the earth, they came to the Americans. They washed our clothes and scrubbed our pots. They manned the bars and brothels. They ate the food brought halfway round the world to feed the most overindulged army in history. Their houses were built of our trash piles. Their bellies were filled with our garbage. And somehow they survived.[26]

What also runs through *Man on a String*, as through the other two middle-brow novels, is the feeling that in Vietnam the civilian is at just as much risk from the American intelligence services as from the Viet Cong. Disguised as Keefe's lover Margaret Eriksen allows him to take all the risks of the recovery of the government money and exposing Colonel Xe's ambivalent loyalties. Like Bailey and Gilroy, Eriksen represents the national interest and shows that it is not necessarily congruent with the interests of the citizen. The spy-journalists' moral fallibility salvages them for the good as, unlike the professionals, they understand both justice and mercy. They are not killing and consuming machines like James Bond, or Sam Durrell in *Assignment Cong Hai Kill*, nor do they indulge in snobbery with violence. In the folk pantheon they would be, in their feeble resourcefulness, tricksters rather than warrior kings. The 'real' spies, the bureaucrats, are mere manipulators who take no risks and are not armed with machine-gun ball-points, or gas-grenade lighters.

So far all of the novels I have discussed have been by and about men. Women are either dangerous seducers, sexual prey, 'nuts', or objects for protection. In novels where the stereotype of the oriental is not used the stereotype of the woman certainly is. In *The Smiling Buddha* Margaret Jones deals with political intrigue in south-east Asia from the viewpoint of an Australian woman. Her nationality is in itself of some significance, for Australian society too was deeply traumatised by the Vietnam adventure and yet the role of Australian troops is barely acknowledged – Karnow's 'standard' history of Vietnam does not even mention their presence. The novel is a 'faction' set in post-war Khamla (Kampuchea) where Gillian Herbert, in the throes of a break-up with her English husband David, meets Peter Casement, an Irish–American adventurer of old Republican stock and 'latter-day Machiavelli' at the court of Prince Soumidath (Sihanouk). She becomes deeply involved in political intrigue through her involvement with Casement by whom she becomes pregnant and even acts as a courier for Harry Greene, a far from innocent photo-journalist and former colleague of the ex-journalist Casement. This last incident results in a failed attempt on her husband's life. Like the hard-bitten journalists of the three novels discussed above Gillian is sucked into the world of espionage but her motivation is not blackmail but the desire to pursue her love for Casement (who spends much of the novel avoiding her).

While the protagonists of the other texts are men of great worldly wisdom, Gillian spends the novel growing up and her estranged husband recognises this: 'I don't like hard, pushy women, and you seemed very young and shy and full of the old-fashioned virtues'.[28] She grows from a child-woman into a woman who will have a child in her quest for 'my own life', from a woman whose life has been circumscribed by parents and husband and into one who is able to choose her own lover and her own employment – working for a news agency.[29] The text carefully distinguishes between the Asian groups, for example between the Khams and the Montagnards with whom Gillian shelters from the civil war (Khmer Rouge take over) but it also presents a range of positive models of femaleness from the grandeur of a dead Kham queen through the delicate sensitivity of the ailing wife of the gentle Kham revolutionary Penn Thioen and her concern for her children, to the taciturn and homely Montagnards.[30] The possibilities for women are thus very different in this text than in those written by men and while Gillian herself to some extent remains a victim of circumstance and is set in the same predicament as the blackmailed journalists her involvement in Kham intrigue is through choice as it furthers her aim of getting close to Peter Casement.

It is Gillian's personal life that motivates her and political intrigue and espionage is entirely subordinated in the text to the exposition of the heroine's growth to emotional adulthood. There is no sense in which Gillian behaves as does, say, Mallory in *A Kind of Treason*; she does develop resourcefulness but she is never a soldier of fortune in the corps of journalism or a Territorial operative of the CIA. The interest is not in the complexity of the espionage (though the politics are complex and authentic) nor in extended action scenes. The novel is, ultimately, a love story which happens to be set against the background of political adventure in south-east Asia.

It is difficult to differentiate the vast range of popular fiction but several things seem to become clear from the study of spy fiction and Vietnam. First of all it is manifest that the pulps try to appeal to the lowest common denominator of populist political myth and they are most unscrupulous in their use of the fear of the 'Yellow Peril'. There is little to be salvaged and the experience of reading novels like *The Dead and the Damned* or *The Noisy American* is one of unredeemed nastiness. In one sense the Vietnamese setting is not especially relevant: the unrelenting deployment of racist and sexist stereotypes sees to that. In the middle-brow novels there is the distinctive voice of a liberal and aesthetically charged concern for the progress of American foreign policy. While none of the middle-brow novelists either condemns the war explicitly or suggests that a unified Vietnam ruled from Hanoi would be desirable there is a continuing disquiet about the situation and this is represented by the unscrupulous agents of the government who initiate the espionage. In the work of Margaret Jones we see the Procrustean nature of the spy genre. *The Smiling Buddha* is certainly a spy novel but Jones uses the form as a vehicle for a fairly conventional type of Romance. The appeal of this book is very different from that of the middle-brow novels but its political orientation seems to be rather similar even though it was written at a much later date.

Vietnam was a vast field of surveillance and the American public was saturated with information from the theatre of combat. The group of spy novels which deal with the conflict represent the spectrum of opinion and attitudes towards the war. In this the novels play the role that spy novels have always played and, indeed, that all popular fiction plays: to mediate the ideology which produces them. We have seen how the role of the journalist is ambiguously portrayed and how this matches the role of the American media during the Vietnam era but, more important, these novels help us to unravel the problems of power when it is exercised over a foreign culture. The novels help to confirm what events have already taught: that for the American policy-makers and military Vietnam was a species of complex discourse and not a real country.[31] The validity of this discourse as a perception shared by the American people is alternately confirmed and denied as we move through the hierarchies of popular fiction. It is almost always erroneous to assign styles of fiction to classes of readers and it would be quite wrong to assume that pulp and middle-brow necessarily have corresponding consumer groups in water-tight socio-economic categories: it is sufficient to say that one way in which America has been able to work out its thoughts about Vietnam is through spy fiction and that a frequent conservative genre has enabled surprisingly critical and even damaging perspectives on the role and integrity of the state.

NOTES

1. Jean Baudrillard, *America* (London: Verso, 1988) p. 49.
2. See J. Hellman, *Fables of Fact* (Urbana: University of Illinois Press, 1981) and J. Hellman, *American Myth and the Legacy of Vietnam* (New York: Columbia University Press, 1986).
3. Quoted in M. Denning, *Cover Stories* (London: Routledge & Kegan Paul, 1987) p. 7.
4. Ibid., pp. 7–36.
5. M. Omi, 'In Living Colour: Race and American Culture', in I. Angus and S. Jhally (eds), *Cultural Politics in Contemporary America* (London: Routledge & Kegan Paul, 1989), pp. 111–22, pp. 116–17.
6. Umberto Eco, *The Role of the Reader* (London: Hutchinson, 1981).
7. George Orwell, 'Boys' Weeklies', in *Collected Essays* (London: Secker & Warburg, 1975) pp. 88–117, p. 101.
8. W. Wu, *The Yellow Peril* (Hamden: Archon Books, 1982).
9. Bill Rekab, *The Dead and the Damned* (London: Zenith, n.d.) p. 44.
10. Ibid., p. 65.
11. Ibid., back cover.
12. Ibid., p. 186.
13. E. S. Aarons, *Assignment Cong Hai Kill* (London: Hodder Fawcett, 1966), pp. 36–7.
14. Ibid., p. 10.
15. N. Elliot, *The Noisy American* (London: Scripts, 1967) p. 17. It is a sad irony that this appalling book should ape the title of Graham Greene's seminal text on this topic, *The Quiet American*.

16. Wu, op. cit., pp. 164–82; Omi, op. cit., p. 117.
17. Denning, op. cit., 91–113.
18. On the press in Vietnam see P. Braestrup, *Big Story* (New Haven: Yale University Press, 1983) and, for an Australian view, H. Lunn, *Vietnam: A Reporter's War* (St Lucia: University of Queensland Press, 1987).
19. R. Elegant, *A Kind of Treason* (Harmondsworth: Penguin, 1980) p. 11.
20. C. Collingwood, *The Defector* (London: Sphere, 1972) pp. 66–7.
21. Ibid., p. 299.
22. Elegant, op. cit., p. 20.
23. Ibid., p. 22.
24. M. Wolfe, *Man on a String* (New York: Manor Books, 1975) pp. 61–2.
25. The views of Be Do and Keefe's thoughts on them make interesting reading when compared with the 'Factual Epilogue' on pp. 271–85 of W. J. Lederer's and E. Burdick's *The Ugly American* (New York: Norton, 1958). Here the faults of the American foreign service, especially in not training its operatives in the language and culture of host nations, are highlighted.
26. Wolfe, op. cit., p. 213.
27. M. Jones, *The Smiling Buddha* (London: Corgi, 1986) p. 20.
28. Ibid., p. 163.
29. Ibid., p. 100.
30. There are some similarities between *The Smiling Buddha* and another text about Cambodia, C. Hudson's *The Killing Fields* (London: Pan, 1984) in that a central concern is the entrapment of friends within a prison-state.
31. This movement has been extensively theorised for the Middle East by E. Said, in *Orientalism* (London: Routledge & Kegan Paul, 1978).

Index